THE ROMANCE OF THE WEDNESDAY.

1867—1926.

Mr. J. C. CLEGG, J.P.
President of the Football Association and the Wednesday F.C.

First published in 1926

This facsimile edition published
in 1997 by
DESERT ISLAND BOOKS
34 Hamlet Court Road, Westcliff-on-Sea, Essex SS0 7LX
United Kingdom

British Library Cataloguing-in-Publication Data:
A catalogue record for this book is available from the British Library.

ISBN   1-874287-17-1

Printed in Great Britain
by
Redwood Books, Trowbridge, Wiltshire

Publisher's note:
The first edition of this book was published
in Crown size (180 x 120 mm).
This edition is published in Demy-Octavo (216 x 138 mm).
The text has been magnified by 5 per cent

The ROMANCE OF THE WEDNESDAY

1867   1926

DESERT ISLAND BOOKS

RICHARD A. SPARLING
Author of
The History of the Sheffield
· · · · City Battalion · · · ·

CONTENTS.

PART I.
IN THE BEGINNING.

PART II.
QUEST OF THE ENGLISH CUP.

CONTENTS—Continued.

CONTENTS—Continued.

PART V.
AN ILLUSTRIOUS COMPANY.

PART VI.
THE MEN AT THE HELM.

ILLUSTRATIONS.

FOREWORD.

Mr. J. C. Clegg, J.P., the President of the Football Association and President of the Wednesday Football Club, Ltd. writes:—

To the Editor,

I have read the manuscript of "The Romance of The Wednesday" with much interest. You must have given a tremendous amount of time in obtaining & tabulating the facts and I congratulate you on the excellent manner in which you have written the history of the Club.

I am satisfied that all who are interested in the Club will thank you for producing such a book.

Mr. Stha? Clegg

June 29th, 1926.

A NOTE TO READERS.

SHEFFIELD.

"THE ROMANCE OF THE WEDNESDAY" is a homely tale for homely sportsmen. It was undertaken because it was felt that the history of the Wednesday Football Club should be embodied in print and because it is a story worth the telling. The Wednesday club has played a conspicuous part in the development of Association football, nationally as well as in Sheffield. One hopes the book will give pleasure to readers.

I am indebted to Mr. J. C. Clegg, J.P., for valuable assistance and advice; and I also acknowledge the aid of Mr. A. J. Dickinson, Mr. R. Brown, Mr. S. P. Stephen, Mr. Tom Cawley, Mr. Fred Spiksley, Mr. J. E. Davison, and Mr. A. Langley. The facilities afforded by the proprietors of the " Sheffield Telegraph " and allied journals, in various ways, are appreciated, too, and sincere thanks are accorded to all.

RICHARD A. SPARLING.

July 7th, 1926.

PART I.

In the Beginning.
Chapter One.

Dawn at Bent's Green: Sheffield's Wonderful Influence on the Game: Magnificent Record: Sheffield Club.

"YE needna' gang back till the Paradise," said the Scottish judge. "Suppose ye begin somewhere aboot the time of Noah's flood." The hint is placed well to the fore, but as the Wednesday Football Club is an institution in Sheffield, the full significance of that distinction would not be appreciated if adequate references were not made to the facts which warrant the great sporting city of Sheffield being known as "The Home of Association Football," the game which grips the world.

So the kick-off is fixed at 1793 at Bents Green. An old chronicle runs: "A great football match took place between Norton and Sheffield. There were selected six young men of Norton, dressed in green, and six young men of Sheffield, dressed in red. The play continued for three consecutive days at the arch which was erected at the ground. There was a hole in the goal, and those on the Sheffield side would prevent the ball from passing through the hole. Then those on the Norton side, not being so numerous as those of Sheffield, sent messengers to the Peak and other places in the county of Derby, and in consequence a great number of men appeared on the ground. Then those of Sheffield sent a drum-and-fife band through the streets of Sheffield to collect recruits and sufficient forces against the Derbyshire men.

"The fashion then was that all respectable gentlemen, tradesmen and artisans of Sheffield should wear long tails; hence that at the close of the third day's play a general row or struggle took place between the contesting parties. The men of Derbyshire cut and pulled off nearly all the tails from the heads of the gentlemen of Sheffield. There were many slightly wounded, but none were killed. Thus ended a celebrated football match, which aroused bad passions in both parties, and the hostile feeling continued, so that several years afterwards the people of Norton felt a dread to come to Sheffield, even about their necessary business.''

In one giant stride the middle of the nineteenth century is reached, and inside a quarter of a century Sheffield's sons exerted a tremendous influence on the game of Association football. Numerous teams sprang into existence, a city Association and many precedents were set up, precedents which helped to mould the play, the laws and the regulations.

Consider some of the phases : Sheffield teams began the great work of charity for deserving institutions, which to-day is a highly commendable feature of football; Sheffielders were responsible for the introduction of inter-city and important representative matches; a Sheffield club '' imported '' the first Scottish footballer; Sheffield teams instituted the corner-kick five years before the Football Association acknowledged its benefits. For eight years the cross-bar had been in use in Sheffield, while the Football Association merely insisted on a tape across the top of the goal; and the size of the goal, which Sheffield agreed upon in 1868, was only slightly different from the goal of the present time. The Sheffield Association realised the necessity of imposing penalties for breaches of the laws long before the rest of the country.

Sheffield had a football cup competition about three years before the famous English Cup competition was inaugurated. That was in 1868, when the Wednesday won the beautiful '' Cromwell '' Cup, the first football trophy ever presented. Again, Sheffield it was which opened the era of local cup competitions by promoting the Sheffield Challenge Cup tournament in the autumn of 1876, and three years before that Sheffield's legislators had realised the need for a Football Players' Accident Fund, which has its like to-day, though on a far greater scale, nationally.

Two Sheffield worthies were responsible for the present system of drawing for the English Cup rounds; previously club representatives met one another and decided the grounds upon which the ties should be played.

And still the end is not yet! Games between Nottingham and Sheffield were so fierce that Mr. S. W. Widdowson, of Nottingham, had the idea of shin-guards forced upon him, and Nottingham Forest's games with Norfolk (Sheffield) were instrumental in the referee's whistle being introduced. Sheffield Club, by an offer of one hundred guineas for a challenge cup for amateurs, was directly responsible for the founding of the present F.A. Amateur Cup competition, although the Association, naturally, could not avail itself of the Sheffield Club's generous offer.

Is there any city in the United Kingdom which has contributed more to the development of the national pastime than Sheffield? And has not Sheffield supplied the finest legislator the game has had in Mr. John Charles Clegg, J.P., the President of the Football Association?

Sheffield Club is the oldest existing football club in the world, and the minute-books go back to 1855. Those pioneers, the Gentlemen of Sheffield, played matches among themselves on the East Bank. Those whose surnames began with letters in the first half of the alphabet faced the other half. Afterwards they played the officers stationed at the garrison, and, before very long, the Gentlemen of Hallam. On February 12th, 1861, Sheffield Club and Hallam played at Hallam for two and a half hours, and Sheffield won by 2—0. The return match, in which Hallam was strengthened by the hamlet of Stumperlowe, lasted three hours, and Hallam won. Those clubs played the first charity match at Hyde Park, fourteen men on each side, and the receipts from 600 spectators were devoted to the Public Hospital and Dispensary.

A year before the Football Association was formed there were fifteen organised teams in Sheffield, though Sheffield Club and Hallam, in December, 1862, had the honour of playing the first football match ever decided on the famous ground at Bramall Lane. It was on behalf of the Lancashire Distress Fund, and no goals were scored in a game which extended over three hours.

In 1866, Mr. W. Chesterman, the hon. secretary of Sheffield Club, proposed to the Football Association that a match be played between the clubs of London and Sheffield. That sporting challenge was accepted, and the game was placed on March 31st, 1866, at Battersea Park. The match must be regarded as the first of a really representative character in the history of football, as the players were drawn from different teams. London won by "two goals and four touches down, Sheffield not obtaining a single point." The teams were:—

LONDON: A. Pember (President of the Football Association, captain), C. W. Alcock, E. C. Morley, E. D. Elphinstone, Hon. A. F. Kinnaird, C. M. Tebbut, J. M. Martin, J. K. Barnes, D. M. O'Leary, A. Baker, and R. W. Willis.

SHEFFIELD: W. Chesterman (captain), H. W. Chambers, F. Knowles, J. Knowles, J. Swift, J. Denton, A. A. Dixon, W. Baker, J. C. Shaw, J. D. Webster, and A. Wightman.

In that particular year Sheffield Club had 260 members, and the year's receipts amounted to £450, so that it was really stronger than it is to-day. It was a notable year in several respects.

Many alterations in the rules of the game were made by the Football Association. "Rouges" (a kind of try) were abolished, also the try at goal from a touch-down, the "fair catch"; the regulation as to off-side was introduced. The Sheffield clubs acknowledged "rouges" for about two more years, however, and they held any player on-side if he had only one opponent in front of him. The Sheffield rule for off-side was a curious one; it read: "Any player between the opponents' goal and the goal-keeper, unless he has followed the ball through, is off-side and out of play. The goal-keeper is the player of the defending side, who, for the time being, is closest to his own goal."

The Sheffielders stuck to their off-side law until 1877, for while the Sheffield Association, formed in 1867-8, linked itself with the Football Association in 1871, it was only on condition that it stuck to its own rules—a request which was granted. Of course, the amalgamation with the parent body considerably strengthened the adoption of one universal code. On the proposition of Pitsmoor in 1868, the Sheffield Association abolished "rouges," and in consequence the goal became a width of eight yards—the crossbar was nine feet high—so that it was not much different from present-day dimensions. The Association consisted of the following clubs: Sheffield, Hallam, Norfolk, Mackenzie, Broomhall, Milton, Pitsmoor, Norton, Heeley, United Mechanics, Firvale, Garrick, and Wellington. Later, Nottingham Forest, Middlesbrough, Derby Town, Rotherham, Chesterfield, Newark, Birmingham, and other centres joined it.

The Sheffield Football Players' Accident Fund, previously mentioned, had 37 clubs and 560 members in 1875, in which year Sheffield played two matches with Birmingham, after having played the first inter-city game with Glasgow in 1874. The games with London in the meantime continued. It was in 1873, by the way, when the Royal Engineers had a little tour, the first of its kind ever undertaken, and on Saturday, December 20th, they defeated the Sheffield Association by 4—o. That was the first defeat of any representative Sheffield eleven at Bramall Lane.

It was in that match that Mr. J. C. Clegg first met Major Marindin, the captain of the " Sappers," and Mr. Clegg once said that the Engineers were the first team to show Sheffield the value of combination. The most important difference between football then and now is in the development of mutual help. Said Mr. Clegg: " Individualism in my early days stands out in marked contrast to the combination of the present. My brother and I began to play together, and we found it a great advantage, but the Royal Engineers proved to us what could be accomplished by unity of action on the part of the whole team."

The season 1873-4 saw Sheffield Club enter the English Cup competition for the first time. They were drawn against Shropshire Wanderers, and the teams met at Bramall Lane and at Shrewsbury without either side notching a point. Accordingly, it was decided to toss for victory. Mr. Chambers, of Sheffield, won the toss, and so Sheffield had to journey to London to play the Pilgrims, whom they defeated with the aid of such splendid players as the Rev. J. R. B. Owen, the brothers J. C. and W. E. (now Sir William) Clegg, and H. W. Chambers. That necessitated Sheffield opposing Clapham Rovers in the next round, and by arrangement the tie was decided on a neutral enclosure— at Peterborough—on January 17th, 1874. The Rovers won

by 2—1. Four years later, Sheffield Club had to play
Darwen in the Cup, and the " Darreners " were beaten by
an odd goal.   The ground at Darwen was in such a shocking
state owing to heavy rains that the Gentlemen from
Sheffield wore white kid gloves!   The gloves had probably
been used at either a ball or concert, for they were mostly
soiled and had evidently been taken for the purpose.   But
the strange innovation was certainly a source of amusement
to the cotton-workers of Darwen.

Another stride—to 1889.   That year was notable for the
formation of the Sheffield United Football Club, and
when we turn to the big League sides, Wednesday and
United, great deeds are noted.   Both have played more than
1,000 matches in the Football League; also, both have
gained 1,000 points.   Each club has provided numerous
International players for all countries, including Fred
Spiksley, Tom Crawshaw, and Ernest Needham—three
players whose names will never be forgotten so long as the
game endures.   Further, Mr. J. C. Clegg played in the first
international match ever contested.

Wednesday and Sheffield United had a great period from
1890 to 1907 ; indeed, from 1893 to 1907 not a season passed
without a League or Cup honour coming to Sheffield.
Together, the Sheffield teams have been English Cup
finalists eight times and have won the trophy six times.
They have been Cup semi-finalists fifteen times.   In addition,
they have won the League championship on three occasions,
and have been runners-up twice, while Sheffield Club won
the F.A. Amateur Cup in 1904.   Thus it has been shown
what Sheffield has done to help the ball game along.   The
part played has been a magnificent one, and unequalled.
Still, whatever honours the city has gained, let homage be
paid to the Gentlemen who kicked off in '55.

Chapter Two.

What's in a name?—Birth and Death of Cricket
Club—Famous Tom Marsden—Glance at " good
old days."

THE story of the Wednesday Football Club, unfortunately or otherwise, starts with an argument. What's in a name? Well, there seems to be a great deal in that of " The Wednesday." One party here objects to the " The," another over there wants to know why and when the " Sheffield " part of the title was dropped ; in short, wherever Wednesday enthusiasts foregather this subject of the correct title of the club, as often as not, crops up. Even that great man of Wednesday authority, Mr. A. J. Dickinson, cannot make men of one mind, for " men convinced against their will are of the same opinion still."

Everyone knows that the Wednesday Football Club was an off-shoot of the Wednesday Cricket Club, and Mr. Dickinson believes that the cricket club was never known as the " Sheffield Wednesday Cricket Club," but just " Wednesday Cricket Club." So when the football section was formed it was entitled " Wednesday Football Club." He showed me the articles of association of the club, and there is plainly printed : " Wednesday Football Club." The word " The " is not embraced, nor is " Sheffield." It is argued by some that the name of the city was tacked on by the Press of the country, and by clubs of other centres when they advertised fixtures with Wednesday. But one may say that when Wednesday won the English Cup in 1896 and 1907 the name inscribed was " Sheffield Wednesday." At all events, " Sheffield Wednesday " appears on the trophy competed for to-day.

People think that the old heads of Wednesday have tripped up, as so many of us do, on a matter of memory. Mr. Muscroft, son of the late Mr. Herbert Muscroft, who was a player and also a director of Wednesday, has an old photograph of the Olive Grove ground. It quite clearly shows the name " Sheffield Wednesday " painted in huge letters on top of the stand. Mr. Muscroft can produce official club notepaper on which his father received intimation

to play, with the heading " Sheffield Wednesday," and also
a season-ticket similarly inscribed.   A member's card of
1883-4 bears that title as well, and Mr. Tom Cawley, the old
forward, has a postcard, dated 1890, and signed by Mr.
H. E. Pearson, the hon. secretary, which has " Sheffield
Wednesday Football Club " printed on the top.

The solution of the matter probably is that while the
club was originally named " Wednesday," the " Sheffield "
was added for a time in deference to the custom of people
outside Sheffield, who called it " Sheffield Wednesday."
After the Owlerton ground was re-named, the club
apparently became particular about its name, but even then
there was a slip, as you will notice at the main entrance.
For while the articles of association give the name as
" Wednesday Football Club," the big title in mosaic overlooking the Leppings Lane entrance is " THE Wednesday
F.C. Ltd."!   And there we will leave it.

The change of the ground's name from Owlerton to
Hillsborough has worried some people.   In newspapers
outside Sheffield, inquirers have been informed that the
Hillsborough ground is a new one, and that Wednesday used
to play at Owlerton!   Before the big development of that
end of the city the locality was chiefly known as Owlerton,
and so Owlerton appeared on the club's bills.   Later, it was
found that people were mostly utilising the Neepsend tram-
way service—a longer route—instead of the Hillsborough
service.   Therefore, as an aid to the convenience of the
public, Wednesday, in 1913, substituted " Hillsborough " for
" Owlerton " on their advertisements, etc.   For a good many
reasons, however, one would prefer the old designation of
Owlerton.   Older followers of the game still call the ground
" Owlerton," and regard it in the same light as the veterans
regard Olive Grove.

Why the name " Wednesday " was chosen is a question
easily answered.   The old cricket club was formed back in
1820 by the " little mesters," who had their " off " day on
Wednesday.   There were existing clubs at the time styled
" Monday Club," " Tuesday Club," " Thursday Club,"
and " Friday Club," so the traders thought they could do
no better than christen their organisation " Wednesday
Cricket Club."   Old score-books give details of matches
between those clubs of the days of the week.

It was with a feeling of regret that one witnessed the last acts in the " burial " of the cricket club, performed in the board-room of the Wednesday Football Club after the Second Division match with Stockport County on Saturday, Sept. 20th, 1924, when the " Cromwell " Cup was presented to the Wednesday F.C., and the " Tom Marsden " Cup and ball were handed over to the then Lord Mayor of Sheffield (Alderman A. J. Blanchard, J.P.), who accepted them on behalf of the city.   Mr. Percy Bowker, thirty-eight years a member of the now defunct cricket club, presented the famous old trophies.   Mr. J. C. Clegg, the Wednesday chairman, graciously received the " Cromwell " Cup, which will be specially referred to later.

It seems necessary to devote a little space to the cricket club and Tom Marsden.   Historians give 1820 as the year of the club's formation, a record of the matches having been kept from that date ; but " Bell's Life," of April 10th, 1842, states that it was founded in 1816.   It was not, however, the oldest cricket club in the world.   The Hallam club is 120 years old.   Still, it endured 104 years.   Then it passed out because the young men of the age could raise no enthusiasm for it.   What a reflection !

The greatest cricketer Wednesday ever had was Tom Marsden, a free-scoring left-handed batsman and a very useful bowler—very fast underhand and medium round-arm. He kept the Cricketers' Inn at Darnall.   Marsden is best remembered because of his wonderful batting display for Sheffield and Leicester—a combined team—opposing Nottinghamshire at Darnall in 1826, when he scored 227 ; he batted for three days before he was caught.   At that period, owing to the rough wickets, heavy scores were almost unknown.   Tom was worshipped, and, as was the custom in those days, every Feast Day saw the immortal thirteen stanzas on his great feat, recited with considerable vigour by the local enthusiasts.   The chorus, " Hey Derry Derry," etc., ended every spasm.   Half-a-dozen of the lines ran :—

Then Marsden went in, in his glory and pride,
And the arts of the Nottingham players defied.
Oh! Marsden at cricket is Nature's perfection,
For hitting the ball in any direction.
He ne'er fears his wicket, so safely he strikes,
And he does with the bat and the ball what he likes.

It was Marsden's first appearance in a match for Sheffield and Leicester against the famous Nottinghamshire cricketers, and he was only 21 years old. He took part in those matches against Nottingham until 1834 inclusive, and his batting was outstanding—806 runs in 20 completed innings, an average of just 40 runs an innings. The match of 1826 ended in an easy victory for Sheffield and Leicester, as Nottinghamshire were dismissed for 101 and 75 respectively. Sheffield and Leicester's innings realised 379, thanks to Marsden's 227, which, by the way, included only two fours. Only one innings of 200 runs had ever been registered in first-class cricket before that feat, and it was William Ward's 278 at Lord's in 1820, and which Percy Holmes, of Yorkshire, surpassed so brilliantly in 1925.

Yes, Marsden was a famous man. In 1831 he was presented with a silver cup of the value of £50 as a testimony of his ability and conduct, from his admirers. A collection had been taken in 1830 at one of the matches with Nottinghamshire, and it was probably the first instance of a collection taken on a cricket ground. That is the cup referred to in the presentations, and the ball there mentioned was the one used in the match of 1826. His relatives had presented the awards to the cricket club, and it had been the custom to drink a silent toast to Tom at the Wednesday C.C. annual dinners.

Here is another example of Marsden's fame :—

> At a meeting of the Leeds Club, March 24th, 1845, Mr. Barrett presented Mr. Clarke with an elegant gold breast-pin (which had been got up by subscription) in token of respect for his services as treasurer. . . . . The pin represented a bat, stumps and ball, and attached, instead of a chain, were *two links of the late Tom Marsden's hair.*

Marsden did not wear well—all his greatest feats were performed before he was twenty-five years old—and he died at the age of 38. His great deeds were confined to Yorkshire, for although he played regularly for some years at Lord's in Gentlemen v. Players matches, he did very little.

Harry Sampson was another great Wednesday cricketer. He was also a member of the United All-England Eleven, and for his height—5ft. 4ins.—he was a most successful batsman, with " extraordinary fine back-play." He beat

Tom Marsden at single wicket in 1841. He kept the Adelphi Hotel, Sheffield, for more than twenty years. He scored the largest innings—162—ever played on the ice, on February 8th, 1841, for Wednesday against Sheffield Town. He fielded at long-stop. Tom Hunt was a third fine Wednesday worthy—a great batsman, said to have played more single-wicket matches than any other cricketer. He defeated George Chatterton and Notts. players, C. Brown and R. C. Tinley. His innings of 165 in the match with Chatterton in 1843 is the record for a single wicket.

Wednesday's first matches were played at Darnall, then at Hyde Park, and afterwards at Bramall Lane. After that other grounds had to be found, including one at Norton. The Darnall ground of 1822 had no superior in the country at that time. The M.C.C. played Sheffield there for the first and last time in 1825. The Hyde Park ground was begun in 1824 and was finished in 1826; it cost more than £4,000, and it soon became the home of Yorkshire cricket. W. H. Woolhouse became the proprietor of it, and in September, 1830, it is reported, nine double-wickets were pitched on the ground, where upwards of two hundred players were at work at one time. It was about 5½ acres in extent, and delightfully situated. Yorkshire played their first county match there with Norfolk in 1833.

Wednesday organised various matches: one in 1829 was styled "Alpha v. Omega." An interesting side-light on the keenness of the players of the period is shown by the following report, dated 1838, of a single-wicket match played at Hyde Park between Hunt and Chatterton, for £50. It lasted two days. Hunt scored 9 and 165; Chatterton 16 and 15. The commentator says:—

> The result will, we trust, have a salutary effect on the loser, and teach him that, though a man may be a first-rate player in an eleven, he may cut a sorry figure in a single-wicket match. Chatterton is a superior player in an eleven, but his superiority consists in that sort of hitting which is of no effect at single wicket. Outside this, he must improve wonderfully in bowling before he engages again with one so skilled in that department as Hunt.

The club's minute-book has a fascination all its own.   In May, 1832, Wednesday resolved :

> 1.—That we shall have two fieldsmen for the ensuing year.
>
> 2.—That the two fieldsmen be Rawlins and Wilson, and to receive two shillings each for each day.
>
> 3.—That if the said fieldsmen be not in attendance upon the ground at two o'clock, they shall not receive the full allowance, but if before four o'clock to receive one shilling.
>
> 4.—That Mr. Hydes have full power to order and arrange the stoops and blocks for the net given to the club by Mr. Wheat.
>
> N.B.—Mr. Woolhouse agrees to give Rawlins 6d. when he attends at 2.0 o'clock.

In April, 1838, it was decided that a couple of brands be ordered to mark the bats and balls belonging to the club. Further, that any member wishing to play in the practice matches must deposit one shilling, and if he be not ready to play at the time appointed he must forfeit his deposit.   The same year Charles Ward and Isaac Hattersley were fined half-a-crown each "for a breach of Rule IX., viz., leaving a ball on the ground after play."

A contrast with present-day prices is provided by a minute of 1841, which states that the club

> gave Job Shaw six bats to repair and ordered two new bats, one at 3s. 6d. and the other at 4s.

How the club treasured the old score-book may be realised from the fact that it was resolved in 1839 that Mr. Croft be allowed the loan of the old scoring-book for seven days on his depositing 50s.

A friendly match between Wednesday and Spinkhill was the means of revealing a man who afterwards became a world-renowned cricketer.   This young unknown player dismissed Wednesday for about 30 runs, and then compiled 100 not out.   Mr. Richard Gillott, who was president of Wednesday for ten years, went up to the fellow and asked : "Would you like to become a professional cricketer?" (Mr. Gillott was a member of the Yorkshire C.C. Committee.) The youth replied, "It's the dream of my life."   He was a collier at Staveley, but a Lancashire man by birth.   Afterwards Mr. Gillott communicated with notable Lancashire

cricketers, and within a year or two R. G. Barlow was introduced into Lancashire county cricket.

One of the most remarkable men who ever played for
Wednesday was Reuben Hallam. He is alleged to have
had 39 trades and professions at his finger-ends ! Hallam,
it seemed, had tried his hand at all the following
occupations :—

> Grinding, professional cricket, Shakespearean
> tragedies, variety singing, double-bass playing, scene
> painting, scene shifting, theatrical manager, adver-
> tising agent, journalist, author (he wrote " Wadsley
> Jack "), reciting, boxing, teacher of singing, operatic
> singer, gentleman beggar, poet, farm labourer, com-
> mercial traveller, raconteur, and a travelling knife
> and scissors grinder.

By " gentleman beggar " it is meant that when his
theatrical company was " hard-up " he would go to big
houses in the country and offer to give drawing-room
concerts.

Mr. Joseph Gillott, by the way, is the well-known com-
poser, who, when in Australia, sent the Commonwealth
delirious with delight with his stirring and melodious
patriotic songs during the Boer War. He composed " Sons
of the Southern Sea," which became Australia's national
song, and was honoured by all the celebrities of Australia.
His songs are the only songs which have ever been sung in
the Parliament House, Melbourne.

Perhaps the most powerful team Wednesday ever put
into the field was when Lascelles Hall were met at Bramall
Lane in 1876. The side was : Tom Brownhill, George
Ulyett, G. Pinder, E. Stephenson, Tom Armitage, W. Slinn,
E. F. Fay, H. Barber, G. Betts, Ralph Crookes, and Harry
E. Pearson. More than half the team represented Yorkshire
at one time or another, and altogether it spells a fine
testimony to the power and importance of the Wednesday
Club. The Wednesday were heavily defeated, for against
totals of 46 and 47 Lascelles Hall scored 190 in a single
innings. In recent years the club had good sportsmen in
Messrs. J. Merchant, F. Nunn, L. Jefferson, W. E. Hurst,
W. J. Biggin, A. T. Biggin, T. West, H. Warrender, J.
Nunn, M. Vernon, E. Pearse, A. Young, R. J. Wales, A. T.

Noxin, T. Sheppard, A. Frost, G. W. Robinson, B. J. Davy, B. Rodgers, R. Tasker, H. Burgen, and Lance Morley. "Lance" was once given out "stumped" at Beighton. He could not understand it, and in his sporting way he said: "I don't know what you do at Beighton, but I would like to know how I'm out." "Stumped," was the response. "You have to have both feet behind t' crease at Beighton."

In another match a terrifically stout man played. The bowlers were in despair. When the "fat old boy" was batting, the bowlers couldn't see the wicket, and they said they'd never get him out. The umpire came to the rescue by saying: "I've a ruling on him. If a ball hits him on the stomach he's out l.b.w.; if a ball hits him on the back, it's a wide!"

Chapter Three.

The momentous decision—Kick-off with victory—
Win first football cup ever offered—Old Bramall
Lane—Men like iron—Striking civic connections.

THE historic special meeting of the Wednesday Cricket
Club, which saw the birth of the football club, was
held on Sept. 5th, 1867, in the Adelphi Hotel, Arundel
Street, and, " in order to keep the members together during
the winter months," it was decided to have a football
section formed. The resolution was put by Mr. J. Pashley,
seconded by Mr. W. Littlehales, and was carried unanimously. Mr. B. Chatterton was elected president, Mr. F. S.
Chambers vice-president and treasurer, Mr. J. Marsh
hon. secretary, and Mr. W. B. Castleton assistant secretary.
The Committee appointed was: Messrs. J. Rodgers, J.
Pashley, W. Fry, W. F. Pilch, W. Littlehales, J. White,
C. Stokes, and H. Bocking, with power to add to their
number. The Working Committee was Messrs. Marsh,
Castleton, Rodgers, White and Fry. In addition, it was
agreed that no body of persons " shall be empowered to
sever the two clubs without the consent of a general meeting,
six days' notice to be given to every member of the two
sections."

Severance came in 1883, but cricket and football had
flourished splendidly for a time under the one control, and
it is believed that but for an improvident cricket secretary
the two sections would never have been split. The football
club was in the habit of earning the money, while the cricket
club spent it. That was the bone of contention, at all
events. Thus we now draw the curtain on the cricketers.

The football club's first ground was near the present
Upper Colver Road. It was called the high field, and the
Highfield Library now stands there. The first match was
played against Dronfield on December 31st, 1867, at Dronfield. The Wednesday won by 1 goal to four "rouges."
Here one should explain the term " rouge." The goal-
posts were four yards apart and had a bar across them
nine feet from the ground. At each side of the goal were

posts at a distance of four yards from the goal-posts, also
with crossbars nine feet from the ground. The outer posts
were called " rouge flags." The total width was, therefore, twelve yards, and a goal was scored only by sending
the ball between the inner posts. If the ball passed between
a central post and an outer one, it was reckoned a " rouge."
In the event of no goal being scored the match was decided
by " rouges," but one goal was worth any number of
" rouges."   " Rouges " were abolished in 1868.

The first serious football competition which Wednesday
ever entered was that for the " Cromwell " Cup early in
1868. That trophy, which Wednesday treasure to this day,
was named after its donor, the late Mr. Oliver Cromwell,
who, it will be remembered by many, was for several years
stage-manager at the Alexandra Theatre, now pulled down,
but which stood at the bottom of the approach to the
L. & N.E. Railway Station, on Blonk Street. He was then
at the Theatre Royal, and he presented the cup for local
clubs which had not been formed more than two years.
Oliver Cromwell was, incidentally, interested in the Garrick
Club, which had its headquarters at the Garrick Hotel in
Sycamore Street—a famous old theatrical house in days
gone by. Garrick was reputed to be the best team in
Sheffield, and it was believed they would win the Cromwell
Cup. Four clubs entered : Garrick (two seasons old),
Wellington (two seasons), Wednesday and Exchange (one
season). The draw paired the Wednesday and Exchange
and Garrick and Wellington.

Considerable excitement prevailed, for after Wednesday
had defeated Exchange on the Mackenzie club's ground on
February 1st, 1868, by 4—o, the Garrick, apparently,
became alarmed, for it is recorded that the following
Saturday, when they had to play Wellington at Norfolk
Park, they induced seven members of the Hallam club to
join them. Garrick, even so, triumphed by only one
" rouge "—the sole score of the game. The Wednesday,
who, by the way, had adopted blue and white for their
colours, .played Garrick in the final at Bramall Lane on
February 15th, and it was the first game The Wednesday
had played for which an admission fee was charged. There
were 600 spectators.

In the first half Wednesday, having lost the toss, faced a strong wind, yet there was no score. The second half was strenuously and evenly fought, but Garrick had their dangerous moods, and that they were held out was due a good deal to the fine work of " little captain J. Marsh (cover goal), Whelan and Denton." With time completed and still no goals recorded, it was decided to continue the play until either Garrick or Wednesday took the lead. After ten minutes of extra time, " Whelan passed to Alf Wood, who placed the ball in the goal-mouth. In the course of a terrific struggle the ball was forced through. Wednesday had won." Skipper Marsh was carried off the ground. Spectators, then as now, had their emotions.

It is worth the effort of younger generations to try to visualise that first cup-tie. Picture the Bramall Lane ground—the range of low wooden sheds which were dressing-rooms for the men, and also licensed premises, where now the John Street stand is; " Donoghue's booths," where folks could get beer, stand about and watch the play; no rails then around the historic playing field; keen sportsmen present, some rough-and-ready, possessing that rich characteristic wit for which crowds at Bramall Lane have ever been noted. Imagine, too, the play and the players. In those early days individualism reigned; no team combination existed as we know it to-day, and there were only one or two definite positions, such as the goal-keeper and the " kicker-in " or " pusher-through."

Goalkeepers had tough times, for the " kicker-in " and a mate or two simply hung around the goal-keeper, determined by hook or crook to get the ball through the posts, goalkeeper and all, if necessary. It was a common sight to see a heap of men with the unlucky goalkeeper at the bottom. The scrimmages were very fierce. Alderman Wardley, a director of Wednesday now, has said more than once that as " kicker-in " the goals he scored and the knocks he received broke all records. The players had to be men of iron.

As a rule the players followed the ball wherever it went, and the rush was terrific. Teams used to play in ordinary boots and trousers, and there were games in which the men were dressed exactly as they had left work, wearing

iron-bound clogs. Players on one side had a handkerchief
on the arm to distinguish them from the opposition. No
team thought of playing without wearing caps of some
sort. There were few rules for the definition of foul play,
and it was quite legitimate to kick a man off his feet or to
hack him to make him part with the ball. The hacking
business was not child's play.

Players found they could get a better foothold with nails
stuck in their boots, so for a time they had special pairs of
boots from the soles of which there were exposed five or
six sharp nails, perhaps half an inch in length. Battle
scars! Few players in those days were without them. It
is easy to understand why studs were introduced and nails
made illegal.

Reverting to the "pusher-through": Wednesday had
in Frank Butler a man who was a perfect adept in the art
of pushing through. Standing little more than 5ft. 4ins.
and decidedly bow-legged, Butler proved himself a positive
terror to opposing custodians. He would stand and chat
with his prospective victim until the ball came within reach,
and then the fun began. Every now and then Butler met a
Tartar, but he used to reckon all his bruises and other
injuries as parts of the game.

From the foregoing, therefore, one obtains a shrewd
idea as to the prevailing conditions when Wednesday won
the "Cromwell" Cup. The cup, incidentally, was presented by Mr. Cromwell on the stage at the Theatre
Royal to the Wednesday players on March 16th, 1868—
Mr. Cromwell's benefit night. A fortnight after the
presentation, Wednesday promoted their first sports,
held at Bramall Lane before about 2,000 people. Stevenson,
of Norton, won the two miles open race, and Donovan, a
prominent player for Garrick, won "the 300 yards steeplechase," was second in the football race (once round the
course), and was third "in the 650 yards steeplechase."

Wednesday, in the following season, played such teams
as Norton, Broomhall, Mackenzie, Pitsmoor, Garrick,
Mechanics, Norfolk (Sheffield), and Heeley.

On April 19th, 1869, they held the second annual sports,
and the boys of the charity schools were invited. Silver
and copper were collected, and squandered amongst the
boys.

The prizes were presented by Alderman Thomas Moore, who was Mayor of Sheffield for four years in succession, and who took a great interest in the Wednesday club. The Mayor, as the Alderman then˙was, urged that after they had done with field sport they should consider the government of the town, and here one takes the opportunity of showing Wednesday's connections in that direction. Alderman Bromley, Mr. B. Chatterton, Mr. J. White, Mr. G. Skinner, of Wednesday associations, served on the Council, and in 1906 the club had a unique record in civic connections. That year Alderman George Senior, J.P., an ex-Lord Mayor of Sheffield, was the chairman of directors; the Lord Mayor for the year, 1906, Colonel H. Hughes, J.P., was a director, and four other ex-Lord Mayors in Alderman Sir William Clegg, J.P., Alderman Sir George Franklin, J.P., Alderman J. R. Wheatley, J.P., and Councillor Sir Joseph Jonas, J.P., were also members of the Board. In addition, the names of another Alderman, three City Councillors, and the Official Receiver, Mr. J. C. Clegg, J.P., were on the roll of directors.

The Board in 1926 had as chairman Mr. J. C. Clegg, President of the Football Association; three ex-Lord Mayors of Sheffield in Alderman A. J. Blanchard, J.P., Sir William Clegg, C.B.E., J.P., and Alderman W. F. Wardley, J.P., and a C.B.E. in Mr. W. Turner, the vice-chairman. In addition, Sir William Clegg and Alderman Wardley are Freemen of Sheffield. No football club in the country can boast a prouder record than this of service to city government and sport.

Chapter Four.

*Rising to power—Matches afield—The first
Sheffield Challenge Cup Final: Lang, the first
Anglo-Scot—" Importations " and a mystery—
Stalwarts of '78.*

THE Wednesday were destined to become a power in
the land; they soon became a power in the city of
Sheffield and the county of Yorkshire. Full of
enthusiasm for the game, the young footballers practised
keenly, and slowly but surely built up their reputation by
battling against numerous local teams. In 1870 the
brothers J. C. and W. E. Clegg joined the club and so
started upon their long and magnificent careers in the world
of athletics. Mr. J. C. Clegg, as a matter of fact, that year
won the 120 yards handicap from scratch and was third in
the quarter-mile handicap, also from scratch, in the club's
sports at the Lane. Mr. W. E. Clegg was second in the
" 300 yards steeplechase," and only a slip at the water-
jump prevented him from being the winner. That season
(1869-70) also saw The Wednesday move to their second
ground at Myrtle Road, where they played on a hilly field
overlooking their future home of Olive Grove.

In that and subsequent seasons, when they played
Pitsmoor, Heeley, Attercliffe Christ Church, Mackenzie,
Albion, Lockwood Brothers, Park Grange, Exchange,
Staveley, etc., there used to be great fun. Of one match
at Staveley a good story is told. There was a fellow keeping
goal for the visitors named " Tottie " Kelvey, a farrier,
who was recognised as a regular " dare-devil " and was
rather feared. But on the Staveley side they had one or
two players just as daring, notably " Lambie " Hay (the
man whose knee-cap slipped regularly and who would just
sit down on the field and put it right again in half a minute
and go on playing). Hay kept going for Kelvey, and the
goalkeeper was told to look out or he would find himself
amongst the spectators. Kelvey turned round to those
behind the goal (several of them were lady relatives of Hay)

WEDNESDAY GROUP TAKEN IN 1874-75.

Standing : W. E. Clegg, J. C. Clegg, W. Wilkinson, E. Bowling, J. Morton and R. Gregory.
Seated : J. Housley, W. E. England, W. H. Stacey, W. Horton, G. Anthony and J. Hunter.

and remarked that the next time their lad tried it on, he would pitch him (Hay) amongst them.   And he did it, too! Hay went dashing in; Kelvey did not bother with the ball, but bobbed down and caught Hay fairly and squarely on his shoulder, and dropped him right amongst his relatives, much to their dismay.

The season 1870-71 was recorded as a brilliant one. The club played 25 matches, won 15, drew 7, and lost only 3.

It is observed that Sir William Clegg's first match for the club was against Attercliffe Christ Church in the season 1871-2, and Wednesday won by 3—0.   Up to that term each winning team had a gallon of beer allowed, the defeated team having to be content with half the quantity. Then it was decided that the " practice of allowing refreshments to players after a match be discontinued."   The season was also memorable for the inauguration of the official matches between Sheffield and London, and for the first, played at Bramall Lane on December 4th, 1871, when Sheffield won by 3—1, Wednesday supplied no fewer than seven players, and Mr. C. W. Alcock captained the visitors.

Wednesday's activities widened.   Season after season they provided men for the inter-city matches, and in 1872-3 they arranged home-and-home contests with the Derby County Association.   The first county match was decided at Bramall Lane on November 23rd, 1872.   The teams consisted of 14 players, though Wednesday were accustomed to fielding eleven only.   As showing how Sheffield has grown, it may be pointed out that Alf. Wood, a Wednesday player, was claimed by Derbyshire, having been born at Heeley, which club had affiliated with the Peak county.   Derbyshire won by the odd goal.

The following year, Wednesday's ranks received a notable acquisition in Bob Gregory, who turned out for the first time in Wednesday's colours against Broomhall.

The season 1875-6 marked the first matches with Nottingham Forest.   The first game was fought at Nottingham on January 8th, 1876, and it was a somewhat furious encounter.   During the first half, Wednesday held their own and by the aid of " Billy " Mosforth scored the first goal.   Eventually they ran out winners by 5—0.

Forest, however, were not at full strength.   The teams were :—

Wednesday: W. H. Stacey (captain), J. C. Clegg,, W. E. Clegg, F. Stacey, W. Mosforth, W. Heath, W. Crofts, J. Hunter, F. Butler, S. Charles, R. Gregory, and H. Barker (goal).

Nottingham Forest: S. W. Widdowson (captain), W. Bevis, J. Wyatt, A. E. Goodyear, A. H. Smith, T. Oliver, S. Rick, J. Richards, H. Rothers, H. R. Gamble, R. P. Hawksley, and J. Brown (goal).

Later, Wednesday visited Nottingham a second time and played a team styled Notts Castle at Trent Bridge, where the result was 1—1.

Following the lead of the Football Association, which had promoted the popular English Cup competition, the Sheffield Association in 1876-7 instituted the Sheffield Challenge Cup competition (the trophy was valued at £50).   For some years that Cup was more highly esteemed than the national trophy.   Twenty-five teams entered the competition, and Wednesday set the ball rolling by meeting Parkwood Springs.   The Wednesday won, and dismissed Kimberworth at Kimberworth by 1—0 in the second round, and in the third defeated old rivals in Attercliffe at Shirland Lane by the odd goal.   The tie with Attercliffe was played during a terrible rain-storm on New Year's Day, 1877, and J. J. Lang donned Wednesday colours.   Exchange were overcome by 3—1 at Bramall Lane in the semi-final amid great enthusiasm.   The brothers Clegg and Muscroft, Lang and Frank Butler played splendidly.   Thus Wednesday had grimly contested their way to the final, in which they had to meet Heeley, another grand club of those days, and powerful.

The struggle between them—12 a-side—took place on March 10th, and it is of importance, hence the teams are given below :—

Wednesday: F. Stacey (goal); W. H. Stacey (captain) and E. Buttery, backs; W. E. Clegg, T. Butler, and H. Muscroft, half-backs; J. Bingley and F. M. Butler (right wing), J. J. Lang and J. C. Clegg (left wing), and T. Bishop and W. E. Skinner (centres), forwards.

Heeley W. Beard, T. A. Tomlinson, P. Andrews, J. E. Deans, R. Martin, Joe Tomlinson, F. Brownhill, T. Leslie, Jack Hunter, J. Thorp, H. M. Barringham, and J. Lindley.

Lindley kept goal for Heeley, but it is impossible to give details of the positions of the other players. It will be noticed that Wednesday had two centres and three half-backs, but one of the latter had a roving commission—either to lay just behind the forwards or fall back and act in the capacity of " cover-goal "—whose duties are clearly outlined in the title given him. Half the Wednesday twelve were three pairs of brothers. The fame of the Staceys was then only second to that of the Cleggs. In the team again mark James Lang, who played with Clydesdale and the Third Lanark, and was a Scottish International.

About 8,000 spectators assembled for the exciting final at Bramall Lane. Heeley began excellently, and took the lead as a result of a scrimmage. Immediately on the re-start they scored another goal: the ball rebounded off the back of one of the Wednesday players. That put the Heeley supporters in high glee, which became almost boundless when Stacey headed through his own goal. At half-time, Heeley were leading by 3—0. However, as on numerous occasions in later days, The Wednesday showed their opponents how to play the uphill game. In a very short time Frank Butler scored a beautiful goal. It was followed by some fine play by W. E. Clegg, who crossed to T. Butler, and that player scored the second goal for Wednesday. With but one goal in arrears, Wednesday played manfully to draw level, and eventually Frank Butler passed to W. E. Clegg, who, with a grand shot, beat the goalkeeper and made the scores level (3—3). That was sensational and full-blooded. Half-an-hour's extra time was played, and Wednesday obtained a fourth goal (through Skinner). In spite of all their brave efforts Heeley had to admit defeat by 4—3 in a thrilling struggle. So did Wednesday become the first winners of the Sheffield Challenge Cup and build up a reputation as cup-fighters. In 1926, the reserve team again won the trophy.

A curious occurrence took place when Wednesday met Heeley at Myrtle Road on January 31st, 1876. When half-time arrived and Wednesday were leading by 1—0 it was discovered that Wednesday had been playing fourteen men and their opponents thirteen. It was agreed to cancel the first half's play and make a fresh start. Heeley secured another player. It was like a Rugby match. Twenty minutes were played in each half, and Heeley won by the only goal scored.

As the season of 1925-26 will always be remembered because so many Scottish International players were obtained by Football League clubs at astonishing transfer fees, it is interesting to note that J. J. Lang was the first Scottish professional to cross the Border for the purpose of playing football. The oft-repeated assertion that J. Love and Fergus Suter, who went from Partick to Darwen in 1878, were the first Scottish players imported is obviously incorrect. The distinction belongs to Lang. Incidentally, Peter Andrews, a Scottish International, was in the ranks of the Heeley team in the afore-mentioned Sheffield Challenge Cup Final.

It is not long since James Lang, who celebrated his 75th birthday in March, 1926, told the story of how he became an Anglo-Scot. First, he pointed out that a colleague in the long since defunct Glasgow Eastern club, Peter Andrews, was the first Scot to play in England, but Andrews—and here is the distinction—did not come to England in order to play football. The Scottish firm by whom he was employed sent him to Leeds on business, and after he had been there for some months he became connected with the Heeley club.

Andrews crossed the Border in the early part of 1876, and in the December of that year he played for Sheffield against Manchester at Manchester. Sheffield won by 4—0. Actually, Andrews was the first Scot ever called upon to play for Sheffield in a first-class match. In the autumn of 1876 Lang arrived south with the sole object of joining Wednesday. He was supposed to work as well, for he was given a post by Mr. Walter Fearnehough in Garden Street, but his time was chiefly devoted to football and reading the news of the day in the papers. His first match for Wednesday was on the first Saturday of October at Myrtle Road, and he says himself that he did not play for nothing. Thus did he light the beacon that was to guide so many of his countrymen towards fame and riches, riches greater than they could obtain at home.

It was in February, 1876, that Lang first visited Sheffield. He played for Glasgow against Sheffield at Bramall Lane, and, apparently, his quickness in taking the ball through the Sheffield defence and his deftness in shooting took the fancy of the Wednesday officials. Glasgow won by 2—0, their first win away from home. In the first half, play was under the rules of the Football Association, but under Sheffield rules in the second. Incidentally Sheffield's team was :—

W. Carr (goal); Jack Hunter, J. Houseley (backs); S. Charles and W. E. Clegg (half-backs); J. C. Clegg (captain) and G. Anthony (right wing), W. Orton and R. Gregory (centre), and W. Mosforth and W. Wilkinson (left wing).

The following April (1876)—the first day of April, as a matter of fact—Wednesday visited the Clydesdale club, of which Lang was a member, and played a match at Kinning Park, Glasgow. It was the ground later taken over by the Rangers. Again Lang put in some of his captivating work, and, as a result, he was invited, and agreed, to transfer his services to Wednesday. On March 25th, 1876, by the way, Lang played for Scotland against Wales at Glasgow, which was the first international contest in which Wales took part.

Lang disclosed to Mr. Dickinson a very interesting personal matter in 1926. He stated that he lost the sight of his left eye owing to an accident in 1869 in the shipyard of Messrs. John Brown & Co., Clydebank, but kept it a closely-guarded secret from his friends in Sheffield. He believed that if the knowledge had spread opponents would have taken advantage of his " blind " side.

He is still on the Government List as " blind."

So much for Lang's story. It is, however, noteworthy that, it is believed, Wednesday have never since gone through a season without having a Scotsman on the books. Indeed, in February, 1911, Wednesday's camp included no fewer than eight Caledonians and three Irishmen—Murray, O'Connell and Warren. It was possible for the Wednesday to field a team of " importations," but they never got to that stage. That year, though, the team against Bury included seven Scotsmen. Paterson was moved to inside-right in order to make room for David McLean, and with Wilson and Robertson as the left wing, the attack was almost all-Scottish. It was a coincidence that while Dowling, who played at outside-right, was an Englishman, he joined the Wednesday from a Scottish club. The total of seven Scotsmen against Bury was not a record for Wednesday, because they had a team at one time in which Fred Spiksley was the only Englishman.

About the advent of the '90's the proportion of six Englishmen to five Scots was generally maintained, and later, too; and the Wednesday did not disguise their opinion that given two men of equal ability they undoubtedly preferred to engage Englishmen as being much easier to manage. Probably that opinion exists to-day, for since the war Wednesday's experience with Scots has been unfortunate, to say the least. It seemed, at one period, as though someone had placed a " black spot " on Scotsmen soon after they had set foot in Yorkshire's biggest city.

In the first post-war season, David McLean played in only two or three matches. Then friction arose, and, within a few weeks, he was signed on by Mr. Tom Maley in a Sheffield cinema-house for Bradford. Then Wednesday had difficulties with James Blair, who had been prevailed upon to leave Alloa only after considerable trouble. At left-back, in which position he was " capped," he played excellently for some months. In October, 1921, there came the rift in the lute, and he was transferred to Cardiff City.

Andrew Wilson concluded his twenty years of service with Wednesday, and he went off to manage Bristol Rovers, a position he resigned at the end of the 1925-26 season. Eggo, the captain of Reading, of the Southern Section of League, came from Heart of Midlothian, with a youngster named Colin Mackay. After a comparatively short stay, Eggo went to Reading and Mackay to Huddersfield Town. To Huddersfield at the same time went Jimmy Campbell, the Scottish international half-back who played so brilliantly for the Wednesday in pre-war times. Campbell died in 1925. George Robertson had knee trouble, and that grand left-winger departed, as did Bob McSkimming, a rare half-back and back. McSkimming never recovered from his disastrous experience in the Darlington cup-tie in January, 1920.

There was also the remarkable case of Fletcher Welsh, secured in January, 1920, from Raith Rovers. He was the leading goal-scorer in the Scottish League, but he struck a bad patch almost as soon as he joined the Wednesday. In short, he was a failure, a distressing failure, for he eventually became the reserve player to the reserve team. He was shortly after transferred to Third Lanark and faded out of first-class football. After Welsh had been signed on, J. McIntyre was secured from Fulham. McIntyre was a half-back, yet had a wonderful rise to fame as a forward. He adapted himself to the centre-forward position and scored 27 goals in that memorable season, 1920-21, when he shot more goals than all the rest of the Wednesday team put together. His scoring prowess was the talk of the country. The next season McIntyre's form declined. Rumours flew about the city and an embarrassing situation arose both for the club and the player. Another cinema-house interview and off went "Mac," transferred to Blackburn Rovers. Wednesday's consolation was a very handsome transfer fee.

By and by, another Scot, William Walker, was obtained from Bristol City. He was an experienced player, who, however, after a few months went to Weymouth as player-manager.

In the 1924-25 season more Scots joined the Wednesday staff—Wm. Inglis and Wm. Collier, from Raith Rovers, who, after they had packed bags to go to America, changed their minds. Their departure from Hillsborough, however, was not delayed many months. In the summer of 1925 Inglis was transferred to Manchester United and Collier became player-manager of Kettering. It was in the dying days of February, 1926, when the Scottish strain was renewed at Hillsborough with the signing on of Tom Walker, the back of Bradford City.

One now hopes the mysterious influence which has spread over the destinies of Scottish footballers in Sheffield no longer exists

Having dealt with ancient and modern Anglo-Scottish football history one must retrace steps and pick up the threads from where one left off in 1877. The season 1877-78 saw the Wednesday with headquarters at Sheaf

House. On February 19th, 1878, they played Glasgow
Rangers at Bramall Lane and were defeated by 2—1, not a
bad performance in view of the fact that the Rangers had
just beaten Nottingham Forest at Nottingham by 4—2.
The Sheffield Challenge Cup provided more spirited fights.
Wednesday repeated their triumph of the previous season
by beating Attercliffe 2—0 in an exciting final tie on March
2nd. C. L. Stratford was in Wednesday's ranks, and F.
Stacey gave a grand display in goal.

That was the season which determined the Cleggs that
Wednesday were too powerful, and that it was for the good
of the game that the Sheffield trophy should be held by
other teams.

In April, 1878, the "All England Cricket and Football
Journal," long since gone to its rest, took pleasure "in
presenting its readers with a photograph of the cup team
of the Sheffield Wednesday Football Club, taken at Bramall
Lane, Sheffield, a few minutes after they had won the
Challenge Cup for the second year, against the Attercliffe
Club, on the 2nd of last month."

At that time, said the old chronicler, the Wednesday F.C.
had become one of the leading clubs in the town, numbering
about 300 members.   He briefly ran over Wednesday's
triumphs up to 1878, and regretted that more could not be
said on the subject, "as we are informed that no record of
its principal matches exists."   However, he drew some
sketches of the players of the 1878 eleven, as under:—

"The captain of the eleven is Mr. W. H. Stacey, who is
a very quick player, generally as back or half-back, taking
the former position in the cup matches.   Mr. Stacey
formerly played for the Sheffield Association, but has not
taken much part in their matches lately.

"Messrs. J. C. and W. E. Clegg are well known as
Sheffield Association players, who, although they, in connection with their father, have a successful business in Sheffield as
solicitors, yet find time to devote to the game they have so
long supported, as well as to one they have recently taken
in hand—lacrosse.   The elder of them is a most excellent
forward, and passes the ball with great judgment, seldom
failing to obtain a goal whenever there is a chance.   His
brother plays well as a forward or half-back, in which latter
position he played in this cup contest.

" J. J. Lang is a very skilful forward, of great energy and power; and, although a member of the Wednesday Club, is a resident of Glasgow, from which place he journeyed to Sheffield to play for the cup. Another of the team—T. Bishop—resides at Chesterfield; and he, as well as H. Bingley and the brothers Butler, play forward, and all are excellent men.

" The half-backs are W. E. Clegg and C. L. Stratford, a young but promising player. E. Buttery, who with the captain played back, has played for Sheffield, and is a useful man. Last, but not least, comes Mr. F. Stacey, whose goalkeeping has won the admiration of the public and the Press; and the best recommendation of which is that in the Cup competition he did not give a single goal to the other side, Wednesday having obtained eleven goals to their opponents' none. His excellent goalkeeping also brought him under the notice of the committee of the Sheffield Association, who selected him to that post in the last two matches—those against Staffordshire and Birmingham, neither of whom obtained a goal, though Sheffield obtained four in one and five in the other."

Chapter Five.

*Novelty Matches—Goals miles apart—Football
in the Night—The noted Zulus.*

PEOPLE have always been fond of novelty. An
example was the girls' football exhibition match at
Hillsborough in 1923, when Dick Kerr's famous
young women's team defeated a Yorkshire set of girls.
Wednesday men took part in striking " novelty " matches
in the '70's. They are often talked about. One was the
fierce game " played " at Sheffield, with the turnpike for
the " ground." It was one of the most remarkable
exhibitions of football which have ever been witnessed in
Sheffield ; so exciting and fierce that it was a wonder no one
was seriously hurt. The match was played on January
10th, 1876. It was between Ecclesfield and Pitsmoor,
twelve men a-side. The distance between the goals was
miles ; there were no lateral boundaries ; men could handle,
kick or deal with the ball in any way they wished.

The scene was the turnpike road leading from Sheffield
to Barnsley, and the goals were represented by the Pitsmoor
and Ecclesfield turnpike bars. Though the affair had not
been advertised there were over 15,000 spectators, spread
over road, field and furrow. W. R. Wake was the captain
of the Pitsmoor team, which included George Ulyett, the
famous Yorkshire cricketer, who later kept goal for
Wednesday, and Tom Beat was the captain of Ecclesfield. A
start was made at Sheffield Lane Top, about midway between
the goals, and if plans had succeeded Pitsmoor would have
been beaten easily. There was a " little mester's " shop at
the corner, and Ecclesfield appointed a friend to sit near
the chimney of that place with the object of giving the side
a helping hand. When the ball reached him he had to fling
it to the other side of the building, where a player was in
waiting, and that player had been instructed to take
advantage of the confusion and set off at full pace for the
Pitsmoor Toll Bar. He was not forbidden to leap on any

vehicle which was likely to assist him in his efforts. The
ball, however, struck the chimney and rebounded to the
road; so the quaint idea failed.

A terrific struggle was waged; kicks and knocks were
given freely. Eventually Pitsmoor took the ball nearly to
the first toll-bar at Ecclesfield, but they got no farther, and
afterwards play went on around Shiregreen, in fact all over
the place; players jumped over hedges, dashed across
ploughed fields, through farmyards and along roads, lanes,
and by-paths. For three hours that sort of thing went on,
and the finish came about 4 p.m., the ball having been
taken to Wadsley Bridge by Beat and William Hague, with
H. Firth, of Pitsmoor, after them. Play actually ceased at
a place called Long Lane, near the " Lopping Stones," so
that neither side could claim a victory.

Many of the players were covered with bruises, and one
fellow, going through a hedge, lost his garments and had
to secure the protection of a woman's apron. Yet he continued to play with the apron wrapped around him. The
grandfather of Harry Johnson, Sheffield United's noted
post-war centre-forward, took part in that memorable
match, for Ecclesfield. The old gentleman died in
February, 1926.

In 1878 came football by night. On Monday, Oct. 14th
of that year, a match was played at Bramall Lane with the
aid of electric light. The teams had been selected by the
Sheffield Football Association. There had been plenty of
athletic exhibitions by the light of gas—notably at the
Agricultural Hall, London, but little of the kind had been
attempted in the open-air. The match was announced to
start at 7.30, and considerably before that hour the roads
to Bramall Lane were besieged. One report reads : " There
seemed no end to the ever-coming stream, and the crowd of
excited people outside the gates struggling to pass in at the
turnstiles created a scene of great animation.

" The vast enclosure appeared quite crowded, so large
was the assembly, and there must have been a considerable
number who failed to get a fair view of the play, as it was
quite impossible to see over the heads of the dense masses
of humanity, all craning their necks towards the debatable
territory. At each corner of the ground marked off for the

players a wooden stage was erected some ten yards high for carrying the lamp and reflector.   Behind each goal was placed a portable engine, each of which drove two Siemen's dynamo machines—one for each light.   The illuminating power equalled 8,000 standard candles, and the cost per head for each light was about $3\frac{1}{2}$d.

" At first, the light was too powerful to be looked at in comfort, but Messrs. Taskers soon got it under sway, and at once gave convincing proof of their ability to regulate the illuminator.   The lights were elevated thirty feet high, and they were most brilliant and effective.''

It was duly noted that the distinguishing colours of the two sides were clearly visible, although it was rather difficult to discern the individual movements on the top side of the ground.   The teams " wore blue and red dresses, Mr. J. C. Clegg captaining one team and Mr. W. E. Clegg the other.'' The Blues won by 2—0.

The following players took part :—

Reds: F. Stacey (goal); J. Housley, J. Hunter, E. Buttery, and F. Hinde (backs); J. C. Clegg (captain), W. Mosforth, A. Woodcock, C. Stratford, H. Barber, and G. Anthony (forwards).

Blues: T. Lawson (goal); W. E. Clegg (captain), R. Gregory, T. Buttery, and W. H. Stacey (backs); G. B. Marples, A. Malpas, J. Tomlinson, E. Barber, T. Bishop, and P. Paterson (forwards).

Umpires: W. Skinner and R. W. Dickinson; referee: W. Pierce Dix.

It was estimated the match was watched by 20,000, for large numbers of people scaled the walls, but the turnstiles recorded only 12,000, with receipts of £300.

The novelty matches remind one of the famous Zulu games, which recall that some people, paying no heed to the Lang case, declare that Sheffield's touring Zulus were responsible for the introduction of professionalism into the game of football.   The Sheffield Zulus were a band of very capable footballers, who began operations in November, 1879, and " carried on " until about 1882.   They toured the country and made quite a name for themselves.   They might very well be classed with the old-time clown cricketers, who about the same period were successful entertainers on the cricket grounds. The painted Zulus masqueraded, they rollicked, they were as clowns, but in spite of their whimsical ways, they played excellent football, and the crowds had capital entertainment for their money.

Although they may be declared the progenitors of professionalism, it should be stated that they started upon their career under good auspices. In 1879 the Zulu War was raging, and the British captured the Zulu Chief, Cetewayo, in the month of October. The first match in which the Zulus played was against a Sheffield Players' eleven at Bramall Lane on November 10th, 1879. The proceeds were devoted to the widows and orphans of the soldiers killed in the Zulu War, and the match was under the patronage of the Mayor of Sheffield, members of the Council, and the officers of the local Volunteers. Both teams included some of the very best football talent in the city and district.

At 3 p.m. the Zulus appeared at the Lane, being driven to the ground in half a dozen hansom-cabs. A big crowd of folk awaited them. Their garb was simply perfection, and it was impossible to distinguish any of them at a distance. The dresses were provided by Mr. W. Barkworth, of Marcus Street. They consisted of black jerseys and drawers, decorated with beads, etc., while the arms and waist were covered with tufts of hair. Barkworth himself, who acted as " chieftain," was like the rest, but had more feathers around his head, and was further set off with a necklace of cockle-shells. Shields and assegais were loaned to the men by Mr. J. Greenwell, of H.M.S. Shah, who had brought them from a recent battlefield. There was a good attendance, and amongst the crowd was a member of the gallant 24th, who made such a name for themselves in the defence of Rorke's Drift.

The Zulus won a fine match by 5 goals to 4. The two teams were :—

Zulus: Ulmathoosi (H. Hinchcliffe); Cetewayo (captain, T. Buttery) and Dabulamanzi (J. Hunter), backs; Sirayo (G. Herring), Methlagazulu (A. Malpas); Umcilyn (A. Ramsden), Ngobamabrosi (G. Butcher), Magnenda (S. Earnshaw), Jiggleumbeno (T. Cawley), Muyamani (G. Ainley), and Amatonga (S. Lucas).

Players: W. Turner; A. Woodcock, J. Slack, G. Harris, E. Lawton, G. Anthony, W. Mosforth, C. Elliott, W. Orton, J. Whitham, and W. Lax.

Umpires: E. Bowling and G. Cropper; referee: W. Littlehales.

A fortnight later, the Zulus played at Chesterfield, and there they wore girdles of white hair and white hair around their calves, which formed a pleasing contrast with the mass of duskiness! They toured the town in a wagonette, and attracted a big crowd. At the match itself much amusement was created during the interval by reason of the Zulus displaying a British love for bitter beer, bottled stout and such concoctions known as " fire-water." The game was drawn. Incidentally that famous Jack Hunter (a storm-centre of attacks on professionalism later), and Jimmy Lang figured in the Zulus' team. Lang acted as secretary at one time.

Subsequently, of course, the personnel changed. The Zulus developed the system of charging fees for playing, though it is open to question whether they made any large profits; and the charge of professionalism came. In 1882, the Sheffield Football Association passed a resolution that " in future any player taking part in a Zulu match, or in any way receives remuneration for playing, be debarred from playing in any Association contest or cup-tie." That was virtually the end of the Zulus. But in '79 such a thing as a professional footballer was a topic never talked about or even dreamt of. No doubt the players thought they had as much right to receive payment for playing as pay for work done in the workshops, and the matter received no attention until the troubles in Lancashire developed.

Well, they made a little fame. They played Aston Villa at Perry Bar, and it is reported that they once had a definite proposal to tour Canada, but that never matured. The Zulus were not once beaten, and Tom Cawley affirms that the senior members of the party took care of the younger players in exemplary fashion.

Wednesday provided a novelty also. To wind up the season of 1878-9 the Wednesday executive announced their intention to give four silver watches as first prizes and four gold lockets as second prizes in a competition at Sheaf

House on April 11th and 12th.   The competition was a
series of four a-side matches.   Twelve clubs entered, and
Hallam and Exchange were the finalists.   Hallam won by
3—0.   Their team consisted of those very fine players—Bob
Gregory, Wm. Mosforth, A. Woodcock, and S. Lovell.

Chapter Six.

Warm City Cup battles—First games with Aston Villa, Preston North End, Bolton Wanderers, Queen's Park—Great Developments — Wednesday's heaviest defeat.

IN those days of yore and until 1888, League football was unknown; hence football programmes consisted of matches for the English Cup, friendly games of various standing, ranging from contests between Aston Villa, Wednesday, Blackburn Rovers, Blackburn Olympic, Nottingham Forest, Notts. County, Preston North End, Derby Midland, Darwen, Walsall, Wednesbury Town, and so on to lesser lights. In addition, the Wednesday had Sheffield Challenge Cup-ties, Wharncliffe Charity Cup games, and days set apart for the various inter-association or inter-city matches. For example, in 1883-4 there were outstanding fixtures—Sheffield v. The North, Birmingham, London, Lancashire, Edinburgh, Notts, Glasgow, Berks. and Bucks., Cambridge and Oxford Universities. Sheffield, incidentally, had two Associations, the original Sheffield Association, and a later body styled " Sheffield New Association." Because of differences and alleged unjust treatment there had been a split, and in spite of opposition the New Association gained recognition from the Football Association. That Association, too, engaged in various Inter-Association matches. Eventually the title was altered to " Hallamshire Association." It was not until 1886 that differences were composed. Then the Associations amalgamated and assumed the name of " Sheffield and Hallamshire County Football Association."

The Wednesday in that season had their ground at Roberts' Farm (or Rustlings Farm), near to where now is the bathing dam in Endcliffe Park, though until Olive Grove was secured, the chief matches were played at Sheaf House or Bramall Lane. Two or three teams were run, and it must not be thought that all Wednesday matches drew spectators or that conditions were ideal. Mr. J. C. Clegg has said more than once that he remembers having to strip under a hedge and give a boy a few coppers to guard his clothing, and Mr. Tom Cawley, the veteran who watches Wednesday's progress so keenly still, and who first joined Wednesday in 1876, says he has played in a Wednesday match when there were no spectators at all; indeed, not a soul present to guard clothing or anything else. Members wishing to play had to inform the club honorary secretaries of their desire. The club subscription, by the way, was 4/6, and that gave members the privilege of competing in the annual sports. Without the latter privilege the fee was 2/-. If a man did not pay his " sub." he was put on a " black list," and often games were stopped in order that a player might be asked to show his membership card and receipt.

In the '70's and '80's players could play for any number of clubs, and there was rare fun at times. There was an amusing occurrence in connection with a Sheffield Challenge Cup-tie between Wednesday and Hallam at Bramall Lane on October 11th, 1884. Rumour had been busy with the names of various players, and it was strenuously asserted that Mosforth would play for Hallam against his old club— Wednesday. Rare excitement prevailed before the match, and there were tremendous arguments as to which team Mosforth would assist. William, who always was a bit of a " wag," minded to shoot folly as it flies, presented himself in the colours of Hallam to the admiring gaze of the spectators. Shouts from the Hallam partisans rent the air. But when Mosforth, after a short visit to the dressing-room, emerged in Wednesday colours, the shouting was the other way round.

While Mosforth had had the Hallam colours on, a fervent Wednesdayite had cried to him: " Ten shillings, Billy, and free drinks all the week, if you will only change your singlet!"

The best bit of fun was that one gentleman was so disgusted by Mosforth changing his jersey that he declared it was an " unprincipled piece of trafficking in professionalism on the part of Wednesday." In the game, by the way,

"The Little Wonder," as Mosforth was called, met his match in a fine player named Powell, who performed splendidly, though Wednesday won by 5—1.

Mosforth first came to the front when playing with Sheffield Albion, who had a ground at Heeley Cross Fields, and also for a time at Ecclesfield. He then had as his partner, as afterwards with Wednesday, Herbert Newbould, now the President of the Hallamshire Harriers and vice-president of the Amateur Athletic Association. They played so well together that they were chosen to play for Sheffield in the inter-city contests with Glasgow on more than one occasion. Mr. Albert Dronfield, destined to become a Wednesday director, was the first secretary of Albion, and was succeeded by Mr. W. Pierce Dix. The Cleggs occasionally played for Albion as well as Sheffield Club, and, I believe, Perseverance, for they held that in the interests of the game no particular club should dominate the rest.

It was in September, 1878, that the Earl of Wharncliffe presented his "challenge prize," the "Wharncliffe Charity Cup," and it was Mr. Dix, the hon. secretary of the Sheffield Association, who proposed that the trophy be competed for every year for the benefit of the medical charities. He based his remarks on the custom in favour at Glasgow. The Wednesday and Heeley—once more—met in the first final for that vase, and Wednesday won by 3—2 amid the usual scenes of excitement. Wednesday regained the Sheffield Challenge Cup in 1881, which they also won in 1883-87-88, and the Charity Cup was won in 1882-83-86-88. Since 1888 the Wednesday Reserves have competed for both these trophies, and won the Sheffield Challenge Cup, now an invitation competition, in 1926, by defeating Doncaster Rovers Reserves at Bramall Lane by 4—2. [Meanwhile, let it be noted that in December, 1880, Wednesday played their first tie in the English Cup Competition, and their great fights for the Cup are embraced in a special section of the book.]

The officials of Wednesday when they first won the Wharncliffe Charity Cup were: President, Mr. H. Hawksley; vice-presidents, Messrs. C. Hill and A. Stacey; hon. secretary and treasurer, Mr. W. Littlehales; assistant

hon. secretary, Mr. A. West; committee: Messrs. W. H.
Stacey, H. Ellis, F. Stacey, W. Crofts, Walter Fearne-
hough, F. M. Butler, J. L. Ward, J. Gascoigne, H.
Muscroft, H. Stratford, H. Vessey, J. Holmes, J. Hoyland,
J. Bingley, F. Sheel, W. Fretwell, Whiteley Fearnehough,
and M. Hall.   In five years there were a few changes, for
in 1883 Messrs. W. Fearnehough, W. H. Stacey, and John
Holmes were vice-presidents, Mr. Littlehales had become
hon. treasurer, and Mr. Jas. Hoyland, the one-time
Yorkshire County Cricket Club scorer, the hon. sec., and
Mr. H. Muscroft, his assistant.   Jack Hudson was on the
committee, so were Mosforth, Herbert Newbould, and
Harry Wilkinson.   Headquarters were still at the Adelphi
Hotel, Arundel Street.

On January 3rd, 1880, Wednesday played Vale of Leven
(who had twice won the Scottish Association Cup) at Sheaf
House.   Unfortunately, play had not long been in progress
before W. E. Clegg fell and broke his arm, and it proved
to be the last match in which he played for the old club.   In
these days of talk about substitutes, it is noteworthy that
the visiting team allowed Wednesday to replace W. E. Clegg
with H. M. Moss, and that this is the first actual instance
of substitutes being allowed.   Vale of Leven won by 3—0.

On October 21st, 1880, Wednesday tackled the famous
Queen's Park club at Bramall Lane.   The Scots, who were
dubbed " The Champions of Great Britain," won by 5—0.
From their first match in 1867, the Queen's Park players had
an unbroken series of victories until February 5th, 1876,
when they sustained their first defeat—the Wanderers beat
them at Kennington Oval by 2—0; but perhaps their goal
record was even more wonderful, for the first goal scored
against them was by the Vale of Leven, at Hampden Park,
on January 16th, 1875—their ninth season.

The season of 1880-81 brought difficulties with the
Zulus to the fore.   The Wharncliffe Charity Cup competition went well until the semi-final tie between Heeley and
Wednesday.   That tie was fixed for January 24th, 1881,
and in the ordinary course the winning club would have
had to meet the Exchange in the final.   However, only a
day or so previous to the day fixed for the semi-final, it was
discovered that several players had infringed the rule of

the Association as to players taking part in Zulu matches,
and notice was at once given to both clubs that no member
was to take part in the tie if he had played in a Zulu match.
The result was that Heeley were deprived of two of their
best men and Wednesday of one man. The other club in
the competition, Exchange, also had in their. Cup team
seven men who would have been disqualified by that rule
from playing.

Heeley before the match handed in a protest against the
rule being thus summarily put into operation, and that was
laid before the Cup Committee, but consideration of the
protest was deferred. In the meantime, the whole of the
offending players from all three clubs sent in apologies to
the Committee, which were accepted, and the players were
reinstated. The Committee decided to reinstate Heeley,
who had been beaten by 7—2 when short of Hunter and
Moss, thinking that a fair decision. So Heeley were given
permission to play Exchange, the winners to meet Wednesday in the final. The decision was arrived at for the reason
that if the Exchange had played in the same circumstances
as those in which the Heeley club had to play, they would
have suffered the loss of seven men, whereas Heeley had
only two members so affected. Unfortunately the Exchange
club declined to fall in with the arrangement, and consequently, were ruled out of the competition. Whereupon
Wednesday followed the lead of the Exchange Club and
refused to play Heeley again. The result was that the Cup
was withheld for that season.

At the close of the Heeley-Wednesday tie, a most
regrettable scene took place. Mr. Dix was hooted and
pushed about by the spectators, and in consequence Mr. Dix
resigned his position as hon. secretary to the Association.
All the foregoing reads curiously in these days of rigid
discipline.

Wednesday's Zulu offender was Malpass, and he paid
more than one penalty later, for he was the source of a cup-
tie protest and of protests from Lancashire when the
Sheffield Association had declared that they would not play
matches with the County Palatine if the latter's Association
included " importations " and professional suspects.
Lancashire bowed to the will of Sheffield, but pointed an

accusing finger at Malpass, who, in consequence, lost important honours.

The next season (1881-2) there was more bother in a Wharncliffe Cup-tie, that time between Wednesday and Staveley at Bramall Lane. The teams met on October 22nd, and Staveley took the lead early on. Then Gregory and Bingley made a splendid run, and the latter shot through. Staveley at once disputed the point, which the referee, Mr. W. E. Clegg, had sanctioned. They first appealed for a foul, and when that failed declared the goal was scored from an off-side position. In vain, however. That so upset the Derbyshire men that eight of the players left the field to the accompaniment of groans and hoots from the spectators. During the next month or so Wednesday had three glorious tussles with Heeley in the second round of the Sheffield Challenge Cup. The first match ended with the score 3—3. In the replay, the score was 1—1 (Mosforth playing marvellously well, likewise Harry Winterbottom, then with Heeley). In the third match the teams were level (1—1) a few minutes from time. Then the ball was kicked out, and Tommy Tomlinson, who took the throw-in, dropped the ball right in front of the Wednesday goal. In a fierce scrimmage, the Wednesday backs were forced over the line, and the ball was banged between the posts, and Wednesday thus lost. Those teams later met in an English Cup-tie (as will be told of later), and also in the Wharncliffe Charity Cup final, which Wednesday won by 5—0. The English Cup-tie went Wednesday's way, incidentally. It is easy to imagine what excitement prevailed in the town over those encounters.

Season 1882-3 saw Wednesday win the two Association trophies again, and on October 14th, 1882, they played Aston Villa for the first time. The match, herald of such momentous games of the future, was played at Perry Bar, and Aston Villa won by 6—1. It is also of passing interest to note that in the third round of the Sheffield Challenge Cup, Pyebank played against Wednesday at Bramall Lane, also George Waller, the grand old trainer of Sheffield United, and Billy Betts, a magnificent half-back and captain for Wednesday later. Waller, too, played for Wednesday afterwards. Pyebank had a strong side that year. They reached the final of the Wharncliffe Cup, but Wednesday beat them by 4—o. Frank H. Sugg, the famous cricketer of many counties, played for Pyebank in that tie. Wednesday's success in the Sheffield Challenge Cup was the fourth in seven seasons—a testimony of the club's great strength.

The next season found them playing Redcar in a Sheffield Challenge Cup-tie and winning by 7—1, and the club provided Sheffield with eight players for the match with Berks. and Bucks. Wednesday were also the first to beat Blackburn Rovers that season. George Ulyett, who had received an injury at Deepcar, resolved to retire from football altogether. Though the season opened brightly, Wednesday had setbacks, for they were dismissed early from both the Sheffield and Wharncliffe Cup competitions. Lockwood Bros. and Park Grange beat them. Furthermore, Staveley whacked them in the second round of the English Cup. Those were nasty blows.

Frank Sugg assisted Wednesday that season, and benefit matches came to be recognised as matters of importance. Bob Gregory (Wednesday's captain) had such a match on April 14th, 1883. The teams consisted of " Over 25 years " v. " Under 25 years." The old 'uns won by 4—o. In 1884 Tom Buttery had a benefit when Wednesday played Lockwood Bros. at Bramall Lane and won by 5—2. Jim Smith, destined to become a great goalkeeper for Wednesday, turned out for the club on New Year's Day, 1884. In the second team, no fewer than 73 players took part in 17 games.

In the season 1884-5, the Wednesday held their annual sports on August Bank Holiday, and Preston North End and Bolton Wanderers paid their first visits to Sheffield. Matches were also arranged with Aston Villa, Notts. County, Nottingham Forest, Blackburn Rovers, Blackburn Olympic, etc. The club, too, sought patrons, some of whom were the Earl of Wharncliffe, Mr. C. B. Stuart Wortley, M.P., Sir Frederick Mappin, M.P., Sir Henry Stephenson, Aldermen Hunter and Gainsford.

" Ike " Swallow played for Wednesday, and the first team was generally : J. Smith ; W. Robinson, G. Wortley ; I. Swallow, C. L. Stratford, E. Brayshaw ; W. Bentley, W.

Harrison, T. E. Cawley, H. Winterbottom, and Walpole Hiller.

Bolton Wanderers' first match in Sheffield took place on January 24th, 1885, when they beat Wednesday by 6—2. Preston's first visit to Steelopolis was on Shrove Tuesday, February 17th, the same year, and Wednesday were beaten by 4—0, and lost the return match by 8—1. On April 11th, Arthur Malpass had his benefit at Ecclesall Road—the match with Lockwood Brothers.

Wednesday won the Wharncliffe Charity Cup for the fourth time in 1885-6, and on October 1st met Notts. County at Nottingham. For Notts, who won by 6—1, Cursham, Gunn, and Moore revealed some wonderful shooting. On New Year's Day, 1886, Wednesday beat Tottenham Hotspur at Bramall Lane by 2—1. Not long afterwards, Mr. W. Littlehales, who had been the hon. secretary of the club for some years, died after a severe illness, and was buried at Intake on January 28th.

It was rather curious that the next season, when Mr. Jack Hudson was the hon. secretary of Wednesday, the entry for the English Cup was forwarded too late, so several of Wednesday's players assisted Lockwood Brothers, which club reached the fifth round. However, the Sheffield Challenge Cup was won for the fifth time, though Staveley beat Wednesday in the Wharncliffe Cup final and won the trophy for the first time.

The season had its features in that Teddy Brayshaw kept goal against Tottenham Hotspur at Sheaf House, where Wednesday won by 4—0; and on January 8th the Sheffield team was trounced by Halliwell at Bolton. The score was 16—0, the heaviest defeat on record for Wednesday. Wednesday, however, were a man short throughout the game, and the ground was like a sheet of ice.

Wednesday met Collegiate in the Sheffield Challenge Cup final, which provided one of the best matches of the season. It was only in the last few minutes of the game that Brayshaw, with a grand shot, gave Wednesday the victory by 2—1. The teams were :—

Wednesday: J. Smith; J. Hudson (captain), E. Brayshaw; T. E. B. Wilson, A. Beckett, J. W. Dungworth; J.

Watson, M. Naylor, W. Mosforth, W. Needham, and T. E. Cawley.

Collegiate: W. F. Beardshaw; W. Robinson, L. J. Clegg; H. B. Willey, T. E. Barnes, A. B. Wood; G. A. Parker, D. Davy, G. H. Aizlewood, A. E. Liddell, and W. T. Wright.

Umpires: Messrs. W. E. Clegg and T. Tomlinson. Referee: Mr. J. C. Clegg.

PART II.

Quest of the English Cup.
Chapter Seven.

*Yorkshire Cup-fighting Pioneers—When leather
knobs beat felt—First semi-final campaign—
Missed appeal which probably cost the Cup.*

NO sports trophy in the world possesses the magic
influence of the Football Association Challenge Cup,
popularly known as " The English Cup." The sons
of Great Britain throughout the world and the Dominions
are fascinated by the competition year after year, and the
interest never slackens. The inexpensive silver vase is a
wonderful magnet, and Cup-winners' medals are the
players' most cherished possession, for while a man may
gain international honours and League Championship
awards, the winning of a Football Association Cup medal
rarely comes more than once in a player's career—if at all.

As will have been gleaned from the preceding chapters,
Wednesday soon made a reputation as Cup-fighters. Their
first quest of the English Cup was in 1880, and their
adventures since make a wonderful and thrilling story.
Wednesday were the first of the big clubs of Yorkshire to
make history in the national competition.

Of Yorkshire clubs they were the first which won the
trophy. They have played in 41 Cup campaigns; have been
finalists on three occasions; have carried off the trophy
twice, and have figured in eight semi-final ties. They have
scored 264 goals in 134 games against 158 goals by
opponents. One tie they won by 12—0, another by 12—2;
on six occasions they scored six goals in a tie; five times,
five goals.

Curiously enough, the heaviest reverse they ever
sustained in a Cup engagement was in a Final, at
Kennington Oval, where they were opposed by Blackburn
Rovers, who won by 6—1. That Final was the first in

which a Yorkshire side played.   In 1882, when they reached
the semi-final, it was only the second year in which they
had competed for the Cup.   Their complete record of ties
is :—

Played.	Won.	Lost.	Drawn.	Goals for.	Goals agst.
134 ...	70 ...	41 ...	23 ...	264 ...	158

The first English Cup-tie was against Blackburn Rovers
on December 18th, 1880.   Wednesday had had a " walk-
over " in the first round; thus the game with the Rovers
was a second round encounter.   They were drawn to play
Queen's Park, Glasgow, at Glasgow, in the first round, but
the match was not played for some reason or other.

Queen's Park then comprised, according to the late Mr.
William McGregor, the founder of the Football League,
more really brilliant footballers than any eleven he had ever
seen, except the great Preston North End combination,
which followed a few years later.   They were hailed as
" Champions of Great Britain," and, consequently, were
much in demand.   Wednesday did play them in the October
of that year at Bramall Lane, but it was a " friendly "
engagement, and the visitors won by 5—0.   What would
have occurred in a Cup-tie on the amateurs' own soil?

The Rovers of Blackburn were tackled on a frosty day
at Blackburn.   Indeed, the ground was so icebound that
the home club placed strips of felt on their boots, in order,
as they thought, to maintain better their foothold, while
they were amused at the Wednesday men, who relied upon
leather knobs—probably the equivalent of the modern studs.
But the laugh was with the Wednesday eventually, for the
felt came away from the soles and the knobs prevailed.
Wednesday won by 4-0—a shock to Lancashire folk.   The
late Mr. John Lewis and other Blackburn people had
suspicions about the Wednesday players' boots—they
thought that they had been " doctored " in a way that the
rules did not permit, but they were soon satisfied that the
regulations had been complied with.

Wednesday's team in that historical game was :—

W. H. Stacey; T. and E. Buttery; Hunter, Hudson
and Malpass; Winterbottom, Lang, Gregory, Mosforth and
Newbould.

W. H. Stacey kept goal exceedingly well for Wednesday, and his club's triumph was a sensational one, because the Rovers were one of the leading clubs in the country. Indeed, that season the Rovers had a brilliant record: they lost only five of 41 matches and scored 214 goals against 52. The team included Suter, M'Intyre, and "Black Jimmy" Douglas, the last-named a forward from Renfrew, who had just played for Scotland against Wales, and who, by some strange chance, had settled in Blackburn about the same time.

Wednesday met another Lancashire club in the third round—Turton, at Turton, near Bolton. Wednesday won by 2—0, and the goals were scored by Gregory, a great centre-forward, and Rhodes, another large-hearted, clever player. Arthur Malpass, Gregory and Buttery were three men who shone particularly, and the tie is mentioned because the Turton team included J. J. Bentley, a half-back, who became an outstanding figure in Association football, and who rose to the presidency of the Football League. The late President had an abiding friendship for Wednesday, which he freely showed. Another point worth noting is the constitution of the teams. According to the "Sheffield Telegraph" of that year, Wednesday had three backs, two half-backs, and five forwards, whereas Turton had two backs, two half-backs, and six forwards. The teams were:

Turton.—H. Brown, goal; W. Turner and J. J. Greenhorn, backs; C. Tootil and J. J. Bentley, half-backs; H. Howarth and T. Scowcroft, centre; J. Howarth and J. Hunter, left wing; T. Gorton and T. Wadiker, right wing.

Wednesday.—H. Ledger, goal; A. Malpass, E. Buttery, and J. Hudson, backs; J. Hunter and H. Fletcher, half-backs; J. J. Lang and W. Mosforth, left wing; E. Rhodes and Bingley, right wing; R. Gregory, centre.

Jack Hunter, who was in Wednesday's ranks, played valiant games for Heeley (as already stated); he was a half-back of genius. William Mosforth has declared that Hunter was the best centre half-back he has ever seen, and, of course, he played for England.

Eighteen months after that tie Hunter threw in his lot with Blackburn Olympic. The Olympic officials got him a licensed house in the town, and by so doing secured his services on the football field—faintly veiled professionalism in those days. The Sheffield critics declared that "the Lancashire money-grubbers" had "shamelessly bought him and carried him off bodily." For a couple of years the departure of Hunter was a sore point.

On Saturday, February 7th, 1881, Wednesday and Darwen met in the fourth round of the Cup. The tie was described as the Final of the Northern Section, and Darwen avenged their neighbours the Rovers, for they won by 5—2. Stacey, who was the goalkeeper, was rendered almost blind by falling snowflakes, and nearly every time the ball travelled straight to goal it went through. Wednesday's side was: W. H. Stacey; T. Buttery and A. Malpass; C. L. Stratford, J. Hunter, and E. Buttery; H. Winterbottom, J. J. Lang, right wing; W. Mosforth and H. Newbould, left wing; R. Gregory, centre.

When Wednesday in their second English Cup season reached the semi-final, the campaign was of exceptional interest. The ties had a quaint opening. Wednesday's first round opponents were Providence, a well-known and strong Sheffield club, for whom Alderman J. Benson, J.P., Lord Mayor of Sheffield in 1925-26, used to play. The game took place on Quibell's Field, near Hyde Park, Sheffield, and had been in progress about ten minutes before it was discovered that Providence had been playing twelve men! A further interesting feature was that after Cawley had scored for Wednesday, Anthony delivered a fine shot; one of the Providence backs stopped the ball with his hands, and the referee, Mr. W. E. Clegg, decided that it would have gone through; consequently he awarded a goal to Wednesday, who thus won by 2—0.

That was the season when the Football Association acted on the suggestion of the Birmingham Association to give a referee power to award a goal in cases where, in his opinion, a score had been prevented through the wilful handling by one of the defending side. The power given to the referee was proved to be too great, and at the next annual meeting the law was repealed.

This is particularly interesting in view of occurrences on football fields in recent seasons, when Cup-ties have been won by the offender's side after penalty-kicks have failed to provide goals. Referees of to-day have said that they ought to have power to award goals immediately, as in 1881-2, but the Football Association has remembered what happened in the long ago.

Following a bye in the second round, Wednesday had three fierce games with Staveley. The first was drawn (2—2) at Bramall Lane; the second (at Staveley) produced no goals, even after extra time, so the teams met a third time— on Lockwood's ground, Ecclesall Road, Sheffield, where Wednesday triumphed by 5—1. Rhodes scored four goals, Cawley the other. Next Heeley were accounted for by 3—1, also at Bramall Lane, no easy accomplishment, for Heeley were a powerful brigade and had previously drawn severe games with Wednesday in Sheffield Challenge Cup-ties.

Heeley had A. Mallinson in goal, W. and T. Moss at back, J. Hunter, T. A. Tomlinson (famous for his throws-in), and W. E. Jacques in the middle line, and forwards were Harry Winterbottom, J. Whitham, I. Swallow, R. Marsh, and J. Wild. The Wednesday had Ledger in goal, A. Malpass and E. Buttery backs, J. Stevens, J. Hudson and H. Wilkinson halves, and forwards were Bob Gregory, Mosforth, Tom Cawley, F. West, and E. Rhodes.

An old-world atmosphere is felt in the fifth round bout with Upton Park, whom they defeated by 6—o at Bramall Lane. The clubs tossed for the choice of grounds. As the Southerners had no Saturday or Monday at liberty, it was decided to play the tie on Tuesday, February 7th, 1882, one of the worst days of the week in Sheffield for such a match, because it was market-day in the town and the majority of the inhabitants were more than ordinarily busy. What a true light these few lines throw on the standing of the English Cup competition at the time, and the generous latitude allowed by the Football Association!

About 3,000 people attended the game. Wednesday's backs played powerfully, "Buttery, Hudson and Malpass keeping the forwards fully employed with good returns." The goal-scorers were Cawley (3), Mosforth (2) and Rhodes. The manner in which Mosforth scored one of his goals was superb: he took the ball from one end of the field to the other and put it between the posts. So delighted were the spectators that "The Little Wonder" was carried off the field at the conclusion of play.

The success was an excellent achievement on Wednesday's part, as the Southern team had beaten several good clubs during the season, including Hotspur (by 5—0) in the fourth round. Records recall how Upton Park played with consummate skill and unflagging energy, but could not score. Wednesday excelled in individual brilliancy. Upton Park had not quite the speed of the Sheffielders, but were superior in combination—"the crossing game," as it was then described. The play of the losers made critics declare that "if Wednesday would go in for the crossing game they would be invincible."

One can scarcely imagine a team to-day losing a cup semi-final because of failure to appeal, but Wednesday did so that season. But for such a mistake Wednesday might have brought the Cup to Sheffield fourteen years before they did.

Once more they came up against their old rivals, Blackburn Rovers, and the game, which was played at Huddersfield, resulted in a goalless draw. Huddersfield then was a Rugby stronghold, and the semi-final had been taken there with a view to popularising the Association game. There was no proper Association ground in the town, so the match was played on the Huddersfield Rugby arena. Goalposts were taken from Sheffield and erected for the occasion!

In those days, there were two umpires and a referee. Only in the case of the umpires disagreeing as to the scoring of goals was the referee called upon to give his decision. In the match at Huddersfield the umpires were the late Mr. C. W. Alcock and Mr. Morton. The referee was Major Marindin. Robert Gregory, who was Wednesday's captain, had the reputation of being unusually keen on appealing, but when the ball went through the Rovers' goal, he for once failed to do so.

Mosforth, who played in the match, in his version of the affair has said that on appeal to umpire Alcock, that official signalled off-side. When Wednesday turned to the other umpire he raised his flag. That was taken as being in agreement with Mr. Alcock, and nothing more was done. However, when Mosforth saw Major Marindin in Manchester before the replay the referee said " Well, Mosforth,

you should not be here to-day." "Why?" queried
Mosforth. "Because you won at Huddersfield. That was
a good goal your side scored, and Mr. Morton did not raise
his flag in agreement with the other umpire. Mr. Morton
considered it a goal, and had you appealed to me I would
have awarded it," replied the major. So instead of going
to London to play the Old Etonians in the Final, Wednesday
went to Manchester and were defeated in the replay by 5—1.
Blackburn Rovers were beaten in the Final by 1—0.

Wednesday put up a plucky fight against the Rovers in
the first half of the replay, which had its exciting moments.
For instance, early on a struggle took place on the
Wednesday's goal-line. About half a dozen players fell on
the ball by the side of the upright, and the Rovers' backs
tried to push them bodily through the posts. However, the
ball was eventually got away. The Rovers then claimed a
goal, but the umpires decided otherwise. The Wednesday
took the lead after twenty minutes' play, when Malpass put
in a fine corner-kick, and C. Suter headed the ball between
his own posts. J. Hargreaves equalised five minutes before
the interval, when Ledger dropped the ball. In the second
half, the the Sheffielders did not play nearly so well. Inside
ten minutes Avory had put the Rovers in front, Strachan
got a third goal, and Wednesday fell to pieces. Douglas
and Suter were the other scorers for the winners.. The
teams were :—

Wednesday : Ledger ; E. Buttery, J. Wilkinson ; J. Hudson,
J. Stevens, A. Malpass ; R. Gregory and F. West, right wing ;
J. J. Lang, centre ; T. Cawley and W. Mosforth, left wing.

Blackburn Rovers : Howarth ; McIntyre, Suter ; F. W. Hargreaves, Greenwood ; J. Douglas and Duckworth, right wing ;
Brown and Strachan, centre ; J. Hargreaves and J. Avory, left
wing.

Incidentally, Mosforth played in two international
matches and two semi-final games in ten days : On March
6th, the first semi-final ; against Scotland the following day
at Hampden Park, Glasgow ; against Wales at Wrexham
the Monday after the Scottish match ; and in the semi-final
replay at Whalley Range on Wednesday, March 15th.

Chapter Eight.

*Travels of a cheque—The days of the protestants
—Sheffield " billed " by Sam Widdowson—Notts.
County follow in steps of the Forest — Derby
County meet their match—Iremonger's dismal
experience—The collapse of Peers.*

WEDNESDAY have had some remarkable experiences in the English Cup campaigns. In
December, 1887, they were drawn against the
Crusaders at Leyton. The total gate receipts amounted to
£15. After waiting several months the Sheffield club
received their share of the proceeds, expenses having been
deducted. The share was 8s. 4d. ! A cheque was forwarded
and made payable to " John Hudson, secretary." As the
match had entailed an expenditure of £24 by the Sheffield
club the tie with the Crusaders was not soon forgotten. But
that is not the end of the story.

The cheque was duly endorsed and paid away with others
to a tradesman in Sheffield. Without having been cashed,
it was passed on from hand to hand, and eventually was
sent out of England. After it had travelled thousands of
miles the little cheque eventually reached the bank on which
it was drawn, when the cashier refused to honour it because
it had been wrongly endorsed in the first instance! " John
Hudson " was not deemed sufficient without the word
" secretary."

So the cheque was sent back the circuitous route it first
went, until it again reached the Wednesday committee, and
its re-appearance aroused the utmost curiosity and evoked
peals of laughter. The late Mr. John Holmes, then the
treasurer, always regretted that he did not buy the cheque
and have it framed.

Just before that, Wednesday had had English Cup-ties
with Long Eaton Rangers, and on one occasion the share
of the gate was £4 15s., which was offered to them in
coppers. Naturally, the Wednesday officials declined to be
burdened with over 1,000 coppers, but accepted silver in

their stead. It was on the occasion of that match that the hungry visitors to the little town could not obtain any food at the inns and the supposed places of refreshment. So Carl Hiller, a well-known forward in his day, went on a foraging expedition, and returned with half a stone of that delicate savoury known as black-puddings, which were cooked and devoured as if the players were trappers on the prairie.

The old days certainly had their extraordinary attractions. Cup-tie football was warfare; no quarter was given or asked for, and protests were almost the rule, not the exception. The state of the ground was often a matter for protest. If the spectators encroached on the playing area there was a protest. If the onlookers caused a bother there was a protest. If the goal was not in accordance with the rules and regulations as regarded the size, a protest. Club officials sometimes went out by night to measure grounds. Quite a common plea was that a player on the winning side was ineligible because he had played in a five or six a-side contest during the close season. That kind of objection invariably concerned a Scottish player. Sometimes the club would keep up their sleeve the knowledge that a player or players had so offended against the laws and would only make use of it in the event of defeat. At others, emissaries would be hurriedly despatched to Scotland in order to investigate a rumour that such and such a player had transgressed by having taken part in a merry little five a-side contest. Clubs would make artless inquiries on the off-chance of finding something out.

Many and varied were the grounds for protesting against a result, including protests against the officials' ruling on time played in a tie. Then would come excited comparisons of watches. Win, tie or wrangle was the order and many a time spectators never knew whether a cup-tie was a cup-tie, a decisive match, or whether a protest had been lodged. Nowadays, of course, all is changed. Promiscuous protests were eventually " killed " by the Football Association.

In those days the great point of clubs was to see that their protests were in order before the day of battle. Wednesday did their bit in that direction, but the two Nottingham clubs were never behind in a thing of that sort.

Wednesday's turn came in January, 1883, in the third round. After they had beaten Spilsby at Bramall Lane by 12—2 and Lockwood Brothers by 6—0, they were drawn against Nottingham Forest. Before the tie began at Trent Bridge the Foresters lodged an objection to Arthur Malpass on the ground that he had been paid for playing. Malpass had assisted a team called Sheffield Wanderers in a game at Bolton and had received 30/-. So Malpass was barred, and Bentley took his place. The match then proceeded and the result was 2—2. Gregory and Harrison scored for Wednesday. Widdowson obtained one of the Forest's goals and the second one came from a mêlée after a corner-kick. Each side gained eight corner-kicks, according to a report of the match, in which, by the way, the famous " Billy " Betts played for Wednesday for the first time.

The following week, Nottingham Forest got to work. Sam Widdowson, the captain, visited Sheffield in search of protest evidence. He asked to see Wednesday's minute-book with a view to satisfying his doubts as to the bona-fide membership of certain of the players. He was not satisfied, though the books revealed no wrong. Sheffield street hoardings were then plastered with placards announcing that the Forest would pay a reward of £20 for the evidence that the players to whom they objected were not members of Wednesday club. However, the men of Sheffield were not communicative and they would not be bribed.

Therefore, on the Saturday following the replay took place at Bramall Lane. Yet was the protest there all right and all in order. It was a rainy day, and Sam declared the ground was not fit to play upon; consequently the tie took place under protest. Wednesday won by 3—2; their goals were scored by Harrison. " Mosforth, by one of the most marvellous screws ever witnessed, brought the ball fair in the mouth of the goal " for Harrison to get his second goal, reads a record of the match.

Strange to say, the Forest did not pursue the ground protest further. They went back on the old tack and objected to several of the Wednesday players. The London Committee of the Football Association dismissed the objection and censured the Forest, who argued that the Wednesday books produced in London were not the same as those that Widdowson had seen in Sheffield.   The books, however, were ruled to be in perfect order.   In a letter afterwards, Sam Widdowson, who was captain of the Forest, wrote : " It is true that the F.A. committee passed a vote of disapprobation, but it was on account of the bills posted in Sheffield, not because of a frivolous protest.   I might add that I had not authority from the Forest committee to offer any reward, and I had not consulted any committee man on the subject.   I am solely responsible for the bills being printed and posted, and I do not regret the steps I took."

Notts. County afterwards offended Sheffielders.   Notts. were Wednesday's opponents in the next—the fourth— round.   It was not a case of a protest, but a matter of procedure.   A   " Sheffield   Telegraph "   scribe   wrote : " Sheffield Wednesday have been served another scurvy trick at the hands of Nottingham players.   The unpleasant squabbling and frivolous objection raised by Nottingham Forest over their defeat by Wednesday has been followed by Notts. County getting on their legs and laying out all sorts of obstacles.   The tie had been arranged for Shrove Tuesday at Bramall Lane, and all Sheffield was agog at the prospect   of   a   great   encounter   between   these   clubs. Wednesday did the thing handsomely and went to much expense in the way of advertising.   On Monday, Wednesday received a curt telegram from Notts. declining to play the tie on Tuesday because they could not raise their team.   The drollest part of the thing is this, that Notts., though unable to send a team to play Wednesday, could yet send an eleven strong enough to beat Sheffield Club by 8—2 the same day. This is something more than odd ; it is an impertinent blunder.   Meanwhile, it is arranged for the tie to be played next Monday.   The hope of every honest footballer is that Notts. will receive such a dressing-down as will adequately atone for the indignities heaped on Wednesday."

However, Notts. were too good for Wednesday.   The County won by 4—1.   The conditions were abnormal, for rain fell for hours prior to the tie.   During the forenoon, it came down in torrents and a terrific wind prevailed.   Old footballers declared the game could not be played, but the F.A. had already granted the clubs an extension of date and the last day had arrived, so the clubs had no alternative but to play. The ground was in a shocking condition, and the appearance of the players at the end was deplorable.

In what is known as the long bar in the tavern at Lord's cricket ground there used to hang, if not now, an old portrait of the Notts. County team which played in that memorable tie. The team was: H. Gillatt, goal; A. T. Dobson, H. Moore, E. H. Greenhalgh, S. Macrae, C. F. Dobson, William Gunn, H. Chapman, A. W. Cursham, H. A. Cursham, and S. Smith. Those fellows were magnificent in the way they rose superior to the conditions. Stuart Macrae, the centre half-back, was a hero in his defiance of the water, the mud and the whole Wednesday eleven.   Most of the Notts. goals were scored almost directly from William Gunn's throws-in. Men could then throw in with a run. Some of Gunn's throws-in from the centre touch-flag were of far more assistance to his side than a corner-kick.

Notts. County in 1883 were quite good enough to have won the Cup in a year which was not notable for teams of exceptional ability; but in that season Blackburn Olympic, a really grand team, made history by taking the trophy into the provinces for the first time.

Great feeling existed at the time and things were not made pleasanter when Notts. had four men selected to play for England against Scotland at Bramall Lane that year, while not a single Sheffield man was honoured.   Sheffield felt that Jack Hunter and William Mosforth were too good to have been left out, and the match was rather boycotted in consequence.   However, the international encounter was the finest game ever seen in Sheffield up to that time.

The Wednesday had a bye in the English Cup competition in the first round in the season 1883-4, and were drawn against Staveley (at home) in the second round.   Great rivalry existed between the clubs, and as neither would agree to the other's nomination of a referee, the late Mr. C. W. Alcock, the then hon. secretary of the Football Association, travelled from London and himself took charge of the tie. Wednesday, though superior, were beaten by 3—1.   Daff James gave a marvellous display for Staveley.   During the last ten minutes James played Wednesday "on his own,"

and the feeling among the crowd and the players became
such that it was just as well that Mr. Alcock was in charge.

The next batch of protests came in 1890, when Wednesday and Notts. County were in opposition in the third
round.   Prior to that Wednesday had defeated London
Swifts at Olive Grove by 6—1, in spite of a display of goalkeeping by H. A. Swepstone which, perhaps, has never
been surpassed ; and in the second round had disposed of the
red-jerseyed men of Accrington (then a prominent League
club), also at Olive Grove. So all was quite ready for the visit
of the Notts. " Lambs " (as they were then nicknamed) on
February 15th, 1890.   However, once again the weather was
" disposed " to interfere, and after Wednesday had rolled
the Notts. men through a dreadful quagmire for ninety
minutes and piled up five goals to none, the " Lambs "
protested against the conditions and obtained a replay.   It
was an exciting business.

The second match ended in defeat for Wednesday by the
odd goal of five—a narrow margin for the County, but quite
sufficient had not Wednesday had a trump card up their
sleeve.   A protest followed—not on the state of the ground,
but on the plea that Notts. had played ineligible men. One
was David Calderhead, the present manager of Chelsea.
He and the Oswalds had played in five-a-side competitions
in Scotland.   Notts. had not a leg to stand on when they
were protested against, and the F.A. ordered the match to
be replayed at Derby on the old Racecourse ground.   That
last fight ended in a victory for the Sheffield team by 2—1.
Jim Smith, Wednesday's goalkeeper, played " the game of
his life," and saved the situation at a critical period.

Wednesday officials had proved themselves equal with
Notts. in the art of protesting, and ultimately saw their team
in the Final for the first time. Of this more anon.

A lapse of three years and more protests after thrilling
play. In the season 1892-3, Wednesday were drawn to
play Derby County at Olive Grove in the first round, and the
tie caused trouble and tremendous excitement. The first
game looked like ending in a certain victory for Derby
County, for with only two or three minutes to go, they were
leading by 2—0 Thousands of people were leaving the
ground convinced that the game was over. One, however,

George Ulyett, remained staunch.   Said he: " I'll goa when
it's ower."   Then Fred Spiksley scored a goal and almost
immediately after scored a second.   He thus made the
scores level, and the spectators were well-nigh frantic, as
there was a chance of an apparently certain defeat being
turned into a wonderful victory.   Extra time was played in
the first matches in those days, not only in replays, and
that additional period was entered upon.   People streamed
back to the ground; many of them could not believe the
news, but returned to " see the fun."   The first quarter of
an hour of extra time was blank, but about seven minutes
before the end, Spiksley scored a third goal.   So the
Wednesday won a memorable match.

Then the protestants appeared on the scene.   An objection was lodged on the ground that Alec Brady, Spiksley's
famous partner, was ineligible.   Brady was suspended; the
game was replayed at Derby, and the County won by 1—0.
Spiksley says that the replay was a most unpleasant affair
for himself, for Hickinbottom had been instructed to look
after him, and he had some rare buffetings.

However, the tie was not yet ended.   The reverse set
Wednesday on the warpath in the protest department, and
they discovered that a young player named " Steve "
Bloomer had taken part in an unauthorised competition.   The
protest was in order; Bloomer was rendered ineligible, and
a third time the teams had to meet—at Olive Grove.   The
Wednesday won the second replay by 4—2.   John and
Archie Goodall, two of the original " Old Invincibles " of
Preston North End, were members of the Derby County
eleven.   A third protest was made.   Derby County objected
to Allan, Wednesday's goalkeeper.   But despite that,
Wednesday played their third-round tie with Burnley, whom
they defeated by 1—0 at Olive Grove two days later, and
subsequently the protest was over-ruled.

Allan, incidentally, was the goalkeeper for whom
Wednesday had no boots big enough.   Before he could
play for them a cobbler in the town had to sit up all night
and make him a special pair.   Wednesday may still have
a pair as souvenirs in the office.

The particular series of protests just recorded led to the
Football Association bringing into operation the rule which

instructs clubs to send to the opposing club so many days before a tie is played the list of players from which a team will be selected.

Another thrilling Cup-tie occurred the following season, when Wednesday overcame Aston Villa in the third round at Olive Grove. Three minutes were left for play, with the Villa leading by 2—1. Once again Spiksley equalised, and extra time was necessary. Harry Woolhouse scored a winning goal for the "Blades" five minutes from time, after brilliant play by Spiksley. Aston Villa protested against the result; the legitimacy of the winning goal was disputed; the Villa claimed that the ball had been "fouled." Even in those days, however, the referee's ruling was accepted as final; protests on any point of fact connected with the play were not entertained; so what was a frivolous protest was dismissed.

Twenty years after there were further appeals to Cæsar. In the first-round tie between Wednesday and Notts. County at Hillsborough in 1914, Wednesday beat their famous opponents by 3—2, and there was bother over the winning goal. Perhaps it was justified. Certainly that goal was the most important incident in the game, important because it gave Wednesday the right to remain in the competition, threw Notts. out,, and converted a brilliantly-fought cup-tie into an uninteresting scramble, which most people were glad to be finished with.

The game had just been re-started after the interval; the score was 2—2. Wednesday advanced on the right; L. Burkinshaw centred, and Tom Brittleton got the ball; a corner was well won, and from the flag-kick the ball was dropped into the goal-mouth. Miller, with his head, turned it towards the corner of the goal; Albert Iremonger, using all his 77 inches, flung himself at the ball, and opponents were soon on him; the spectators lost sight of the ball and the goalkeeper; all they could see was a heaving mass of blue and white shirts and the referee standing with his gaze attracted towards the middle of the struggle. Suddenly, the referee shot his hand up in the air and blew his whistle. Most onlookers expected that a foul had been committed— dangerous play—and that Notts. were being given a free-kick; but to their amazement they saw the Wednesday players dashing towards the centre of the field congratulating each other as they ran. A goal had been awarded; how the Sheffield section of the crowd cheered! Meanwhile, Iremonger, still grasping the ball, had been raised to his feet by his backs, and for a moment he stood in the middle of the goal like a man in a trance. Then he dropped, and after a little delay he was carried to the dressing-room, where for some time he lay unconscious, suffering from concussion.

The following Monday, Notts. sent a protest by telegram to the F.A. and declared that the third goal to Wednesday was not a legitimate one, that Iremonger when he fell was kicked several times on the head in the scrimmage, and that the ball had not been over the line. However, the protest was in vain. Wednesday never had any fear, for, as Mr. A. J. Dickinson put it, "they relied on the rule-book."

The next tie produced a protest, too, for after Wednesday had drawn (1—1) at Wolverhampton, the replay took place at Hillsborough on February 4th, 1914. That was the day when the wall collapsed twelve minutes from the end, and when the casualties numbered about 80 injured. The match was finished, but the Wanderers protested. They pleaded that their goalkeeper, Peers, was incapable of playing on after having seen the injured people in his dressing-room, and that the referee had played five minutes short of the regulation time. The protest went the way of the other. Wednesday won by 1—0.

Chapter Nine.

Grave Crisis—Adoption of Professionalism—The move to Olive Grove—Amazing experience of Mr. J. C. Clegg—" The Invincibles " and small-pox scare.

D ARK days have Wednesday experienced just as those of glorious light, and the club, severed from the cricket club in 1883, then began to undergo trials. The professionalism rampant in Lancashire caused unrest. Tom Buttery went to play for Preston North End, Hunter went from Heeley to Blackburn, other men left for towns where football was more profitable. Wednesday frequently travelled to Lancashire to play, and their men had to listen to alluring tales from Scots and others, who told them, in short, what fools they were. As fortune would have it, the club had unequal times on the field.

A crisis was approaching swiftly, when, in 1886, the club sent in its entry for the English Cup tournament too late. Lockwood Bros. had entered, and Wednesday players, Jack Hudson, Tom Cawley, Harry Winterbottom, Ted Brayshaw and William Mosforth, assisted them. The works club was so successful that the team reached the fourth round. They defeated Long Eaton Rangers by 2—0, then Cleethorpes at Cleethorpes by 4—1, Nottingham Forest at Bramall Lane by 2—1. The next round saw the " Factory Lads " oppose West Bromwich Albion at Bramall Lane. Having played the allotted time, during which period neither side had scored, it was agreed to play an extra half-hour, and the Albion scored the only goal of the match. Afterwards, Lockwood Bros. lodged a protest against the referee's decision, claiming that a shot by Cawley had gone between the posts when a goal was disallowed. The objection was sustained, and the teams met again at Derby—the " Throstles " would not agree to play at Bramall Lane. At Derby, the Albion won by 2—1. Soon afterwards, Ted Brayshaw was selected to play at Bramall Lane against

Ireland, and he acquitted himself well. England won by
7—0.

The foregoing is given because the performances
inspired ambitions in the minds of the players. The banding
together of good players in one team had carried Lockwood
Bros. to the fourth round, and it was believed that if the
cleverest players in Sheffield could be drawn together a
team capable of challenging any combination in the country
could be built up. Professionalism had come to stay, but
Wednesday were against it, and the outcome was that a
team known as Sheffield Rovers was formed. That team
had the opportunity of playing a match against Eckington,
and one with another club before the season concluded, and
those matches made them eligible to enter for the English
Cup the following season. The application was sent in, and
Mr. C. W. Alcock, then the secretary of the Football
Association, accepted the entry. Wednesday were sorely
troubled.

Those footballers and interested folk who had founded
the Sheffield Rovers were not keen on embracing professionalism, yet they held the view that if players desired
pay to help meet expenses they should have it.

Tom Cawley is one of the men who saved Wednesday
from disaster—possibly from extinction—in 1886-7. He
has recalled in conversation the important meeting of the
party forming Sheffield Rovers held at the Brunswick Hotel,
Haymarket, Sheffield. The assembly included Mr. Jack
Harvey, then the secretary of Sheffield Association, Sam
Hetherington, Harry Winterbottom, William Mosforth,
Jack Hudson, Albert Chapman, Albert Marples, Tom Cawley
and G. Cropper. Before the critical motion was put, Cawley
said that he thought that the Wednesday club ought to
have the option of saying " Yes " or " No " on the subject
of payments referred to. As the majority of those present
were members of the Wednesday club, he proposed that
they sign a requisition for a general meeting of Wednesday
to explain the exact situation. That resolution was accepted
and Wednesday held a meeting at the Garrick Hotel in
Sycamore Street.

A great discussion took place, and pungent comments
were made on professionalism. It was pointed out, how-

VIEW OF THE OLD OLIVE GROVE GROUND.

ever, that the Rovers would " carry on " if the conditions were not accepted, and that would have meant all the best players throwing in their lot with the Rovers. Obviously, that would have broken the backs of the clubs of any standing, even Wednesday's. So Wednesday capitulated, and the wages of 5/- for a home match and 7/6 for away games were agreed upon. Those amounts really only compensated for loss of wages in the workshops when absent playing football and for expenses in the matter of refreshments. The players found their outfits, save jerseys, while the committee generally subscribed for new boots needed. The jerseys, by the way, were then in blue and white quarters (like Blackburn Rovers'), not the present stripes. What a contrast with the fees present-day players may receive!—£6 a week in the summer and £8 a week in the winter, plus £2 when the team wins, and all expenses paid.

That meeting at the Garrick proved a turning-point in the history of the Wednesday club. Professionalism adopted, important steps had to be taken, especially as the Bramall Lane authorities did not look very favourably on football. The latter thought more agreeably of cricket, and stiff conditions were imposed on the football clubs which played outstanding games there, if permitted. As an example, one may quote the case of the Cup-tie with Notts. County in the '82-83 season. For every sixpence taken at the gates, Notts. County took 3d. as their right, the Bramall Lane authorities 2d., Wednesday having to be content with the remaining penny. Professionalism made it necessary to obtain a ground where results financially would be more beneficial. So Wednesday secured a field (through which a stream and a footpath ran) off Queen's Road. It was obtained on a seven years' lease from the Duke of Norfolk. The path was diverted, the brook covered over, the field enclosed and drained, and the pretty name of Olive Grove bestowed upon it.

The Olive Grove enterprise probably cost Wednesday £5,000, the ground proved so difficult to drain. Prominent in shouldering the burden were Messrs. Walter Fearnehough (whose son is a director at the present time), Alfred Holmes, Arthur Nixon, John Holmes, Herbert Nixon

THE ROMANCE OF THE WEDNESDAY. 77

and A. J. Dickinson, all of whom, except Mr. Dickinson, have " crossed the bar."

The new ground was opened on Monday, Sept. 12th, 1887, with a match against Blackburn Rovers, and nearly up to the time of the kick-off it was doubtful if the modest guarantee of £10 would be realised; but it was. It was not exactly an ideal enclosure, with its undulating surface and no covered accommodation except a small shed along the railway side. The men who represented Wednesday on that notable occasion were:—J. Smith; F. Thompson and J. Hudson (captain); E. Brayshaw, W. Betts, and A. Beckett; H. Winterbottom, G. Waller, T. E. B. Wilson, T. Cawley and W. Mosforth.

Blackburn Rovers were represented by: H. Arthur; A. Chadwick and J. Beverley; J. Hayes, J. Hunter (formerly of Heeley), and J. H. Forrest; J. Douglas, N. Walton, J. Berisford, R. Rushton, and L. H. Heyes. The umpires were Messrs. H. Muscroft and T. B. Mitchell; the referee, Mr. J. C. Clegg.

All Wednesday's players had not turned professionals—Talbot Wilson and Fred Thompson continued to play as amateurs. In that first game the Rovers, at one time, led by 4—1, but Wednesday rallied and the match ended four goals each. Afterwards the teams dined together at the old George Hotel in High Street, which occupied the site of the present Bodega, and many good wishes were offered by the Rovers for the success of the new venture of their old friends The wishes were realised. That season Wednesday played 45 matches, won 32, lost 7, drew 6, and scored 158 goals to 62. They reached the sixth round of the English Cup, and were then beaten by Preston North End, the " Invincibles."

Thus had been made evident the influence of the English Cup competition in Wednesday's career.

Having conquered Belper and Long Eaton Rangers, Wednesday also triumphed over the Crusaders at Leyton, and thus earned the right to play old rivals, Nottingham Forest, in the fifth round in 1888. It was an exciting match on the old Gregory ground, Lenton, Nottingham, which Wednesday won by 4—2. William Ingram obtained three of the goals, two of them with beautiful long shots.

Tinsley Lindley (now a well-known barrister), then holder of a bundle of international caps and England's prized centre-forward, led the Forest's attack, yet it counted for little, even though he scored a fine goal after two minutes' play. Betts had the centre-forward completely under his thumb, and the great work of Ingram at inside-right, and his partner, Harry Winterbottom, was an equally outstanding feature. Wednesday's backs, E. Brayshaw and Fred Thompson, also were brilliant. Brayshaw, by the way, wore his international cap on the field, a point which is of interest to modern followers of football.

The Sheffielders were next drawn against Preston North End—a mighty side—and one may be pardoned on referring to a remarkable experience of Mr. J. C. Clegg in connection with that team and Aston Villa. On the day that Wednesday had met Nottingham Forest, the North End were in opposition to Aston Villa at Perry Barr. The tie was an amazing fiasco. Both teams were in magnificent form at the time. The Aston Villa team at the period was a most brilliant one, with Archie Hunter the captain. They had played 29 matches, lost only one, and had scored 168 goals against 23. Preston North End had a reputation quite unique. They had played 24 matches, won them all, and obtained 189 goals to their opponents' 27.

The Villa had a well-appointed ground, as football enclosures then went, and every effort was made to cope with an abnormal rush of spectators. As much as ten shillings was charged for some of the seats; such a price was unheard of in connection with football of that day. The Villa really thought that they had made adequate arrangements, but the match stirred the pulse of the Midlands, and, indeed, the football public generally, as no game had ever quickened it before. The prospect of witnessing the two greatest teams of the year compelled everyone's attendance. It is computed that 27,000 people were present, and the receipts were £1,100, the greatest sum taken at a football match in the country up to that year. Whatever the number of people, not more than half of them saw the play. The stands were soon crowded, and brakes, waggons, lorries and traps were all utilised as temporary stands. Plenty of folk paid up to half-a-crown for the privilege of standing on a lorry to get a reasonably good view of the match. But the pressure from the rear occasioned by those who could not get a glimpse of the players, and who only knew that the game was going on by the occasional skying of the ball, became too great, and the onlookers were soon swarming over the touchline. The game had to be repeatedly stopped before it was finished. North End, who scored three goals against one, were the cleverer team, yet grievous dissatisfaction was caused.

When the first stoppage occurred the Villa were leading by 1—0. Nicholas Ross lodged a protest on the grounds that in the circumstances the match would not be a fair test. However, very naturally, Archie Hunter did not acquiesce in the protest. Mr. Clegg, who was the referee, noted the protest, but expressed no opinion on its merits. After the match, it was alleged that the two captains, the umpires and the referee had agreed to let the game proceed as a " friendly " match only.

North End claimed the match, long epistles were written on the subject of protests and the alleged agreement, which North End denied. Major Sudell pleaded North End's right to withdraw their protest, as the home club was responsible for maintaining law and order. Ultimately the Association ruled that Aston Villa were disqualified because they had failed to take adequate means to keep the crowd in order.

Some of the newspapers had startling bills in connection with the event. " The military called out !" was one. When it was seen that the crowd was becoming unmanageable, mounted police were asked for, but they could not be obtained quickly enough. A couple of dragoons who happened to be on the ground were, therefore, placed on horses, and they trotted up and down the touchline near the goal at the Perry Barr end. The animals were not military horses; they were taken from some cabs which were standing on the ground. However, there were mounted soldiers before the gaze of the people, and their presence gave rise to the sensational phrase, " The military called out !"

After all that excitement Preston North End visited Olive Grove to play Wednesday in the first English Cup-tie played there. There was great wrangling about the date of the tie, however, for there had been unfounded, yet alarming, stories of small-pox in Sheffield, and the North End were fearful of spreading the disease in their district. Indeed, a Preston doctor declared that he would pour scorn upon them by means of bills posted all over the town if they played in " the plague spot " !

They came eventually (on January 30th, 1888), William Mosforth's benefit match having to be postponed. Wednesday had made extensive preparations. A stand to accommodate 500 people was erected, the brook was covered over to make room for 1,500 more folk, and on the bridge side of the ground omnibuses, with drags and drays in front, were utilised as stands. Strong wire ropes were placed around the pitch, too.

Unfortunately, snow began to fall before the play began, but 8,000 people paid to see the tie. Ingram scored for Wednesday, but the North End won one of the best matches seen in Sheffield by 3—1. Their scorers were Thomson (2) and Ross. The teams were :—

Wednesday : Smith ; Thompson and Brayshaw ; Dungworth, Betts and Waller ; Winterbottom, Ingram, Hiller, Cawley and Mosforth.

Preston North End : Mills-Roberts ; Howarth and Ross, sen. ; Robertson, Russell, and Graham ; Gordon, Ross, jun., Goodall, Drummond and Thomson.

Chapter Ten.

An impressive record—A friendly snowflake —
Semi-final conquest over Bolton Wanderers—
The Final tie disaster at Kennington Oval.

WEDNESDAY played at Olive Grove for twelve seasons, and during that period contested 23 English Cup-ties on that ground. Only four times were they defeated, namely, by Preston North End in 1888, Notts. County in 1889, West Bromwich Albion in 1891, and Nottingham Forest in 1897. In addition, they made a draw with Stoke, 2—2, and lost the replay by 2—0. The Notts. County game was the subject of a protest, as already indicated. The defeat by the Forest was sustained in the first round of the season following that in which they won the Cup. Wednesday became noted for striking successes in Cup-ties, and their record was ·outstanding. Nothing helped the club more to establish itself on a sound financial basis and gain the enthusiastic support of the Sheffield public so much as the team's ability in that sphere of football activity.

From the opening of Olive Grove to the day they won the trophy nine seasons afterwards, they were always among the last eight clubs in the competition. They won the Cup, were finalists on another occasion, and in other seasons reached the semi-final three times—in successive years, 1894, 1895, and 1896. In 1896 ambitions were realised : Wolverhampton Wanderers were defeated by 2—1 in the Final at Crystal Palace. Thus, Wednesday were the first to have their names inscribed on the new Cup, which had been provided because the original trophy had been stolen from a tobacconist's shop-window in Birmingham, where it was on view while the holders were Aston Villa.

Among their victims were some of the finest teams in the country—Aston Villa, Bolton Wanderers, Woolwich Arsenal, Notts. County, Middlesbrough, Sunderland, Derby County, Everton, Small Heath, West Bromwich Albion and Burnley.

It was a sign of the times when in the Spring of 1888, Wednesday's first professional team had a few days' special training at Brigg for the semi-final tie of the Sheffield Challenge Cup, with Wilf. Muscroft as the trainer.   The spell at Brigg apparently did the players much good, for Wednesday went on and won both the Sheffield and Wharncliffe Cups.   Staveley, Rotherham and Ecclesfield were three of the smartest teams in the district, and Wednesday's superior staying-power proved to be an important factor in their operations against them.

In February, 1889, occurred an adventurous English Cup-tie with the youthful Notts. Rangers, a band of players who had a big share in the football honours of later days. It is not generally known that Notts. Rangers were Sheffield United's first opponents in a club match.   Wednesday's tie with the Rangers was played in a field surrounded by hedges—no other fencing—and probably one-half of the spectators entered without paying.   The spectators were divided from the players by means of a loosely-hung rope, and a consequence was that before the tie was far advanced the touch-line had been well crossed by the crowd.   But that did not appear to worry anybody, for all were willing to make a lane through the ranks for the half-back to throw in the ball from the line!

Wednesday might have joined in the fashionable protest had the game ended as looked probable at one time, but Fred Thompson, a hurricane of wind, and a friendly snow-flake in the eye of George Toone gave Wednesday an equalising goal in the closing minutes.

Fred Geary, afterwards of Everton, and England's centre-forward against Scotland in 1891, was the Rangers' pivot of the front line; the brothers Shelton, who became possessors of no fewer than eight caps between them, were at half-back, and Toone (the father of the half-back who played for Wednesday in the season 1924-25, and who was destined for the Scotland match), stood guard over what was then the unnetted goal.   Toone always vowed that the ball did not pass between the posts on that stormy day.   But then he did not really know for certain, as the snowflake interfered.   However, the four goals that Wednesday got past him at Olive Grove on the following Saturday settled the affair from the Sheffield point of view. Wednesday beat Notts. County by 3—2 in the second round, and fell at Wolverhampton by 3—0 in the third.

The season 1889-90 witnessed the protests by Notts. County, the counter-protests and Wednesday's second appearance in a semi-final. That season Bolton Wanderers made their first effort to secure the elusive trophy, and they were Wednesday's opponents in the semi-final at Perry Barr. Wednesday won by 2—1. It was said in Lancashire that the Wanderers had been beaten by the " Darren " rush and that they spent too much time protesting instead of looking after the play.

A writer, " The Grumbler," of the " Bolton Field," said : " I did not like the look of the Wanderers before the departure from Bolton. They sat in the saloon with faces pale, drawn and anxious. They might have been a Sunday-morning congregation in the Scotch kirk, with the worthy Councillor (Horrocks) as precentor, and where it was an offence to smile and a heinous crime to laugh. This is no exaggerated picture. Then take them a little later on at the luncheon with the Three Thin T's—Tea, Tongue and Toast! At Birmingham, hurried forward to the Colonnade, and thence to bed. Great Scott! They might have been convalescent influenzas. Had the Wanderers met the Wednesday in an ordinary fixture they would have licked their heads off, but because it was a Cup-tie and because they were coddled up into a state of high-sprung nervous-ness, they were beaten."

However, it was a day of rain, sleet and hail, and Bolton Wanderers, though they won the toss, elected to kick against the elements. There was no score at the interval. When they had re-started it was seen that while the Bolton men were still wearing wet and clammy garments, Muscroft had clad Wednesday in fresh, dry shirts. Cassidy gave the Wanderers the lead, but within a few minutes Winterbottom and Mumford secured an equalising goal, and eventually Mumford scored the winning goal.

Thus did the Wednesday reach the Final of the Cup for the first time. Alas! they had a sorry experience. In a very one-sided game at Kennington Oval, they were defeated by 6—1. That disaster was a great shock to Sheffielders, for the Wednesday team of local players, skippered by Hadyn Morley, a Derby amateur, had raised enthusiasm for football in the city to a pitch that it had never reached before.   The men had played excellent, dashing football in order to qualify for the Final.   What could their feelings have been, when, afterwards they read in the papers that the Final tie had been " the worst Final on record!" ?   For all that so glorious a defensive game did Morley play that he was carried off the field shoulder-high, surely an occurrence unique in the history of Cup Finals.

Blackburn Rovers were basking in a blaze of Cup glory at the time.   Three times winners of the great trophy, they included in their ranks seasoned Cup-fighters and several international players.   Only two players, indeed, were unable to claim international honours; even then Horne, the goalkeeper, had twice stood as reserve for England.   The Rovers would have presented a stiff proposition to the strongest eleven in the country, and Wednesday were anything but that.

Wednesday had prepared for the tie at Matlock, but half the side was lame from the effects of a terrific gruelling in an Alliance match against Grimsby Town on the previous Saturday; the other half was low in spirit in consequence. It was in that Alliance match that Ambrose Langley, later to become so doughty a back for Wednesday, made his presence felt in material fashion.   Wednesday won the game, however, and the success virtually gave the " Blades " the Championship of the Alliance.   But at a price!

Harry Winterbottom had a foot injury, and Woolhouse was introduced into the attack at the Oval.   In consequence, a complete alteration of the line had to be made.

Bennett headed Wednesday's goal, and William Townley, of the Rovers, established a record for Cup Finals by scoring three goals.   The teams were :—

Blackburn Rovers: Horne; Forbes and Southworth; Barker, Dewar and Forrest; Lofthouse, Campbell, J. Southworth, Walton and Townley.

Wednesday: Smith: H. Morley and Brayshaw; Dungworth, Betts and Waller; Ingram, Woolhouse, Mumford, Cawley and Bennett (" Micky ").

The umpires were Messrs. R. J. Smith (Derby) and M. P. Betts (Old Harrovians), with Major Marindin, then President of the Football Association, as referee.

Several of the players have passed away, but most of them are still alive and interested in the good old game. George Waller, left-half in that Final, is one of the best of trainers and has had a remarkably successful career with Sheffield United.

Chapter Eleven.

" Play Up, Wednesday Boys!"—Record victory over Halliwell—" Toddles " scores five goals— Spiksley Pluck and Influence — Sensational tie with Aston Villa.

JUST as there are famous marching songs, so are there football chants which are said to inspire teams on whose behalf they have been written. At all events, when Huddersfield Town won the English Cup in 1922 they had a Town Club " anthem," which was presumed to have given them good luck as well as good cheers. Wednesday have one of the oldest football songs in existence, but owing to the passage of years the verses have become strangely mixed, and each old Wednesday stalwart knows but one verse and that different from the one known by his neighbour. In 1924, the " Sports Special " (Sheffield " Green 'Un ") tried to revive the old song and a good deal of interesting correspondence followed.

The origin of the " anthem " was never really proved, though it seems certain that it came into existence between 1890 and 1892. A Worksop contributor declared that it was first sung at the Alexandra pantomime of 1889-90 by Harry Fischer, who took part in the pantomime, but the first notice of the show, which appeared in the " Sheffield Daily Telegraph " of December 26th, mentions many songs, but not that about Wednesday.

Probably the song was introduced during that memorable season dealt with in the preceding chapter, for the association between the two events should have been obvious. The pantomime of that year was full of good songs, and old theatre-goers recall such favourites as " Young Men Taken In and Done For," " The Whistling Wife," " Across the Bridge," " Love's Golden Dream," " See Me Dance the Polka," " Good Old Mother," and " Quite English, you know."

Mr. Albert Wilkinson, the well-known Sheffield steeple-jack, says: " I was at the pantomime when this song was

sung by Teddy Coleman, the Wassby Man. I was quite a
boy at the time, and it would be about 1892. The pantomime was ' Aladdin.' The words were:

> Play Up, Wednesday boys, no matter where'er you go;
> For we wish you all good luck, and we hope you'll win
> the Cup,
> And it's Play Up, Wednesday Boys!"

Mr. G. E. Nicholson, of Ruth Square, Sheffield, has
stated that the correct chorus words were:—

> So Play Up, old Wednesday boys,
> For you'll win whene'er you can,
> And we wish you all good luck;
> For you'll bring us home the Cup,
> So play up, old Wednesday boys.

Mr. Nicholson puts the date as 1890.

Mr. Walter Hutton, of South Street, Sheffield, suggested
that the words were changed every night by the singer, so
that in the course of the week every player was mentioned.
Mr. Hutton's recollection of the song is as follows:—

Verse.

There's a good old Wednesday captain,
Fred Thompson is his name,
And on each side of him are heroes of great fame:
There's Morley, Smith and Dungworth,
There's Betts of great renown,
There's Ingram, Woolhouse and Mumford,
They will never let him down.
For they're good 'uns one and all
No names I need to call.

Chorus.

So play up, my Wednesday boys,
They try to win where'er they can.
By a little bit of luck,
They will bring us home the Cup,
So play up, my Wednesday Boys!

Another old Wednesday follower thinks that the song
was written for a special occasion at Olive Grove, when a
match with Bolton Wanderers had the Royal patronage of

the Duke of Teck. He says that the words were sung to
the tune of "I shall never let our Jane try the parachute
again!" His version of the chorus is:—

> Play up Wednesday, White and Blue,
> I shall always stick to you;
> And when the season's up,
> I hope you'll win the English Cup.
> You're playing up in splendid style;
> At the game you are no strangers.
> Play up, my lads, you're all their dads:
> You're the Duke of Teck's own Rangers!

Mr. H. Glew, of Sharrow Vale, Sheffield, gives the date
of the original song as Christmas, 1891, and the New Year,
1892, and the place Alexandra Theatre. The title of the
pantomime, he says, was "Sinbad the Sailor," and the
most popular song was "The Man who broke the Bank at
Monte Carlo," sung by Mr. Wilfred Shine. Miss Vesta
Victoria was also a character in the same pantomime.

Mr. R. Richford, the veteran conductor of the Danne-
mora Band, up to the end of the season 1924-25, regularly
had the heart-warming chorus, "Play Up, Wednesday
Boys," played at Wednesday's matches at Hillsborough,
but good luck did not attend Wednesday. The extraordinary
thing was that in 1925-26, when a new band appeared at
Hillsborough, the "anthem" was never played and
Wednesday won the championship of the Second Division.
When a blind musician travelled to Derby and played the
melody on a concertina outside the Baseball Ground,
Wednesday were well beaten by 4—1. What fanciful
superstitions there are in connection with football!

It was the season after the disastrous Cup Final of 1890
that Wednesday gained their biggest Cup victory of their
career. They overcame Halliwell by 12—0 at Olive Grove.
Halliwell, it will be remembered, had defeated Wednesday
by 16—0 in 1887 at Halliwell; so that the Lancashire club
had the rare distinction first of having inflicted Wednesday's
heaviest defeat, and four years later provided Wednesday
with their biggest victory! It was by a private arrangement with the Halliwell club that the Cup match took place
at Olive Grove, but there was also a Cup-tie at Bramall

Top Row : W. Muscroft (Trainer), Mr. H. Vessey, T. Brandon, J. Smith, J. Darroch, Mr. John Holmes.
Middle Row : Harry Brandon, A. Mumford, G. Thompson, T. E. Cawley, F. Spiksley.
Bottom Row : D. Gemmell, W. Betts, —. Richardson.

Lane between the newly-formed Sheffield United team and
Notts. County, and that fact kept the attendance down to
about 2,000 people. The Bramall Lane game also resulted
in a high score, as Notts. County defeated the United by
9—1; consequently there was the unparalleled event of 22
goals scored in Sheffield on one day in English Cup-ties in
which the city's two leading teams were concerned.

The Olive Grove ground was covered with snow, but
nothing came of a protest by Halliwell on that account.
Cawley scored within three minutes of the start, R. Brandon
after eight minutes, and at half-time Wednesday were five
goals up. The complete list of goal-scorers was:—

Woolhouse	...	5 goals.	Mumford ...	1 goal.
Cawley	...	2 ,,	Ingram ...	1 ,,
R. Brandon	...	2 ,,	H. Brandon .	1 ,,

Wednesday's team were:—J. Smith; F. Thompson and
E. Bradshaw; H. Brandon, W. Betts, and T. Cawley; H.
Winterbottom, Mumford, R. Brandon, H. Woolhouse and
W. Ingram.

Previous to the event just reviewed, Wednesday had
scored a dozen goals in a Cup-tie against Spilsby, also in a
first round, on November 4th, 1882, at Bramall Lane.
Wednesday played the present formation of team, while
Spilsby played two half-backs and two centres in the
forward line. Wednesday won by 12—2 and it was a
notable success, because Spilsby were then the holders of
the Lincolnshire Association Cup and had been unbeaten;
moreover they had scored 37 goals against only 3.
Newspapers in those old days did not give full details of
scorers. In the first half Malpass, Gregory (2), Anthony
and Cawley scored, but the names of second-half scorers
were not given or noted. Perhaps it was because the play
was so one-sided, for Ledger, Wednesday's goalkeeper,
handled the ball only once after half-time.

In 1891, Wednesday were defeated in the third round
by West Bromwich Albion, though in the second round they
had overcome Derby County by 3—2 in a great game at
Derby. J. Goodall scored both Derby's goals. Wednesday's
scorers were Hodder, H. Brandon and Winterbottom.
Betts played a magnificent game on that occasion, and

Cawley and Winterbottom were sterling forwards. The narrowness of the margin was interesting, for the reason that there had been very heavy scoring in previous ordinary matches. In 1885, Derby beat Wednesday by 8—2, the following year by 7—0, and on Christmas Eve, 1887, the " Blades " had turned the tables by winning 8—0.

It was after the Cup-tie with Derby that Winterbottom had a benefit match. Stoke provided the opposition at Olive Grove. Mr. W. E. Clegg was the referee, and Wednesday won by 4—1. The gate receipts were £79 9s. 2d., but tickets and subscriptions made the total award £142— a sharp contrast with figures which prevail to-day in connection with benefit grants to first-class players.

The 1890-91 season, however, brought numerous difficulties to Wednesday and many criticisms, and it was made prominent because of the acquisition of the wonderful winger, Fred Spiksley.

Spiksley was destined to make great history for Wednesday and even England. The protest matches with Derby County in 1892 revealed his worth, and the second round Cup-tie with Burnley on February 4th, 1892, after the Derby County series of games, proved his pluck. In the course of that Burnley tie, Spiksley was hurt as a result of a charge by Nicol, the Burnley back. He was knocked out and had to go off. There was no score at the interval. Spiksley felt very ill, but Tom Brandon persuaded him to turn out. Says Spiksley: " Tom said to me ' Try and get one goal, and we will keep them out at the other end.' " Spiksley, who must have scored more goals during his career than any other outside-left, scored the goal, and the tie was won by virtue of that success. For weeks, Spiksley had a damaged side and had to report to a doctor every day. Very little sleep he had, too. Still, he never missed a match, for he had been assured that his injury was nothing serious. Eventually the nature of the injury was revealed to him. He had had two ribs broken. Wednesday had continued to play him because of League anxieties and because of his great influence on the team.

The next season, 1893-4, Wednesday again qualified for a semi-final, and Spiksley, selected to play for England against Wales and Scotland, did the " hat trick " in each match. That feat of scoring three goals in successive international matches has never been equalled, and Spiksley is the only man who has done the " hat trick " for England in a match with Scotland.

In the first round Wednesday played Woolwich Arsenal, and in that particular tie Langley fell on top of the ball in the Wednesday goal-mouth—right on the goal-line. He must have thought he was playing Rugby, as he kept his arms round the ball and stuck to it for quite a long time. And on top and about him were Wednesday players and a good half-dozen of the Arsenal fellows.

It was a terrific scramble, but finally he managed to get the ball out of the ruck and it was kicked clear. When he got to his feet he was covered with sand and whitening. But the situation had been saved. Wednesday were very fortunate to have won that day by 2—1, for about three minutes from the end, as the back stumbled across the goal, the ball struck him on the elbow, and it was surprising that the referee did not give a penalty-kick against them.

Wednesday beat Stoke at Olive Grove by 1—0 in the next round, and in the third round played Aston Villa at home. The Villa tie was one of the most exciting Cup-ties seen in the city. There were about 25,000 people present, which was a tremendous " gate " for Olive Grove then, and it was remarkable how the folk got into the ground. Two minutes from time Aston Villa were leading by 2—1, and thousands of people had left the ground, believing that Wednesday would be bound to lose : the match was as good as over.

At that moment Spiksley received the ball, and working his way through the Villa defence, he pushed—he did not shoot—the ball by the side of the Villa goalkeeper, Dunning, equalising the scores. Pandemonium ! It is easy to picture little Spiksley running up to the goalkeeper, who stood 6ft. 2ins., and beating him so gently. The cheers which went up brought those who had left the ground rushing back again, and the excitement was intense. The teams had an extra half-hour to play.

In the second half of the extra time Spiksley worked his way through from the wing, drew out the Villa goal-keeper, and then passed the ball right back into the middle for Woolhouse to shoot into the untenanted goal. It was the winning shot. Langley told Athersmith at the time that they had got them beaten, but Charlie said " Not yet," whereat the answer was: " The Wednesday haven't got enough balls in the club to keep the game going!" The ball was kicked out of the ground over the railway-lines and into the gardens time after time, and four balls were in use altogether! What were the feelings of the Villa men as the ball kept whizzing over into the gardens?

That was a match of many in which Spiksley's value to Wednesday was illustrated. The spectators hung about the ground for a long time afterwards, so great was the excitement and so unexpected was Wednesday's final triumph. The victory took the club into the semi-final, in which Bolton Wanderers were met at Fallowfield.

It is popularly believed that black cats are a sign of good luck, but some of the old Wednesday men are sceptical. For the tie at Fallowfield Wednesday travelled from Manchester to Fallowfield in a drag drawn by four horses, and on the way a black cat ran right in front of the leading pair of horses. Everybody cried: " That's good luck for us to-day!" But they were that afternoon about the unluckiest team that ever played. Fred Spiksley, taking the ball on the run at top speed, scored two magnificent goals, and they were disallowed for off-side. Mr. T. Armitt, of Leek, was the referee, and he, like other referees, did not calculate Fred's speed which carried him into the position to receive the ball. Mr. Armitt had a consultation with the linesmen, but the verdicts were unaltered. Those were not the only strokes of misfortune.

Bentley, the outside-left of the Wanderers, drove in a ball from a free-kick, and in the sunlight, Allan, Wednesday's goalkeeper, missed it, so that the Wanderers led by 1—0 at the interval. Then in the second half the same player sent in a ball which swerved into the goal. Allan, instead of catching it, tried to fist it away, with the result that he sent it into his own net. Woolhouse got a goal for Wednesday before the end, but they were beaten by 2—1, and poor Allan's heart was nearly broken. In the Final, Notts. County beat Bolton Wanderers by 4—1, on Everton's ground.

Chapter Twelve.

*Cup brought to Yorkshire for first time—Onions
and Grand Opera—Partisans—Spiksley's sensational goals—Sheffield excitement.*

FOR the second successive season, Wednesday reached
the semi-final in 1895. In the first round, they
defeated the Cup-holders, Notts. County, by 5—1 at
Olive Grove; in the second, Middlesbrough by 6—1, on the
same ground; and then Everton by 2—0, also in Sheffield.
The triumph over Everton was a magnificent one, for Everton
were a grand side in those days; moreover, for an hour
Wednesday had only ten men. Davis had been badly
injured, and Ferrier was dead lame owing to a kick received
very early in the game. Thus, with nine men virtually,
Wednesday accomplished a great performance.

The semi-final tie with West Bromwich Albion, on the
racecourse at Derby, was a memorable one, and it was
estimated that Wednesday took a crowd of about 8,000
supporters. Many people said at the time that Wednesday
lost because of bad refereeing, as a penalty kick was
awarded to the Albion and against Langley for an alleged
foul on William Bassett, now one of the leading officials of
the Albion club. Langley has said:—

"Most of the old Wednesday supporters will remember
that Bassett was a great thorn in my side and always seemed
to come out on top. In this particular instance, however,
he didn't, and a penalty kick was given against me; I say
for no infringement whatever. In those days the penalty-
line went right across the ground. The ball was close to
the corner flag, when Bassett and I turned sharply to go
for it. Bassett slipped, and in my eagerness to reach the
ball I accidentally trod on his foot. The penalty-kick was
awarded. As soon as the decision had been given Bassett
was so delighted that he jumped about and danced like a
marionette. His recovery was so complete and instan-
taneous that it would have been difficult for him to account
for his previous 'agony.'"

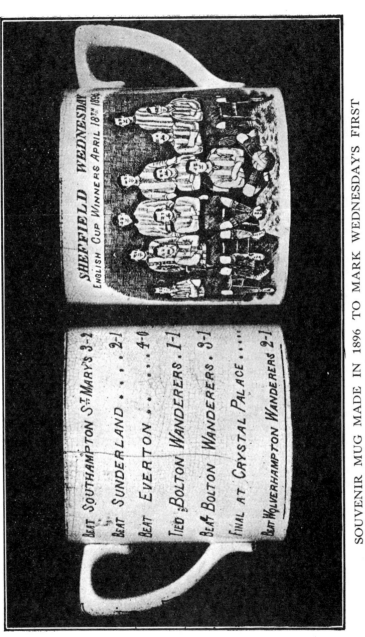

SOUVENIR MUG MADE IN 1896 TO MARK WEDNESDAY'S FIRST
ENGLISH CUP TRIUMPH.

"Williams, the back, scored with the kick, and, no doubt, that goal lost Wednesday the match, for it took the heart out of us. Albion won by 2—0. The business worried me for a long time afterwards. No one knows the feelings of a player after he has been unfortunate enough to be the means of his side being beaten in an important match."

In those days, keenness and enthusiasm were extraordinarily high, and the anxiety for the favourite team to win is as deep-seated to-day as ever it was. There are partisans who will absolutely refuse to drink out of a blue and white mug or a red and white one, and the rival supporters of Wednesday or Sheffield United will argue about results all the week through There are wives who are on tenterhooks the whole of a Saturday afternoon. They stand about trying to learn the results of the matches at the earliest possible moment, and fear destruction of furniture, etc., if the teams their husbands support have gone down!

These extraordinary supporters would be in the seventh heaven of delight if it were possible for them ever to have a short conversation with a Wednesday or a United player— nay, the chance of a handshake!

When Wednesday won the English Cup in 1896, the excitement in Sheffield was tremendous. Great days, indeed, those. A few words about the training preparations, as told by one of the team, will come not amiss. Wednesday always used to train at Olive Grove and Owler Bar, and it was a rare pleasure to them. At the ground in the morning they got all the hard work done, and then took train to Dore and Totley. From there they walked to the "Peacock," where the catering was good. After the mid-day meal they traversed the moors and filled their lungs with grand fresh air. As a rule they got back to the ground at Olive Grove for tea about six o'clock, the food consisting mostly of ox-tail soup and roast chicken.

They were all healthy lads with healthy appetites, and that mid-day meal at the "Peacock" was a mighty business. The party would number about fifteen, and the late and highly-respected "Plumstick" Davis, who acted as honorary trainer to the Wednesday club for many years, always preceded them with the fare, which was: Steak, 14 lbs.; onions, 16 lbs. Cooked, with mashed potatoes, it

was a dinner fit for a king! How they enjoyed it! Never
was there anything left.

When the players got back to the ground they stayed
there most nights until ten o'clock and entertained themselves as best they could. However, to relieve the
monotony, they were occasionally entertained by being taken
to the theatre, on a Friday generally. The Wednesday men
thought that a real luxury at the time, but once they caused
consternation at the theatre. They had been up to the
" Peacock," and had made short work of the steak and
onions. At night they went to see grand opera and sat in
the orchestra stalls amongst the ladies and gentlemen in
evening dress. Phew! All the good people felt like saying
that after the footballers had arrived, for sixteen pounds of
onions would make their presence felt anywhere! In short
the " gas " attack was so severe that instructions were
issued that onions were to be knocked off the diet list the
day a visit to the theatre was intended.

In the early rounds, Southampton St. Mary's were beaten
3—2 at Southampton; Sunderland by 2—1 at Olive Grove,
where also Everton were dismissed by 4—0. The receipts
at the Everton tie were £889 6s. 9d.—a record for the Olive
Grove ground. Wednesday met Bolton Wanderers in the
semifinal at Goodison Park, and the result of the first game
was 1—1. The goals were scored by Brash and Tannahill—
both outside-rights. Wednesday were fortunate to have
the chance of a replay at Nottingham, because Archie
Freebairn missed a glorious opening. The Wanderers' half-
back got right through in front of Massey, but when about
two yards from goal he made a wild kick at the ball, which
struck Massay on the legs and came out into play again.
Wednesday's Cup career ought to have ended then.

However, they had the luck and a replay on the Forest
ground at Nottingham. There was a dispute between the
County and the Forest clubs as to which should house the
game. The Forest, who at that time had no dressing-rooms
on the ground, objected to the County taking the match,
because they had already had a full share of the football
plums, and the County, who required money, rather than
let the match go elsewhere, agreed to the Forest taking it

and sharing the proceeds. The F.A. manage things better
nowadays.

Langley was selected to play in the replay. Just before
the kick-off, Crawshaw went to him and said: " You can
look out to-day, old lad, as Johnny Somerville has told me
they have got a centre-forward who is going to put ' that
big Langley ' fellow through it." That centre-forward was
Vail, who stood 5ft. 10ins. and weighed 13st.   He and
Langley dusted each other's jackets pretty well.

Half-an-hour before the close the Wednesday back came
into collision with him, and was badly lamed; his knee was
so much hurt that it was only with great difficulty that he
was able to go on playing. By the time the game had ended
he had a knee of enormous size.   However, Wednesday
pulled through by 3—1, Spiksley scoring two of the goals.
Thousands of Sheffielders went to Nottingham, and in the
evening they almost took possession of the town.

Really Wednesday were never expected to reach the
Final, for there were clubs considered much stronger and
more likely to be Cup winners than they; moreover, they were
not exceptionally strong in the League.   Still, in the Cup
the Blue and Whites managed to rise to the occasion, and
at Olive Grove they were reckoned invincible in a Cup-tie.
Their opponents in the Final were Wolverhampton Wanderers, at Crystal Palace.

When Wednesday left Sheffield for London, on the Friday
before the match, the constitution of the team to play was not
known. Some of the players were left in a most uncertain
state of mind. It leaked out that Langley would play if
the ground was on the light side; if heavy, Jamieson at half-
back and Brandon in Langley's place.

" I shall never forget that Friday night's experience at
the Queen's Hotel, Upper Norwood," Langley once said.
" Spiksley was my sleeping partner, and he, like me, did not
have more than two hours' sleep the whole of the night.
Coming from the same county as myself, Spiksley was
anxious that I should play. First he would get out of bed
and look out of the window to see what the weather was
like. Then, after he had got back into bed it would not be
long before he would nudge me and say : ' You go and have
a look, Mick, and see if it's fine.'   He used to call me

FIRST CUP WINNERS.

Top Row: Mr. J. Holmes, Crawshaw, Langley, Jamieson, Petrie, Mr. A. J. Dickinson, Mr. A. Nixon.
Middle Row: W. Johnson (Trainer). H. Brandon, Brash, M. J. Earp, Davis, H., Spiksley.
Bottom Row: Brady and Bell.

Note.—Jamieson did not play in Final.

' Mick.' And so it went on through the night. You may
think it ridiculous conduct, but, recollect, a Cup medal was
at stake. The ambition of all players is to get an English
Cup winners' medal—the value is beyond price.

"There were one or two other fellows as restless as I
was—Jamieson, for instance. I believe he played in nearly
all the rounds, and yet, owing to the weather, was denied
his chance of a medal. It was hard luck. I played, as it
happened. I shall always think, however, that, when
possible, players' minds should be set at rest early; it means
a lot."

In the Final all the players rose to the occasion, and it
was really a good Final—one of the best for several years.
Wednesday won by 2—1. Massey, who had caused some
people anxiety as to his goalkeeping, gave one of the best
displays he ever produced for Wednesday. The side had a
good send-off, for Spiksley had put on one of his brilliant
goals within the first minute. That success gave them heart,
as a goal lead in a Final tie is a tremendous advantage.
Black equalised soon afterwards with an overhead kick, but
Fred Spiksley came again and scored a second goal, and the
" Blades " held out, though Massey was plied with innumerable shots in the last few minutes.

Excitement got the better of some of the fellows towards
the end of the game, and Wednesday deteriorated a bit,
having to defend for the last quarter of an hour. Yet they
made two breakaways in that period, and Brady hit the
crossbar.

Spiksley was always doing something; always getting
goals. Consider what he did in the Cup competition that
season. He had a hand in the goals scored at Southampton;
against Sunderland he made the opening for Bell and scored
himself; and against Everton was the chief means of two of
Wednesday's four goals. It was his clever touch-back to
Brash which enabled that player to equalise in the first semi-
final game with Bolton Wanderers, while in the replay he
got two goals, and the goals in the Final. Spiksley is the
only player of a Yorkshire team who has scored two goals
in a Cup Final. What a winger!

The late Lord Kinnaird, then President of the F.A.,
presented the Cup to Jack Earp, and the medals, and those
were great moments.

Discussing the goals against Wolverhampton Wanderers, Fred Spiksley has since said : " I have a very vivid recollection of the Final, not so much because of the keenness of the game, but because of a rather funny incident associated with' it. I happened to score the winning goal, ' hitting ' the ball with such force that it rebounded into the field, while the goalkeeper, a man named Tennant, was still wondering where the shot had gone. Seeing the ball lying in front of him, however, the Wolves' goalkeeper kicked it up the field under the impression that it was still in play. In the excitement—and players do get excited in Cup Finals— Tennant apparently did not notice the subsequent kick-off from the centre, and after the final whistle had been blown said to our captain : ' When do we replay?' ' There's no replay, old man !' our skipper remarked ; ' we won by two goals to one, as you will see when we take the medals !' ' You can't have,' said the astonished goalkeeper, ' for only one shot passed me.' "

Wednesday had a drive on the Sunday and came home on the Monday. All the way from Derby folk lined the sides of the railway to cheer them as they passed.

In Sheffield, the scene was bewildering almost. There were tens of thousands of people to welcome the team, a mass of faces right along from the station to Commercial Street and so on. The streets were packed with excited people, and the players had extreme difficulty in getting on to the coach. There were four horses attached to it, but every two or three yards the crowd stopped progress, and some believed that the team would never be able to get up Commercial Street. What a tumult ! A band attended the home-coming, but the bandsmen became all mixed up with the surging throng—a cornet-player there, a man with a trombone over yonder, and the drummer struggling somewhere else. The route was cut short, and the happy party proceeded to the Royal Hotel (at the corner of Exchange Street and Waingate, but since pulled down). Later, a tour of the town was made and the Empire visited. So ends a great Wednesday chapter.

Wednesday's Cup-winning team were :—

Massey ; Earp and Langley ; Brandon (H.) Crawshaw, and Petrie ; Brash, Brady, Bell, Davis, and Spiksley.

Chapter Thirteen.

*When players did their own washing—Duels with
West Bromwich Albion—Vivian Simpson's great
tie—Some great Wednesday rallies.*

WEDNESDAY had won the English Cup for the
first time, and it had come to the county for the
first time, too. What heroes players are after
a triumph such as that! But only for a while. Players
should thoroughly enjoy always the pleasures of success,
for they do not know how soon they may be down and
practically out. The season following the Cup glories
(1896-7) Wednesday were unluckily beaten by 1—0 at Olive
Grove by Nottingham Forest in the first round; and the
curious thing was that the Forest had not previously won
at Olive Grove, and they had not won a League match away
from their own ground for over two years!

It is rather singular, also, that in the year following that
in which Notts. County had won the Cup, Wednesday had
knocked out the Cup-holders in the first round at Olive
Grove, and now Wednesday were themselves knocked out,
while Cup-holders, by the other Nottingham team on the
same ground. When the Forest were played, Spiksley was
unavailable owing to some injury, and the ground was in
a treacherous state because of frost, thaw and snow—hard
underneath with a layer of half-melted snow and ice on top.

Albert Kaye, a Sheffield native and a splendid centre-
forward, scored the one and winning goal in a celebrated
first-round tie at Sunderland in January, 1898, the year
Sheffield United won the League championship for the first
and last time, and when Sunderland had a great team.
Sunderland, indeed, were then calculated to have the finest
team in the country. In that game Bob Ferrier made his
first appearance as a half-back; he dropped from inside-
right to right-half. It was a gruelling match, fought at
a terrific pace, and there was one amusing incident. A
Wednesday defender raised the ire of the crowd, and one
individual so far forgot himself as to throw his breakfast-

can at the player. A policeman picked it up and stolidly carried that breakfast-can in his hand for the rest of the match! It was the occasion when Langley had to get out of the ground by a back door.

Wednesday had trained at Saltburn for the tie. The late Mr. John Holmes, who was with them, was so extremely anxious that they should win, that he kept producing a piece of rope which he always carried and said. "If you don't win this Cup-tie, John Holmes will be no more, for he will hang himself."

It was all fun, of course, yet a strange spur to use.

At one time at Olive Grove, Wednesday had as trainer W. Johnson, of Stockton, formerly a great sprinter; in fact, it is on record that he once did 130 yards in $12\frac{1}{8}$ secs. with the wind. He was a "character." When the boys used to go out on to the field of play he would murmur: "Go on, my little beauties, you are sure to win." If they didn't win, well, you couldn't see him for "sulphur," as one of the men put it.

Then, the players didn't get massage, etc., as do players of to-day. They had to look after themselves a good deal. They had to wash their shirts and knickers and buy their own stockings. The latter explains why the stockings of the team were sometimes black, sometimes speckled, and so on. The men were to be seen on their knees scrubbing shirts, even at Owlerton. They weren't woollen shirts; they were made of cotton.

If the team had to have luncheon on the train when going to fulfil an away engagement, it consisted of sandwiches and a bottle of ginger-beer. Later, the fare improved. Now, of course, hot lunches are served. Thus you get an idea how expenses of clubs have increased.

After the conquest of Sunderland, Wednesday had to face West Bromwich Albion again, this time at Stoney Lane. In a way history was repeated, and Langley certainly cannot look back on the match with any pleasure. It was Wm. Bassett once more who was partly responsible for his virtually losing that tie for Wednesday. Here was a game which was lost when they looked to be certain winners. It was said in Sheffield that the back had thrown the Cup away.

The ball was kicked out of play, struck the boards
which were on the side of the pitch, and bounded back on
to the field. The player picked it up for the half-back to
take the throw-in. Bassett, however, argued that it was
Albion's throw-in. Langley said it was Wednesday's The
result was that the linesman stepped in and gave the decision
in favour of the Albion. Langley threw the ball sharply
to Bassett, who cried to the linesman, " He's thrown the
ball at me!" The linesman waved his flag and placed the
ball for a free-kick. That was taken like lightning by
the Albion, and the ball was immediately scrambled through
Wednesday's goal. That was how Langley lost the tie
for Wednesday.

He always had the most trouble with Bassett and his
partner, McLeod. Those two men, indeed, formed a
superb wing. Their understanding was so great and they
were so clever that one never knew what they were going
to do. When Bassett got the ball you could never tell
whether he intended to back-heel it to McLeod, who was
ever hanging on ready, or to go on and make a good centre.
He varied his work so much that he was a sore trial to
backs.

By and by, Langley was brought up before the club
directors and severely reprimanded, and he protests it was
poor refereeing that placed him in that embarrassing
position.

If anything out of the ordinary took place, it always
seemed as though Langley was in at it. For some reason
or other a publican once became disgusted with him.
Something the player had done had not suited him, and
he went home in a rage, vowing he would cut the player's
head off! He had at his home a group photograph of
Wednesday. To this he immediately went on his arrival,
took it from its place on the wall, removed the photograph
from the frame, and with great relish cut Langley's head
off. Then he put the picture right, hung it up, and there
stood Langley—beheaded!

In the last season at Olive Grove (1898-9) Wednesday
had sundry misadventures. They passed out in the first
round to Stoke, after drawing 2—2 at Olive Grove. The
following season, the first at Owlerton, saw the great clash

with Sheffield United (dealt with later); then in 1901
Wednesday were beaten in the first round by Bury at
Owlerton.   An odd goal was enough, but it was a tragedy.
Everybody agreed that the Sheffield side were greatly
superior in general work, but Bury had a superb defence
and they got the goal.   What a goal it was! Poor Massey!
Eight minutes after the interval, Bury made a breakaway
through Sagar, who passed the ball to Wood.   The latter
ran on and put in a slow oblique shot, and Massey tamely
allowed the ball to pass between his legs into the net.
Wednesday were prevented from equalising, and Bury had
much to thank Thompson, Darroch, and McEwen for in
the defence.

About that time Wednesday had one of their best
trainers in Paul Frith.   He trained the team that won the
Second Division championship,   the League championship
two years in succession, and also the English Cup (in 1907).
That was a rare record.

Wednesday were not long before they made their
presence felt in the Cup tournaments again.   They had a
magnificent team in the seasons 1902-3 and 1903-4, when
the First Division championship was won twice in
succession, and in 1903-4 they reached the semi-final of the
Cup competition, a feat that they repeated in 1904-5, and
in 1905-6 they reached the fourth round.   The trophy was
won a second time in 1906-7, which was the last occasion
on which the " Blades " prospered so mightily.

In 1903-4 they defeated Plymouth Argyle by 2—0 at
Owlerton after a drawn game (2—2) at Plymouth in the
first round.   They did themselves greater justice in the
second venture, when they routed Manchester United at
Owlerton by 6—0, and it will be remembered because of
the brilliance of Vivian Simpson, who, incidentally, was
killed in action in France in 1918.   Simpson scored three
of the goals in spite of gruelling experiences   As he had
succeeded in the first minute, a Manchester defender who
was absolutely merciless got to work, so the amateur was
badly' knocked about, though never completely knocked out.
In most plucky style   the amateur led attack after attack
against the Mancunians.

In the third round, Wednesday's opponents were
Tottenham Hotspur. At White Hart Lane the result was
1—1, and Wednesday survived the replay by 2—0. That
second encounter, on March 9th, 1904, was one of the finest
matches played at Owlerton. The football was magnificent
from beginning to end, and the right wing, Davis and
Chapman, excelled itself. Those two men scored the goals.
The duel between Tom Crawshaw and Vivian Woodward
was a glorious one.

The match at Tottenham is worth noting because so
many people stayed away in fear. In the previous round,
the 'Spurs had been drawn at home to Aston Villa, and
the match had had to be abandoned owing to the crowd
having broken on to the field.   Early on the game had
resolved itself into a " friendly," and things became worse,
so that the police had to rush on to the playing-piece. The
upshot was that Tottenham Hotspur were fined £350,
which was devoted to charity.

That season, Manchester City had been Wednesday's
greatest rivals for the championship, and though Wednesday thwarted them of League honours, the City beat them
by 3—0 in the semi-final of the Cup at Goodison Park,
Liverpool, where Wednesday played badly.

The " money in the Cup " is often referred to nowadays,
and not without some justification, even though the profits
are not so large as are popularly imagined. On sixpenny
" gates " of yore, clubs did well. At random, one gives
crowds and receipts at Cup-ties which Wednesday played
in 1904-5, when they reached the fourth round. The
figures are interesting :—

	Attend'ce.	Receipts.
At Blackburn v. Blackburn Rovers...	20,723	£511
At Hillsborough v. Portsmouth ...	36,413	£1,238
At Preston v. North End	11,000	£625
At Hillsborough (replay)	24,848	£950
At Manchester v. Newcastle United (semi-final)	40,000	£1,379
Totals ...	132,984	£4,703

One or two points concerning them may be given. The Portsmouth tie provided the greatest "gate" taken on the ground at Owlerton up to that time, and 1,200 people travelled up from the port. The poor figures— comparatively speaking—at Deepdale, Preston, were due to a protest against increased admission fees.

From 1902 to 1908 no team in England could organise and carry out so successfully fighting rallies better than Wednesday. They were the rallying days, indeed. In the first round at Blackburn in 1905 Chapman scored within the first five minutes, but for two-thirds of the game the Rovers were superior. They drew level and would have won but for the superb play of the defence. In the second half, Wednesday did not get to the Rovers' goal more than three times, but one of the three rallies was so strong that Hemmingfield scored the winning goal. It was in that match that Harry Burton was twice kicked. The excite- ment of the game kept him going, but as soon as he reached the dressing-room he collapsed and fainted. Crawshaw, too, was hurt, for he had collided with Slavin and had an eye completely closed.

The match with Portsmouth was very exciting. "Pompey's" defence was remarkably tough, and Harris gave a splendid display in the goal. First, he stopped a penalty-kick taken by Chapman, and when Chapman made a second shot he tipped the ball over the bar. The score was 1—1, Stewart and Cuncliffe respectively having netted the ball, and only two minutes remained for play. The sands of time were fast running out when Davis and Chapman made a great effort, and Davis snatched the victory with a capital goal. After a draw at Preston, Wednesday played superbly against the North End in Sheffield, and famous Peter McBride had a bad day. It was always said of Peter that he never relished the presence of Andrew Wilson; was always nervous when the Scottish centre-forward was anywhere about. In the replay McBride, who had been thoroughly beaten by Wilson at Preston, yielded Wednesday a goal by a faulty save, and then witnessed an extraordinary goal. Indeed, it was a sensational goal! Wilson sent in a terrific shot, the ball struck the cross-bar, bounded yards into the air and fell just in front of the bar; McBride pinned it beneath the bar but could not grip it firmly enough; Stewart rushed it into the net as Andrew hurled his 13 stones of weight into McBride's frame of 14 stones, and Peter floundered humiliatingly in the back of the goal.

Wednesday were next in the semi-final against Newcastle United, who were then regarded as the cleverest team in the whole of the country, and they made great history. They beat Wednesday, and appeared in the Final for the first time.   In seven seasons, by the way, the United played in five Finals, but won the Cup only once (against Barnsley in 1910); in addition they were thrice League Champions. They won the championship for the first time in the particular season under review.

Earlier in the season they had defeated Wednesday by 6—2 in a League match, but in the semi-final, played at Hyde Road, then the ground of Manchester City, Wednesday were admittedly unlucky. Newcastle won by 1—0.   The victors were more fascinating in their style and more polished in their movements; yet Wednesday's ruggedness and battling efforts appealed.   Wednesday displayed thrilling dash and enthusiasm, and the issue was ever in doubt. They made a glorious rally in the second half and in the course of it McCombie palpably handled in order to prevent Wilson getting the ball. A penalty was claimed, but the referee deemed the occurrence an accident, and so Wednesday were defeated.

Howie, who scored Newcastle's goal, played a charming game, as did Gosnell, whose speed was too much for Slavin. Of Newcastle's men Appleyard was the one commoner in a team of "stars."   Davis played brilliantly for Wednesday, together with Crawshaw and Bartlett. However, such was the sterling quality of Newcastle United's defence that Wednesday could never break right through. The teams were :—

Newcastle   United : Lawrence ; McCombie and Carr ; Gardner, Aitken, and McWilliam ; Rutherford, Howie, Appleyard, Veitch and Gosnell.

Wednesday : Lyall ; Slavin and Burton ; Ruddlesdin, Crawshaw and Bartlett; Davis, Hemmingfield, Wilson, Stewart and Simpson (G.).

The season 1905-6 was another excellent one for
Wednesday, although it brought no special distinction.
The team finished third in the First Division and qualified
for the fourth round of the Cup. For that season the
competition proper for the trophy had been enlarged, so
that there were four rounds prior to the semi-finals.
Everton, Wednesday's conquerors, ultimately won the Cup.
The match at Goodison Park was a most thrilling one, and
revealed to the full the grit and the ability of Wednesday to
play an uphill game. Enthusiasm was at fever-heat.
Nearly five thousand supporters went to Liverpool to see
the tie.

A sensational burst by Everton put Wednesday in the
shade immediately, for Everton scored twice within the
first six minutes. H. P. Hardman, the Everton outside-
left, contributed some magnificent football, and the
Wednesday backs could not control him. Soon after the
start he got away and centred beautifully, and Jack Sharp,
the famous Lancashire and England cricketer, and also
one-time international forward, scored. Then Taylor, from
twenty yards out, beat Lyall with a powerful drive—the ball
slipped just the right side of the post. Wednesday had a
chance of wiping out a little of their deficit when R. Balmer
" handled " and a penalty was awarded the Sheffielders.
Davis, however, failed with the kick. Wilson opened
Wednesday's account near the interval, but Everton
added two goals (Bolton and Booth). In the case of
Bolton's effort, the Wednesday men stood still and appealed
for a foul on Layton, and, as often happens, suffered
through their own inattention.

Thus the score at the interval was 4—1 against Wednesday, and defeat stared them in the face. Very clever
football had Everton played, but they fell back before the
terrific assaults of Wednesday in the second half.
Wednesday became almost irresistible. The forwards never
quite reached their best standard, but the halves were
wonderful. Bartlett, indeed, scored a goal which will never
be forgotten by those who saw it. The left half-back alone
eluded four men in a glorious dribble, and the stirring
climax was a clever and successful shot past Scott.
Seldom was Lyall troubled; Wednesday won corner after

corner. Ten minutes from the end Stewart was clearly pushed in the back, and from the penalty-spot Davis registered a third goal, making the scores 4—3. In a tremendously exciting finish Wednesday almost equalised, for a shot from Davis just skimmed over the bar. Thus Everton were lucky.

The match had a lot of "ifs" about it, when summed up. If Wednesday's backs had not opened shakily; if Davis had not failed with the penalty-kick in the first half; if Wednesday's men had not stood still appealing when Bolton scored, and if Lyall had not let the ball from Booth's foot slip out of his hands and over his shoulder into the net, they might have won!

The teams were:—

Everton: Scott; W. and R. Balmer; Booth, Taylor and Makepeace; Sharp, Bolton, Young, Settle and H. P. Hardman.

Wednesday: Lyall; Layton and Burton; Ruddlesdin, Crawshaw and Bartlett; Davis, Chapman, Stewart, Wilson and Simpson.

Chapter Fourteen.

Storming Finishes—English Cup won a second time—Dramatic goals by Wilson—Campaign of thrills.

THE season 1906-7 saw Wednesday's third appearance in the Final tie and their second English Cup triumph. Everton, against whom they had fought the great fight just described, were again their opponents, and on this later occasion Wednesday defeated them by 2—1.

A curious coincidence occurred. When Wednesday won the Cup in 1896 their various opponents were Bolton Wanderers, Everton, Sunderland, Southampton St. Mary's and Wolverhampton Wanderers. In the second Cup-winning campaign all the same clubs were opposed, with the exception of Bolton Wanderers. It was rather extraordinary after a lapse of so many years that the Cup winners' programme was so very similar.

In 1907, Wednesday met Wolverhampton Wanderers, then a Second Division side, in the first round at Hillsboro'. The "Wolves" were not expected to push Wednesday very hard, and the public was apathetic over the tie. In size and bulk, however, the "Wolves" had a pull over their rivals, and they were quicker off the mark than Wednesday. They opened their score with a goal by Pedley, and Wednesday had a slice of luck almost on the interval, when Lyall fell full length and the ball driven hard half-a-dozen times cannoned back from the legs of the other defenders. The whistle blew for half-time just as Lyall was picking himself up and a goal seemed certain.

After the rest period Wolverhampton maintained the pressure with splendidly-combined football, and inside three minutes Wooldridge, one of the cleverest forwards of those times, scored a second goal for them. All seemed over then. Burton, who had been ill, was below par, but Layton and Lyall performed wonders in the defence. The forwards, however, could not get going. Suddenly there

came a change, and Wednesday felt the benefit of their
training at Buxton.   Midway through the half, Wednesday
threw combination to the winds and dropped into the
traditional Cup-fighting style.   Layton, with two goals
already lost, joined the attack, Crawshaw went further
forward, and the whole set of forwards, with Stewart, the
stylist among them, became galvanised and swarmed
around the visitors' goal.   For some time the fort was held ;
the " Wolves " retaliated with swift raids ; then Tummon,
who played many good games for Wednesday, scored with
a shot which had just a little luck about it.   That goal fired
the crowd and the team, and the end was dramatic.

Every shout and every hand was for Wednesday.
Stewart equalised and George Simpson, with one of the
finest shots of the game, gave Wednesday the winning
goal.   There was not much time when all that storming
work was begun by Wednesday's forwards ; there was no
time at all when the crowd had done cheering.   Wednesday, by virtue of their magnificent dash, characteristic of
the team for many years, had prevailed.

Thrills abounded in the next round with Southampton
at The Dell.   Andrew Wilson has since said that
Southampton were a better team by three goals on the day's
play, and they actually led by 1—0 until twenty seconds
from the close of the match.   Then Wednesday got a
corner and in the last ten seconds Wilson equalised.   He
had forced a corner off Clawley, and from the flag-kick
Crawshaw headed the ball down to Wilson, who, with his
back to the goal, hooked it over his shoulder into the net.
The replay at Hillsborough was won comfortably by the
Sheffield team by 3—1 ; the goal-scorers were Wilson (2)
and Stewart.

Wilson's goal at Southampton gave satisfaction.   After
the match a reporter visited the hotel at which Wednesday
were quartered, presented Wilson with a valuable pocket-
knife, and expressed the opinion that he really deserved it.
To this day Wilson does not know who sent him the knife.
Such an exceptionally fine specimen of workmanship is it
that he has never had the heart to use it.   The same season
another beautiful pocket-knife was given to " Andra."
It was handed to him as he left the playing pitch, and folded

around it was a hastily-written note reading: "For the pleasure you have given me in watching you play." Again, Wilson never discovered the identity of the donor.

Wednesday next had to tackle Sunderland at Hillsboro'. They were handicapped because Wilson could not play. He had had a kick over the eye, and the wound had festered. The match was drawn (o—o). The replay was one of the greatest Cup-ties Wednesday have ever taken part in. It was memorable on account of its quality and the accident to Harry Davis, who broke his leg. Davis really never quite got over that injury; he did not recover his old brilliancy, and it was not long before he dropped out of the game.

At Hillsborough, Bradshaw had taken Wilson's place at centre-forward, and for the replay there was talk of Vivian Simpson or Tom Brittleton occupying the position. However, Andrew Wilson took risks; he turned out, and his presence in the side helped the team in a match simply crammed with tense moments.

It was a gruelling struggle, and half-way through the second half Wednesday held a goal lead. Within five minutes from that stage they lost Davis, and for the last seven minutes they had to withstand a hurricane bombardment.

Possibly no match in which Wednesday have played has provided more thrilling incidents than occurred in those last few minutes. A writer after the match referred to the phrase "Curfew shall not ring to-night," and observed that Wednesday must have said to themselves: "Bridgett shall not score to-day!" But Bridgett was in wonderful form at outside-left. He headed advances galore, spun the ball towards Lyall, and scraped the cross-bar with shots, feats which Hogg and McIntosh also performed. Lyall had one of his hottest times, but Wednesday survived.

When the Davis incident occurred, the winger was running at full pace; his feet caught the outstretched boot of McConnell, and there was an ominous sound. The cry for a doctor went up, and Dr. Bishop, of Buxton, went on to the field and attended to the injured player, who was carried off by Layton and Burton.

The goal was scored by G. Simpson.

Wednesday overcame Liverpool by 1—0 at Hillsborough in the fourth round. Liverpool took a lot of beating in those days. Harry Chapman scored the goal, and the crowd was so excited that he was carried off shoulder high. In the semi-final, Wednesday were in opposition to Woolwich Arsenal on the Birmingham club's ground, St. Andrew's, which then had a pronounced crown on it. Arsenal were at that time enjoying one of their best seasons. Wednesday played badly for half-an-hour, but afterwards returned to their highest form.

Andrew Wilson tells a pretty story anent that match. Dr. Bishop, previously mentioned, and his wife were staunch Wednesday supporters, and on one occasion the Wednesday players had presented Mrs. Bishop with an umbrella. She used to take the "gamp" to all Wednesday's matches, and it came to be regarded as a mascot. On the day of the semi-final Mrs. Bishop was late in getting to the ground owing to the train having been delayed, and Wednesday were a goal down. When Mrs. Bishop took her seat on the stand she waved her umbrella, and immediately after-wards Wilson scored. Wednesday did not look back after that goal, and they won by 3—1. One of Wilson's shots struck the cross-bar and the ball flew back towards him. He caught it on the run and slammed it into the net. The ball could not have fallen into a better position, and it travelled into the net at a terrific pace. It only just missed Ashcroft's face, and one of the Arsenal players remarked to Ashcroft: "It's a good job that didn't hit you on the jaw, for it would have taken your head with it!"

There were selectors from Scotland and England at that tie, and they must have been impressed with some of the players, for Stewart was awarded his England cap and Wilson was selected to play for Scotland against England.

Wednesday won the Cup almost sensationally at Crystal Palace. Only a very few minutes remained for play when the ball was suddenly flung towards the corner-flag, with Wilson in pursuit. As the ball approached the touch-line, Wilson was impeded by Jock Taylor, the Everton centre centre half-back. But Taylor was beaten, and Wilson, in a desperate effort, secured the ball almost on the line. Swiftly he put in a great screw shot, without a falter in his

ENGLISH CUP WINNERS, 1907.

Back Row (left to right): Messrs. A. G. W. Dronfield, J. Holmes, A. J. Dickinson, J. C. Clegg, H. Nixon, J. Thackray, — Ellis, T. Lee, W. Turner, W. F. Wardley. *Middle Row*: J. Davis (asst. trainer), H. Newbould, H. Davis, Brittleton, Layton, Lyall, Bartlett, Slavin, Burton, Foxall, P. Frith (trainer). *Front Row*: Bradshaw, Chapman, A. Wilson, T. Crawshaw, Stewart, G. Simpson, and Maxwell.

stride. As the ball went over, George Simpson nodded it into the goal. There were four minutes left for play. So Wednesday won in a finish quite in keeping with their progress to the Palace.

Wednesday had not been regarded as favourites for the Cup. Everybody was then talking of Everton's brilliance, style, polish, shooting ability and superior speed. But there were two essentials in which Wednesday were Everton's equals—in grit and determination. They put every ounce of energy they had into their play, and ran themselves almost to a standstill. Yet there was always that wonderful reserve for a rally. In that Final, Chapman's loose cartilage came out twice; he slipped it back on both occasions without anyone knowing and played on as if nothing had occurred. For well-nigh three years Harry Chapman played football with that weakness threatening to cut short his career, but he never gave in, and every man in Wednesday's team in those days was possessed of the same quality of pluck.

Stewart scored the first point in that Final. There had been a hot assault on the Everton goal, engineered first of all by Chapman and Stewart. Scott fisted the ball out twice, and there was a mix-up. A scramble in the goal-mouth followed. Scott was in it, so were the Everton backs, the brothers Balmer; also Wilson; he crashed into the lot and down the men went. The next thing the ball was in the net, neatly placed there by Stewart's head. The game was twenty minutes old. It was a grim fight afterwards, and at one period Everton nearly overwhelmed Wednesday. Miskicks seemed to have the same effect as missed catches in Test matches, and Everton drew level. Both Layton and Burton missed their kicks when attempting to clear a centre from Hardman, and Sharp trapped the ball skilfully and shot into the corner of the goal with excellent judgment.

Afterwards Lord Alverstone, the Lord Chief Justice, presented the Cup to Tom Crawshaw, and the home-coming on the Monday was an event the nature of which, because of the intense excitement associated with it, is often recollected.

The teams were :—

Wednesday: Lyall; Layton and Burton; Brittleton, Crawshaw and Bartlett; Chapman, Bradshaw, Wilson, Stewart and Simpson (G.).

Everton: Wm. Scott; W. and R. Balmer; Makepeace, Taylor and Abbott; Sharp, Bolton, Young, Settle, and H. P. Hardman.

The attendance at the Palace on the occasion of the Final between Wednesday and Wolverhampton Wanderers in 1896 was 48,836, and the receipts £1,824; in 1907, the respective figures were 84,584 and £4,302.

At Sheffield Town Hall, Wednesday had a civic reception, at which the Cup and the ball were decorated with the colours of the club. Most of the players were good cricketers, and George Robey invited them down to Queen's Club to play his theatrical cricket team, and he also invited them to make their appearance on the stage during his turn at the music-hall. They had a magnificent reception.

Chapter Fifteen.

*" Tummon's   Match "—McConnell's   monkey—
Disastrous   experiences—A   bonus   story—When
the wall fell.*

THAT year, 1907, was the last in which Wednesday
made really notable history in the Cup competition
in the matter of marked successes, though they
achieved prominence of a different kind.   Particulars should
be given first, however, of one more magnificent rally.   It
occurred in " Tummon's match."   In 1909, Wednesday
opposed Portsmouth in the second round on the southern
team's own pitch.   The game was a nerve-racking one for
Wednesday, as they did not equalise until the last minute.
Most folk had thought Wednesday would have a safe
passage to the third round, and the players themselves felt
confident that victory was assured.   They had a shock,
though.   Had it not been for Oliver Tummon's two goals
in the last twelve minutes they would have suffered an
undignified defeat.
    Wednesday did most of the attacking; in fact, they were
superior in nine positions, but nothing went right with their
finishing work.   Portsmouth took the lead in the first half,
and within a couple of minutes after the interval they were
two goals in front, and that quite upset Wednesday's
calculations.   They changed their formation.   Layton was
moved to outside-right to strengthen the attack, and Lloyd
made a fourth half-back, but that did not mend matters, so
back Layton went to the rear division.   Then Wilson was
hurt, and he crossed to the extreme wing and Brittleton
became the centre-forward.   The forward line then was:
Wilson, Chapman, Brittleton, Bradshaw, and Tummon.
Twelve minutes from the end, Wednesday gained a corner.
Lloyd dropped the ball in front of goal; the goal-keeper
should have cleared it, but he did not, and Tummon rushed
in and scored.   It was a pell-mell struggle afterwards and

in the last half-minute Tummon banged the ball into the goal. Wednesday won the replay at Hillsborough easily by 3—o.

Wednesday had known disastrous days in the tournaments, for the year previous they had been ruthlessly beaten by Norwich City on the Norfolk club's ground. The "Canaries" won by 2—o. The narrow ground and the prevailing conditions had as much to do with the reverse as anything, perhaps, though Wednesday's forwards admittedly played badly. They had plenty of chances really, but Stewart, for example, made one or two of the worst "misses" of his career.

It was after the Portsmouth affair that Wednesday sustained probably the severest mishap of their career in the Cup. They were beaten in the third round by Glossop, of all teams—at Hillsborough! The result confounded all. Glossop never had a luckier day, yet their defenders worked like giants and kept Wednesday out when they made sortie after sortie. Perhaps, if Wednesday had remained calm they would have won, but they were so anxious that they made a mess of things.

They were not all fit. Rollinson could not play owing to influenza, Bradshaw had only just recovered from a damaged foot, Weir was feeling the effects of an illness, and "Irish" McConnell had been on the sick-list.

Still, that was no excuse. The story of the penalties is the point of the game, though one ought to lead off with the experience of the mascot. At the Portsmouth cup-tie, a friend who had returned from India gave McConnell a monkey, which was accepted as a mascot. Decorated in the colours of the club, wearing a jacket and carrying a small flag, it was led on to the field immediately prior to the kick-off in the tie with Glossop. The result killed the mascot craze at Hillsborough.

In the first half Grechan was fouled, and from the penalty kick he scored, and Glossop led by that goal at half-time. Afterwards, Bradshaw had virtually dribbled through the defence when he was brought down, and Brittleton was entrusted with the penalty-kick. Realising his great responsibility, Brittleton was particularly anxious to place the ball out of the reach of Butler, but the goalkeeper got

to it and saved, though there was a great scrimmage. Then
Wednesday were awarded a second penalty. That time
Harry Burton was deputed to take the kick. He had a
distressing experience! The ball struck the cross-bar, and
Glossop stemmed the danger. Fury possessed the Wednesday players after that, and they fought hard for an
equalising goal. However, Glossop held on, and Butler,
who afterwards went to Sunderland, wore a big smile when
the whistle blew for time, with Wednesday beaten.

More trouble came in 1910, when Northampton beat
Wednesday in the first round in a replay at Hillsborough by
an odd goal. It was election time, and Sheffield was supposed to be strong in Tories. Northampton was a
stronghold for the Radicals. There were a lot of political
folk present, and Wednesday were much amused in the first
match when a fellow yelled " Free Trade 2, Tariff Reform
0!"

No goals were scored at Northampton. The forwards
were faulty, though Northampton were a good side and
stronger than Wednesday had bargained for. After that
knock-out blow, it was said that entering the Wednesday
office was like entering a duke's house with the duke lying
dead upstairs!

Northampton had bestowed on Wednesday the " Order
of the Boot," and in the following year another Southern
League side whipped Wednesday—Coventry City, at
Hillsborough, by the odd goal of three. That year was the
first when bonus was offered in connection with Cup-ties ($£2$
per man for a win). It was not known what the actual
eleven would be, and about sixteen Wednesday players had
been preparing for the event. During the week the question
arose amongst them as to who should get the bonus money :
Should it go to the men who played or be shared amongst
the sixteen? Ultimately it was decided to " share and share
alike." The only fly in the ointment was—Wednesday did
not win the right to bonus!

In 1912, for the third season in succession, Wednesday
were dismissed in the first round. Middlesbrough
triumphed over them. After a goalless draw at Middlesbro',
the teams met at Hillsborough, and the visitors' defenders
gave one of the finest exhibitions seen on that ground.

When the wall fell at Hillsborough on February 4th, 1914, the day of the Cup Replay with Wolverhampton Wanderers.

"Tim" Williamson, the Tees-side goalkeeper, was magnificent. It was a sensational game, in which Williamson, McLeod and Weir were heroes. Their understanding was extraordinarily good, and they were clever, resolute and fearless. (Williamson was regarded as the greatest goalkeeper of the season.) Middlesbrough won by 2—1.

Brighter days arrived in 1912-13, when Wednesday finished third in the First Division. Grimsby Town were beaten 5—1 in the first round of the Cup; McLean scored four of the goals. Then they drew (1—1) with Chelsea at Stamford Bridge, and won the replay in Sheffield by 6—0. At the latter match the attendance was 37,000; receipts, £1,248. After two minutes McLean scored with a penalty-kick; ten minutes later Kirkman scored the second goal, and Wilson registered the third just before the interval. There was "only one team in it," and Wilson (1) and McLean (2) added the other goals. After those big successes dismay was occasioned when Wednesday failed by 2—1 at Park Avenue, Bradford, in the third round. Bradford was just an ordinary Second Division team, but they rose to the occasion finely.

The following year provided the two "protest" matches, one with Notts. County, the other with Wolverhampton Wanderers, and also supplied Wednesday with a fine centre-half, David Parkes, who, by virtue of his excellent play for Brighton and Hove Albion in the third round at Hillsborough, was almost immediately signed on by Wednesday. The Brighton brigade had been defeated by 3—0, but Aston Villa dismissed Wednesday in the next round, the fourth, by 1—0.

The encounter with Wolverhampton Wanderers at Hillsborough was one of the most remarkable games witnessed. February 4th, 1914, was the disastrous day. Events, though, might have been more serious. That was the day "when the wall fell down." The game was a replay and tremendous interest was shown. The attendance was over 43,000, and the receipts were £1,669. The "popular" admission fee was 6d. then, remember. The number of people present was regarded as phenomenal at the time.

One of the most tragic accidents in football history occurred, though, happily, no deaths resulted. The wall

gave way owing to the pressure of spectators upon it.   In
its fall it carried people with it, throwing them to the ground
on a lower level, and, still worse, fell with smashing force
on to those who were packed below, dealing out broken
bones and injuries withal.   There were twelve minutes left
for play when the accident occurred.   Altogether nearly
eighty people received injuries which were sufficiently
serious to require attention at the medical institutions of the
city, and a number of others sustained minor wounds.

The accident was not only the first of its kind in Sheffield,
but the first recorded in England.   It would not have been
surprising if many people had been killed.   The wall was at the
Penistone Road side of the ground, on the same side as the
old stand.   It was three or four feet above the higher level
of the embankment and about ten feet above the lower, and
had been built in connection with the improvements to the
ground.   It was not buttressed from below, and was about
nine inches thick, twenty yards long, and coated with
cement.

It fell in great heavy masses.   Those spectators on the
top side found themselves precipitated to the lower level,
while those below were plunged into semi-darkness and
overwhelmed by the succession of falls.   All beneath became
confusion.   People were hit on the head, ribs, legs and
various other parts of the body.

Immediately those on the lower side had recovered from
their amazement, there was a wild rush for safety.   People
streamed over the rails adjoining the playing-pitch.   It was
that that gave the other spectators and the players the
intimation that something serious had happened.   It had
not been realised at first, and the game had continued for a
minute while the people were struggling to free themselves
from the weight which pressed upon them.   But then the
spectators ran to the spot, players and medical men, too.
Nurses were quickly available, and all responded to the
demands admirably.   Andrew Wilson, Dr. Bruce Wilson,
Dr. Husband, Dr. Bissett and Nurse Tait, the last-named
the wife of Mr. C. E. R. Watson, did excellent work.
Several ambulances were quickly on the spot under Supt.
Frost, and the injured people were attended to and removed
as quickly as possible.

The game was suspended, of course, but was later completed. It was a heartrending experience for all concerned, and Peers, the Wolves' goalkeeper, was unable to continue to play, so overcome was he by the grim sight.

Wednesday won by a goal scored by Kirkman in the first half. The teams were:—

Wednesday: Davison; Brelsford and Spoors; Brittleton, McSkimming and Campbell; Kirkman, Glennon, McLean, Wilson and Gill.

Wolverhampton Wanderers: Peers; A . Brook and Garretty; Price, Groves and Crabtree; Harrison, Howell, Hughes, Needham and Brookes (S.).

THE ROMANCE OF THE WEDNESDAY.   125

Chapter Sixteen.

*Post-war triumphs and disappointments—Beaten
by North Eastern League team — Tremendous
crowds—The Cup-tie with Barnsley—New
Brighton's shrewd blow.*

THE European War overshadowed the ties of 1915, and 1919-20 saw Wednesday suffer chiefly for loyalty to old players, many of whom had been on active service. The club was relegated to the Second Division, and also had the humiliating experience of failing against a North-Eastern League Club, as Darlington then were, in the first round of the Cup. The first match at The Feethams, postponed from the original date because the ground was flooded by rain, will always be recalled because of the heroic defensive game which James Blair played. Blair has since declared that that day he played the finest game of his excellent career. He was, indeed, truly great at Darlington. The result was a draw. Team changes were made for the replay at Hillsborough, and Wednesday created dismay by going out deservedly by 2—0.

In the season 1920-21 Arthur Price, a Sheffield recruit obtained from the ex-Leeds City club along with Edmondson in October, 1919, when the startling wholesale disposal of players took place, scored a goal with a shot made from the half-way line. Hufton, another Sheffield man, who was in goal for West Ham United, failed to hold the ball. It was a golden goal, as will be seen.

Wednesday were paired with Everton in the next round, and the teams had to meet twice before the tie was decided. Over 100,000 people watched the two games, and the receipts amounted to £7,632. The attendance at Hillsboro' was a record one at the time, 63,000; the receipts were £4,445. Wednesday had all the worst of the luck in the first match, at Goodison Park. They put up a glorious fight and Everton never deserved the privilege of a replay. But the type of incident which weighs down the scales against any amount of good play occurred. Jack Bellas, who had played splendidly, had the misfortune to turn the ball into his own goal when endeavouring to clear, and thus the scores were levelled.

What fortunes depend even on a single kick at a ball! Everton won the replay by the odd goal. There can hardly have been a greater or more exciting rally than that of Wednesday in the closing stages. It was terrific, and it was hard luck that McIntyre, with a wonderful shot, hit the outside of the post and cut into two a blue-and-white umbrella. If that shot had scored Wednesday might have won.

At Bradford in 1922, Wednesday failed rather badly. In that match the forwards neglected to take their chances. The campaign of 1923 saw Smailes and Henshall shine, also Sidney Binks, later with Blackpool as captain and centre half-back. Smailes scored a magnificent goal against New Brighton in the first round, and fifteen minutes from the end Binks scored the second goal, which he followed up two minutes afterwards with a superb third point for the team. He had obtained the ball in midfield, made a swift dash, ran through the whole of the New Brighton defence, in which effort he beat one opponent by speed and two by cleverness. Finally, he drove the ball out of Campbell's reach, and so crowned one of the great features of the tie.

Then came the great conflict with Barnsley, also at Hillsborough, where gathered a record crowd for any match in Sheffield up to the end of the 1925-26 season. That day, February 3rd, 1923, the people who paid were 66,250 and the receipts were £4,911—over £600 more than the receipts at the Cup Final of 1907, when Wednesday won the Cup. It was a wonderful sight—the sea of faces, and people perched on all perilous points of 'vantage. It was estimated that nearly 10,000 people had to be turned away from the gates.

Barnsley, who had longed to pit themselves against one of the Sheffield clubs in a Cup-tie, acquitted themselves admirably, particularly in the first half. Three minutes before half-time, a miskick by Bellas gave Barnsley a corner. That flag-kick was well taken by Curran, and Baines, who headed beautifully, scored. Barnsley deserved the lead,

Scene outside Hillsborough Ground on the occasion of the record attendance of 66,000 at the Cup-tie with Barnsley, on February 3rd, 1923. Note people stood on top of the shed.

though Bellas, Wilson and Blenkinsop (the last-named was making his first appearance for Wednesday at Hillsboro') resisted valiantly.   However, in the second half, Wednesday revived, and the enterprise of Lowdell led to a couple of goals scored by them.   On the first occasion, Beaumont, who had vied with Wilson for honours as centre half-back, in trying to clear kicked the ball high in the air; it fell in the goal-mouth, whereupon a fierce struggle ensued, and Smailes forced the ball through.   Six minutes afterwards, Gale ran out to catch the ball, which was bouncing; Lowdell bumped into him; the goalkeeper dropped it and Binks pounced on to it and scored with a grand cross-shot.

It was a match full of thrills and excitement, and Barnsley gave as much as they received.   There was credit due to every man.   George Wilson, Wednesday's captain, played a magnificent game that day.   He was in his best form.   Sykes, in his first big Cup-tie, played admirably at left-half, and no doubt the experience stood him in good stead in 1925-26, when, as captain, he led Swansea Town into the semi-final stage of the Cup competition.

The teams were:—

Wednesday: Davison; Bellas and Blenkinsop; Kean, Wilson and Sykes; Williams, Lowdell, Binks, Smailes and Henshall.

Barnsley: Gale; Armstrong and Gittins; Fletcher, Beaumont and Baines; Curran, Hine, Wainscoat, Halliwell and Newton.

Wednesday passed out in the next round, when, in another battling tie, Derby County scored four minutes from the end.   The match took place on the Baseball ground. From a free-kick, taken by Plackett, Moore headed in rather dramatically, taking advantage of a temporary lapse on the part of the Wednesday defence, which resulted in Davison being deceived.   The ground was in a shocking condition owing to snow and rain, but a wonderful pace was maintained despite the conditions.

On January 12th, 1924, Wednesday beat Leicester City by 4—1 at Hillsborough and recorded their biggest Cup win since the triumph over Chelsea in 1913.   Wednesday scored three goals in eleven minutes just before the interval and then led by 4—0.   Sam Taylor was a " star " turn in

that match, in which there were three penalty-kicks awarded
—two to Wednesday and one to Leicester. Hebden saved
Binks' second penalty-kick, but not the first. Wednesday's
scorers were Taylor (2), Binks and Petrie.

Then came another of the unsatisfactory reverses.
Bristol City, the "wooden spoonists" of the Second
Division, who were eventually relegated to the Third
Division, drew 1—1 at Hillsborough, where Wednesday had
an invulnerable home record, and won the replay at Bristol
by 2—0. Wednesday played much below form in both the
matches, and Bristol City, the captaincy of whom by Fred
Hawley was so praiseworthy, were entitled to the reward
they gained. Wednesday played much too closely, especially
in the first match.

The latest stunning reverse in the Cup was at New
Brighton in the first round in 1926, when they fell by 2—1.
If Wednesday had kept their heads, had not been so anxious
and excited, they would no doubt have won. The narrow
ground had something to do with their failure, for their
forward operations were cramped—playing down the slope
the Sheffield men frequently misjudged distances. On the
run of the play they did not deserve to lose, but all matches
are decided by goals. For three-fifths of the time, Wednesday were on the offensive, but the waves were broken on a
defence excellent for its pluck and resistance. The Northern
Section team revealed unexpected stamina, and created the
sensation of the round. They were gay adventurers. In
the first half, Brown saved a penalty-kick finely, but for an
infringement of the laws it was re-taken, and then he was
beaten. Thus was nullified the lead, which Wednesday had
taken after thirteen minutes' play through Trotter. A
mistake by the defence allowed Broad to score the winning
goal for New Brighton half-way through the second half.

The previous season had seen Wednesday conquer
Manchester United, a distinctly creditable feat. Hill headed
one of the greatest goals seen at Hillsborough. Actually he
headed two goals, but the second was the better, the result
of wonderful anticipation. He was the hero of the tie.

PART III.

Great Battles with Sheffield United.
Chapter Seventeen.

*How the pendulum has swung—The battles of
1900—Charging " Bill " Foulke — Mumford's
benefit match.*

MAYBE tempers are more strictly controlled nowadays
than in times gone by, and partisanship does not
blaze so riotously as twenty and more years ago ;
nevertheless, the fervour remains very real.   In Sheffield
still it seems as though one is either a follower of the Blue-
and-White or of the Red-and-White. But in the case of
the Wednesday supporter, his enthusiasm appears to be of
a more profound type.   Partisanship is very human and
most of us fall to the temptation of " taking sides."   When
the teams meet on the field, players are tuned up to highest
tension, and the excitement is usually tremendous.

The names " Wednesday " and " United " stir the
memories of all enthusiasts, and in their mind's eye they
see a succession of pictures ; pictures of struggling players,
tense crowds, games full of colour and incident, and old
heroes of the fields seem to live again.   They stir the pulse,
those pictures, yet also make one rather sad.   So many of
the great stalwarts of both clubs lie at rest beneath the turf.
Among the departed are Herrod Ruddlesdin, Walter Bennett,
William Foulke, Harry Thickett, Fred Priest, Harry
Hammond, Harry Chapman, and " Toddles " Woolhouse.

To the end of season 1925-26 Wednesday and Sheffield
United had opposed each other in 106 games. Of those,
Wednesday had won 42, United 36 ; the remaining 28 were
drawn. No fewer than 39 of the matches had been won

by the margin of one goal only. The pendulum has swung
first one way, then the other. United created a rather
remarkable record, considering the good men Wednesday
had at the time, when from 1893 to 1900 they were only
once beaten by them in League matches. It used to be said
then that " as soon as the red-and-white shirts came on the
field United had won." As a matter of fact, of course, it
never was a walk-over for the United, though somehow
Wednesday were unable to get the whip-hand. Yet, on
the other hand, it can be pointed out, from October, 1910,
inclusive, to September 27th, 1919 (not including war-time
football), United did not once defeat Wednesday. From
October 4th, 1919, to May 3rd, 1926, however, Wednesday
triumphed on only one occasion over their city rivals—in
George Waller's benefit match at Bramall Lane in 1923.

The match on October 4th, 1919, at Bramall Lane, was
the " century " match, and the last First Division game
between the sides, for that season we witnessed the relegation
of Wednesday to the Second Division. After six seasons in
the lower Division, Wednesday return to their proper
sphere this year—1926—and were scheduled to open their
1926-27 camapign with a match at Hillsborough with the
United.

That " century " match, by the way, was won by United
by 3—0, despite the fact that they had George Utley injured
and Joe Kitchen off the field for a considerable period.

Naturally, great crowds have witnessed the matches.
On Boxing Day, 1897, at Bramall Lane, there was a crowd
of 38,000; and the receipts, which amounted to £960, were
a record for the time. Then a record League attendance at
the Lane was created on October 25th, 1913, when there
were 42,912 spectators, and the takings were £1,192 5s.
Since the war, of course, those figures have been surpassed.

At the second round English Cup-tie between the teams—
in 1925 at Bramall Lane—in spite of the terrible weather
which prevailed, the attendance was 40,256, the gate-money
totalled £2,756 17s. Another splendid set of figures was
provided on May 3rd, 1926, on the occasion of the Sheffield
County Cup Final at Bramall Lane, when the attendance
was 39,698; and the admission fees were £2,158 18s.—a
record for that competition.

Battles between Wednesday and United! Great battles!! Who can say that this or that was a greater battle than any other? To the players they have all been grim struggles. Perhaps the play in some of them did not come up to the expectations of the onlookers, but they have been hard-fought. One of the best games, from the spectators' point of view, was that in 1897 at Bramall Lane, when each side scored a goal. Probably, however, no League or club matches have ever yielded the same excitement or had the same effect on the players as the engagements in the English Cup. The series of Cup-ties in 1900 will probably never be forgotten; nor will the fight of 1925. Wednesday were in the Second Division in each of those years, and it was a remarkable coincidence that they were the only seasons in which they were ever drawn against United in the Cup. The Cup tussles of 1900 were some of the severest it has been the lot of football followers to see; they savoured of Donnybrook Fair, and the late Mr. John Lewis always maintained that the third match was one of the two most difficult games he had to control in the course of his long and famous career as a referee.

The tie was in the second round of the Cup competition. First, the teams played on Saturday, February 10th, at Bramall Lane, on a ground as hard as iron, before about 34,000 people. United had trained for the match at Lytham, yet they could not strike their best form; but, a trifle fortunate, they got through successfully. They were largely indebted for that to a snowstorm which arose, and as it got worse and worse, Mr. Lewis stopped the match soon after the second half had begun. No goals had then been scored, though Wednesday had had most of the play. United, however, were short of Fred Priest, and Harry Hammond played back, with Ernest Needham at outside-left.

The teams were due to meet a second time on the following Thursday, and United went to Matlock meanwhile, but the weather was fearfully bad and the ground impossible, so the game was postponed until the Saturday. Then they had another try, and again the ground was in an awful condition, inches deep in mud. Spiksley returned to the Wednesday's team after an absence due to knee trouble, and Wednesday started off very strongly. Sheffield United first put the ball into the net, but a goal was not allowed as the referee held the opinion that George Hedley had handled before he shot. Off dashed Spiksley and made a grand centre, from which Brash easily scored. Play was swift and strenuous. United retaliated valiantly to get on level terms, and yet Wednesday had bad luck; for when Massey, Wednesday's goalkeeper, went down with the ball, Beer (now manager of Birmingham F.C.), in his excitement, kicked at it to try to score. A goal was prevented, but Massay was hurt, had to leave the field, and Layton went into the goal. Massey eventually returned to the field, but at the finish of the match he had to be taken home in a cab and was unfit to play again for some time. Spiksley also had to go off awhile, owing to his knee troubling him, and, ultimately, Bennett slipped by Ruddlesdin and centred, and Almond obtained the equalising goal with a sharp drive. The end came with the score 1—1.

The third meeting, which took place at Hillsborough on the Monday following, was a match which those who attended will never forget because of the wild excitement which prevailed, the fact that one player had his leg broken, that two Wednesday men were ordered off the field, and that, after all, it ended in a somewhat farcical win for United.

Before the match began, Mr. Lewis visited both dressing-rooms and cautioned the whole of the players. Stories had been going about as to what might happen, and he warned every man in the match that anybody whom he detected in the act of foul play, no matter who it might be, would get marching-orders straightaway.

The first unfortunate incident was the bad mishap to young Lee, who turned out at centre-forward for Wednesday, Millar having strained himself on the Saturday. Wednesday were also without Spiksley and Massey. The injury to Lee was quite an accident. Thickett and he tried to trap the ball together, and Lee had his leg broken. The mishap occurred shortly before the interval, and thenceforward United were superior. Not long after half-time Langley tripped Bennett, and the referee awarded United a penalty-kick, which Needham took and so scored the first goal.

Pryce, of the Wednesday, was next ordered off the field for having fouled George Hedley, United's centre-forward, who likewise had to leave the field for a time; and, as if that were not enough, Langley also got marching-orders for an offence against Bennett. Thus Wednesday finished up with eight men. There could be only one conclusion. Towards the end Beer ran through and scored a second goal, and so United won by 2—o. The majority of the players had painful knocks.

The teams in the match in question were as given below, and the receipts as follows :—

First match, £1,183 12s.; second match, £917 17s.; third match, £641 18s.; total, £2,743 8s.

Teams :—

Wednesday : Mallinson : Layton and Langley; Ferrier, Crawshaw and Ruddlesdin; Brash, Pryce, Lee, Wright and Topham.

Sheffield United : Foulke; Thickett and Boyle; Johnson, Morren and Needham; Bennett, Beer, Hedley, Almond and Priest.

Wednesday had many exciting games with United. A lot of merriment was created once when little Brash somehow or other knocked Bill Foulke down. How he did it no one ever knew. One of the greatest games was that played on December 27th, 1897, at Bramall Lane. There was then a record crowd, about 38,000, and £960 was taken at the gates. The result was 1—1. It was a grand match, and the play swung first one way and then the other. Before the game started the band played " Auld Lang Syne," the spectators joining in, and also " Lead, Kindly Light," which, of course, captivated the people. Whether the melody was for United's benefit or Wednesday's, or whether it was a plea to refrain from vigorous play, does not matter. Jack Earp scored United's goal for them.

What happened was that in the first half McKay sent in a shot from fairly long range. It was greasy and difficult to reach, and Massey did not fist away as well as he might have done. Earp, in attempting to clear, put into Wednesday's net. At that time Wednesday and United were next to the Villa in the League table, with equal points, the Villa being at the top.

The same year, on Shrove Tuesday, Needham scored one of his best goals against Wednesday. It was a windy day, and Wednesday were having the better of the argument, which pleased the folk at Olive Grove. They looked like beating the United, when Bennett was fouled. Massey punched out from the free-kick, but the ball landed in front of " Nudger," who made a dash and collared it. He " hit " the ball truly. It never rose an inch, and Massey probably never saw it until it was in the net. The shot was one of about thirty yards' range.

Another good game was that played on Sept. 1st, 1902, and it is recalled because it was in that match that Herbert Chapman (now the manager of Arsenal) made his first appearance in League football for Sheffield United as an inside-right. He had been obtained from Northampton, and he played because Alfred Common was not fit. Although Fred Priest scored inside five minutes, Wednesday won by 3—2. Jack Lyall played extremely well in goal. Herbert Chapman's brother, Harry, played for Wednesday in the same game.

Mumford's benefit match at Olive Grove in 1895 was a poor affair. A great Wednesday man was Mumford, yet for that match between Wednesday and United there were only 2,000 spectators. It was not a League game, and United won by 5—0. The players had been instructed not to take any undue risks. It was more of a walking match than a running match.

One Wednesday-United match which is not mentioned on most of the records was an interesting game. The two clubs put their players together for the selection of two teams—" England v. Scotland "—to play a benefit match for Jack Dungworth, who was a big favourite then, both as a footballer and as a mile runner. The Scots had such men as Hendry, Jack Drummond, Tom and Harry Brandon, Alec Brady and Bob Cain, while the English side had Spiksley, Hammond, Dobson, Billy Betts, Mumford and Lilley. " England " won by 3—1.

Chapter Eighteen.

" Funeral " cards—When Spiksley scored four goals—Lievesley's thumb broken—Davison as " George Washington " — Greatest post-war struggle.

ON October 26th, 1891, at Bramall Lane, Sheffield United defeated Wednesday by 5—0 in a club match, and it was notable not only because it ranks as one of the biggest victories of the series, but also because two players destined to make history for England in International football had their first experience of Sheffield " Derby " matches. One was Ernest Needham, who became known as " The prince of half-backs "; the other, Fred Spiksley. Wednesday had Jim Smith in goal, Tom Brandon at back and acting as captain, partnered by Darroch. The halves were H. Brandon, William Betts, and T. E. Cawley, with Gemmell, Mumford, Thompson, Woolhouse and Spiksley as forwards. United had Howlett, the goalkeeper who wore spectacles and who used to lean down and fist away ground shots right off the turf; Bob Cain, who had just come from Bootle; Harry Lilley, of Staveley, who got his " cap " against Wales the same season and who was a fine, clean kicker of a ball, and half-backs " Rab " Howell, Hendry and " Mick " Whitham (the last-named secured a " cap " against Ireland the same term). Needham played at outside-right, Sammy Dobson at inside-right, Hammond at centre-forward, Arthur Watson at inside-left, and Drummond outside. The feature of the game was the magnificent shooting of Dobson. He had been deputy for Jimmy Ross at Preston, and he was one of the best shots football has known.

Fred Spiksley says that he got such a heavy charge from
Bob Cain shortly after the start that everything was a blank
to him afterwards.

As Wednesday were considered the premier team, the
defeat caused no little consternation in the ranks of their
followers. At all events, Spiksley has contended that as a
result of that match the Wednesday directors had their eyes
opened as to the value of systematic training, for they
decided that all players not otherwise employed should put
in an appearance at the ground for two hours' training each
morning.

The return match was played at Olive Grove on Nov.
16th, 1891, and it provided quite a reversal of form, for
Wednesday won by 4—1, and, though the newspaper
reports do not credit him with the feat, Spiksley
emphatically declares that he scored each one of
Wednesday's goals. The match was played on a pitch like
a bog.

"Funeral" cards are not published broadcast in present
times, but in 1891 they were in fashion, and vendors did a
roaring trade. After United's conquest referred to a
Wednesday card was on sale. It read :—

In loving remembrance of

the

SHEFFIELD WEDNESDAY FOOTBALL TEAM,

who were safely put to rest on Monday, Oct. 26th,

at Bramall Lane.

Poor old Wednesday were fairly done,
When United beat them five to none;
Although they lost they did their best,
So let them quietly take their rest.

(Friends of the above club kindly accept this
intimation.)

United did not escape, however, in the following
November. Their "notice" read :—

In pitiful remembrance of
our Idol, the
SHEFFIELD UNITED FOOTBALL TEAM,
who departed their football life, struggling to the
end, at Olive Grove, on Monday, November 16th,
1891.

> When United died, they struggled hard
> Enough to live a brighter and a longer life:
> Do as they would, they could not ward
> Neat kicks by Wednesday; and thus the strife
> Ended. Thus closed famous United's reign.
> Sheffield now mourns their death the more,
> Dying as they did—ne'er to rise again
> And kick for fame at Wednesday's door.
> Yes, United have lost 4 to 1.

How quaintly they read to-day!
For many years now the meetings of the two Sheffield
teams have been characterised by a spirit so admirable as
to be as near to brotherly love as is possible to find on a
football field. Serious efforts have been made to place good
football first, last and all the time. Once, though, the fires
of ill-feeling burst out anew—in the match at Bramall Lane
in 1913, when Wednesday won by 1—0. The players were
excited and overwrought from the very beginning, and they
allowed their excitement to interfere with their ability to
such an extent that the game was hardly worth watching.
There was a record crowd, over 42,000 people, and spectators
rushed over the cricket section of the field and lined the
touch-line, thereby fanning the passions of players by their
proximity.

Glennon was one of Wednesday's storm-centres and
W. H. Brelsford was a rare United character, also Albert
Sturgess.

Two years before (February, 1911) there had been a
spirited contest at the Lane. Wednesday won by 1—0, and
the goal was noteworthy because David McLean was the
scorer, and in trying to stop the ball Joe Lievesley,

Sheffield United's goalkeeper, broke his thumb.   In the November that followed, on the same ground, the teams drew (1—1).   Andrew Wilson scored in the first five minutes and Joe Kitchen equalised in the last minute. Davison, Wednesday's goalkeeper, who protested against United's goal, declared that Kitchen had taken the ball forward with his arm.   A critic, speaking of the incident, said: " If Davison said so, it was so," and the next day was sent an anonymous postcard addressed " George Washington, Wednesday Football Club, Owlerton." Davison duly received it !   Davison, by the way, was never on the losing side in a League match against United.

The war came in 1914, and the match played on Sept. 5th at the Lane is mentioned because addresses for recruits were made.   There was a patriotic demonstration.

On May 4th, 1926, United defeated Wednesday by 3—1 in the Sheffield County Cup final—and for the third time in a County Cup final since 1920.   The match was at Bramall Lane.   The result disappointed Wednesday's followers, as Wednesday had just won the Second Division champion- ship, and they thought it an opportunity for Wednesday to prove their right to be in the First Division.   Wednesday, however, though they played hard football, were deservedly beaten.   They had not the pace, the combination and ability of their opponents.   Of course, it had to be remembered that the men had undergone a severe strain for several months.   Still, the club got a friendly warning of what would be needed in the way of resources for 1926-27.

The greatest post-war struggle between the rivals was the second round English Cup-tie played on January 31st, 1925, on United's ground.   Memories of it will long endure. United beat Wednesday by 3—2, but only after a glorious struggle in mud and rain.   A record attendance had been expected.   On the day, however, rain poured heavily and continuously, and rendered conditions for play absolutely wretched.   Yet 40,256 people paid £2,756 17s. to see the match, and 33,103 of the onlookers were shilling patrons.

An hour before the kick-off the pitch was almost inundated with water.   A party of men went out with forks and tried to perforate a way through for the water, but their efforts met with little success until the rain slackened in force at the time of the kick-off. By that time, however, the ground had become a quagmire.

The tie will always be considered as one of the finest games played between the clubs. It was amazing how the players triumphed over the conditions: they provided sensations and thrills, even brilliant football. Moreover, the contest was cleanly fought. Not a single player was hurt, and the few fouls committed were only of a minor description. The referee was Mr. W. E. Russell, of Swindon, the English Cup Final referee of the previous year.

A sensational start was furnished by Wednesday, who scored two goals in the first nine minutes. They were attacking the Shoreham Street goal and had the wind and rain behind them. Trotter scored on both occasions. Five minutes from the start he received a good pass from Hill, which followed enterprise by Wilson, and darted for the goal. When challenged by Birks he turned the ball to his right, and it rolled slowly into the goal close to the right post. Four minutes later, Green misjudged a centre by Lowdell, and Trotter easily recorded the second point.

However, United, led by that grand captain and player, Gillespie, never wavered. Within nine minutes Tom Sampy had scored for them, and two minutes later Green made the scores level. From that point it seemed fairly certain that United would win, for they took command of the game, and the second half had been in progress only a minute and a half when Tom Sampy scored again with a superb cross-shot—the best goal of the match.

The United's superiority lay in their team-work and stamina. Wednesday had not the cohesive strength and reserve power of the winners, who had an outstanding general in Gillespie.

The teams were :—

Sheffield United: Sutcliffe; Cook and Birks; Pantling, King and Green; Mercer, Sampy (T.), Johnson, Gillespie and Tunstall.

Wednesday: Brown; Inglis and Felton; Toone, Wilson and Powell; Lowdell, Hill, Trotter, Taylor and Richardson.

Incidentally, United, who possessed one of the finest attacks in the whole of the country, went on and won the trophy, and Wednesday had the distinction of being the only team which had scored against the winners in their excellent Cup campaign.

Arising out of the Bramall Lane match, Wednesday raised the point about the referee having ordered the teams to play on without an interval, and obtained the official ruling that the captains must agree before an interval can be dispensed with.

A good deal of comment was made on the subject of Wednesday having lost the tie after having held a two-goals lead. That position had seemed a winning one, and in most Cup-ties a two-goals lead usually spells victory. Tactics had not a little to do with the result. Gillespie was a master strategist and Wednesday's half-back policy was faulty. A defensive policy was adopted, and as the wing halves concentrated on Mercer and Tunstall they left the United inside forwards any amount of room in which to operate. Whatever opinions may be, the fact remains that that United forward-line in form was hardly ever held up by any side, and the display against West Bromwich Albion in the fourth round was an object lesson.

Chapter Nineteen.

Sheffield United stalwarts—Power of Foulke—
Genius of Needham—" Cocky " Bennett—
" Star " players old and new.

SHEFFIELD United have had numerous magnificent and famous players in their service, and reference to some of them can hardly be omitted. Many old players and followers of football have declared that William Foulke was the greatest goalkeeper who ever lived. The contention is based on the facts that Foulke could fist a ball further than any goalkeeper known, throw it further than anyone else, and certainly could kick a ball a greater distance than any man who has played football. Foulke also had a tremendous reach. It was nothing in the old days to see him save a terrific drive with one hand as though he were catching a cricket ball.

Many people have said that they do not recall seeing a goal scored against Foulke from a corner-kick, as all players were afraid to go anywhere near him to use their heads with " Big Bill " ready to shoot out his fist to punch the ball away. He could pick a ball up and punch it to the half-way line—as far as most goalkeepers of to-day can kick it.

Foulke, so much resembling Porthos, of " The Three Musketeers " fame, had tremendous strength. In one game Andrew Wilson drove in fiercely from six yards' range. Foulke simply put out his fist, and the force of the ball made absolutely no impression. The ball rebounded and the outstretched arm had not moved an inch. Many will remember what a help he was to his side when opponents were given off-side. Foulke used to advance from the goal and take all the free-kicks anywhere within twenty or thirty yards of his goal. All the Sheffield United players would get down towards their opponents' goal and wait for Foulke's kick, which invariably placed the ball near the goal and was the cause of fierce mêlées there.

He represented England in only one international match (against Wales), for there were some great goal-keepers in his day: L. R. Roose, Hillman, Robinson, to name but a few.

He had wit, too. Numerous stories are well known. A particular United player once asked Foulke how it was he (the player) was always in the second team. To that Foulke answered " Well, if tha wants to know, it's because there isn't a third team to put thi in !"

Foulke, Thickett, Peter Boyle and Bob Cain formed a defence which often appeared unbeatable. All were big, strapping fellows. Thickett was one of the fastest backs then playing, while Boyle was of the " devil-may-care " type. Boyle never worried whether the ball came to his foot or his knee. Frequently he was seen to knee a ball as far as a back could kick it with his boot !

In marked contrast with those hefty, powerful stalwarts, were the midget half-backs: " Rab " Howell, Tommy Morren and Ernest Needham formed a wonderful half-back line; in fact, that line of diminutive halves has never been surpassed in quality of play by little men. Harry Johnson and Bernard Wilkinson maintained the splendid standard set. A son each of Johnson and Boyle are members of Sheffield United first team now.

Hendry, the stoutly-built, bonny Scotsman, was a price-less half-back for United just before " Nudger " Needham began his memorable career of twenty seasons at Bramall Lane. It has been said that Hendry was the making of Needham. While he aided genius, it is probably true to say, Needham, who played sixteen times for England, would have gained renown without any coaching, for he had football born and bred in him. It is doubtful whether he ever had an equal at left half-back. He was an artist; in short, a " prince of half-backs."

Bernard Wilkinson was a " pocket Hercules," who had a happy knack of bobbing up when quite unexpected.

Langley and Walter Bennett, the latter better known as " Cocky," provided some rare bouts. Bennett was a superb right-winger, very fast and a terrific shot. His partner was Beer, another capital forward.

George Hedley, who was obtained from South Bank, was one of the few forwards who could put Crawshaw off his game. He had a habit of doing it when the ball was in the air. Crawshaw would stand waiting to head the ball, while Hedley would back into him and so push him away from the object. Hedley was a big fellow and a good centre-forward, who, incidentally, won three English Cup winners' medals.

United also have had a clever left-wing in Fred Priest and Bert Lipsham, from South Bank and Chester respectively; and they were a "rattling" pair. Indeed, all the players named were first-class and were men who caused enormous excitement in Sheffield by winning the League championship, gaining magnificent Cup triumphs, and creating the wonderful record of playing 22 matches without sustaining a reverse. The last-named record stood until Burnley, in their championship season after the war, played 30 games without a defeat.

Jack Drummond was another clever forward; also Alfred Common, the subject of the first record transfer fee of £1,000, and who scored goals from seemingly impossible positions. He shared in many of United's triumphs; likewise Cunningham, the inside-right, who materially helped United to win the championship by scoring two glorious goals in the last three minutes against Aston Villa at Aston in a vital match. "Mick" Whittam was a strong, dashing back or half-back who was "capped," and Arthur Watson, a fast and clever outside-left.

Then there was Arthur Brown, who played for his country when only 17 years of age, an opportunist of the first water and a grand marksman. He was from Gainsborough, the place which provided Wednesday with Fred Spiksley. A fine centre-forward was Brown. Harry Hammond, who died at Bolton three years ago, was a player capable of filling any position from goal to the extreme wing with every credit. Jack Jones, a Welshman, also takes his place in football history.

In later times was Smith, the right-back, of whom it was said that if he did not kill someone else first he would end by killing himself, so fearless and acrobatic was he in his work. Bob Benson, another outstanding player, was a wonderful taker of penalty kicks. A perfectly-built athlete, and a man of moods, he died at Highbury from a heart attack after a football match during the war.

Joe Kitchen, centre-forward, possessed remarkable dash and secured many goals by the result of his own efforts. In 1913, William Cook joined Sheffield United, and he and English became one of the best pairs of backs in the country. Though neither of them was very weighty, they feared no foe in football armour, and their kicking was delightful. Cook, by the way, might have made a living on the music-hall stage as a contortionist, 'tis said. Certainly, he could kick a ball from any position, and no one could kick a flying ball better than he in his hey-day. That same season, 1913, United obtained Harold Gough, another goalkeeper of great ability, who was awarded international honours. The fee paid for Gough was £30. He succeeded Joe Lievesley, a very capable custodian and very consistent.

Picking out the noted players at random, one recalls Walter Hardinge, the Kent cricketer and ex-international football forward, who, on his day, could be remarkably clever; Fred Hawley, a talented centre half-back; Stanley Fazackerley, a most artistic inside forward; and George Utley, a splendid general and a powerful battling half-back. Utley arrived from Barnsley at a time when United seemed unable to get out of a ruck, and his influence was remarkable, for immediately United began to make progress reminiscent of former times. Utley was remarkable at throwing in the ball.

Albert Sturgess, at one time a " potter," was a rare utility man. If ever a sudden vacancy occurred, Sturgess could be relied upon to fill the breach efficiently. Sturgess, Brelsford and Utley were a formidable line of halves, and charging one of them was like heaving oneself against a brick wall.

Masterman was a splendid forward, and Jimmy Simmons was a dainty player of distinction, though he never gained any official honours. Bob Evans, who played for both England and Wales, had a remarkable scoring shot from the wing. Tall, and with a long, raking stride, he is entitled to be ranked with the rest of United's " star " players.

Scorers in Wednesday and United matches in the English Cup and the League are of considerable interest, so below is given a list of them, embracing the two competitions named and the competitions decided in war-time. The distinction of being the leading scorer is held by Glennon, always a thorn in the United side. He obtained 14 goals. He is closely followed by Andrew Wilson, another Wednesday favourite of old-time; then follow the late Harry Chapman and Joe Kitchen.

THE WEDNESDAY.		SHEFFIELD UNITED.	
Glennon	14	Kitchen	7
Wilson	12	Priest	5
Chapman	7	Needham	4
McLean	5	Brown (A.)	4
Brittleton	4	Hill	3
Stewart	4	Bennett	3
Burkinshaw (J. D.)	3	Lipsham	3
Kirkman	3	Hardinge	3
Spiksley	3	Simmons	3
Davies	2	Masterman	3
Davis	2	Tummon	3
Hemmingfield	2	Hammond	2
Maxwell	2	Howell	2
Simpson	2	Beer	2
Trotter	2	Donelly	2
Miller, Bell, Ferrier, Brandon, Brash, Bradshaw, Robertson, Capper, Islip, Buddery, Armitage, Pearson, Gill, Campbell, each	1	Drake	2
		Utley	2
		Gillespie	2
		Charles	2
		Sampy (T.)	2
		Drummond, Watson, Earp (own goal), Morren, Field, Levick, Peart, Brelsford, Evans, Wilkinson, Davies, Buddery, Johnson (H.), Salt, Brown (F.), Handley, Green, Almond, each	1

It seems to be a clear fact that Glennon is the only man of the two clubs who has ever done the " hat " trick in such encounters. That feat he performed on March 16th, 1918, when United were defeated at Bramall Lane by 5—0; Glennon scored four goals and Burkinshaw the other.

In recent years, the magnificent forward-line of Sheffield United has been the dominating feature of the team. On the left, the speed, skill and grand shooting of Fred Tunstall; the latter and Gillespie (who has played for Ireland about twenty times) comprise one of the finest left wings in the country. Gillespie is a superb footballer, a master tactician and the thinker of the team. In the centre, Johnson's electrifying spurts always stir the crowd, and frequently he scores goals by his dash when many players would never espy the opportunity. Mercer is one of the prettiest purveyors of football in the game, an artist from tip to toe, and a delightful right-winger.

In short, the Cup-winning team of 1925, consisting of Sutcliffe; Cook and Milton; Pantling, King and Green; Mercer, Boyle (T.), Johnson, Gillespie and Tunstall, were a formidable combination, and very whole-hearted, as were those efficient principal reserves at the time—Tom Sampy, Birks, Waugh, Menlove, and Partridge.

PART IV.

A Thousand Games in the League.

Chapter Twenty.

*Formation of the League and the Alliance—
Creditable Record—Experiences in the Alliance—
Going afar for Players.*

IT might with safety be said that the creation of the
Football League in 1888 led to a complete
reorganisation of the national game in administration.
In the two or three seasons immediately prior to the
momentous meeting held in Manchester senior clubs were in
serious difficulties. Professionalism had been introduced,
and with the professional came the weekly wage-bill. The
late Mr. William McGregor, of Aston Villa, realised that
the only way to meet the wages account was to obtain consistently good "gates." The latter had become
imperative. It seemed to him that if they could get twelve
of the leading clubs to pledge themselves to play each other
a regular course of matches, such arrangement to be
regarded as inviolate, they would get the crowds regularly.

Clubs had frequently cancelled engagements at the last
moment owing to cup-ties, national and local, and fixtures
were thus thrown into the utmost state of confusion. Weak
teams were sometimes sent, with the result that matches
became farcical; there were late starts and variations of
time in the duration of games, too. In such conditions
inter-club matches could not command sustained success;
in fact, the patience of the sporting public was severely
tried, and enthusiasm was somewhat on the wane.
Stability was needed.

So on April 17th, 1888, the Football League was founded at the Royal Hotel, Manchester, and the twelve clubs elected were :—

Preston North End.	Derby County.
Wolverhampton Wanderers.	Notts. County.
Bolton Wanderers.	Burnley.
Aston Villa.	Stoke.
West Bromwich Albion.	Accrington.
Everton.	Blackburn Rovers.

Those clubs never dreamt that the League would become the power it is to-day, nor did they think the League system would be copied virtually throughout the country, indeed the world, in nearly all the realms of sport.

They were all professional clubs and each was bound to play its strongest eleven in every match, or be liable to a penalty of forfeiting its position. There were only five rules, with an additional two in relation to referees. The competition had been running some weeks before it was decided to introduce the award of two points for a win and one for a draw.

Football thus had a new lease of life. People knew what to expect from League matches: Regular conduct, strongest teams, and grim struggles for supremacy and points. Competitive football fascinated the public, and it has never looked back.

At that first meeting of the Football League, Wednesday, along with Nottingham Forest and Halliwell, made personal application to be admitted to membership, but were not successful. The League could then only see 22 vacant dates during the season on which engagements could be fulfilled, and it was not thought advisable to make the membership larger.

On Friday, May 3rd, 1889, Wednesday again made application for admission; also several other prominent clubs applied, but not one application succeeded. The decisions so annoyed the rejected clubs that at the Douglas Hotel, Manchester, on Thursday, May 9th, it was agreed to form a Northern Counties' League, afterwards called the "Football Alliance." Mr. John Holmes, the President of the Wednesday, was elected President, and the following clubs were admitted as members :—

Nottingham Forest.	Bootle.
Wednesday.	Darwen.
Crewe Alexandra.	Birmingham
Walsall Town Swifts.	St. George's.
Grimsby Town.	Small Heath.
Sunderland Albion.	Long Eaton Rangers.
Newton Heath.	

In May, 1890, Sunderland managed to enter the League to the exclusion of Stoke, but in the following year began the series of extensions, which have taken place from time to time since. The League was enlarged to fourteen clubs. It was at that meeting of the Football League that Wednesday were found " guilty " of poaching—their offence was the acquisition of Tom Brandon from Blackburn Rovers. Wednesday were therefore placed beyond the pale, and the League decided to boycott them (also Stockton and Walsall Town Swifts for similar offences) by refusing to play matches with them or to recognise them in any way.

As one author put it, " The League reserved to themselves the right to carry off the men of any team, but they denied others the privilege of returning the compliment. Once enrolled, their playing members must be held sacred, and on July 3rd, 1891, the League resolved that once a man belonged to a League club he was for ever a League player, and could not move either hand or foot without the sanction of the team for which he had signed." However, the Football Association eventually asked for the withdrawal of the boycott resolutions and they were duly rescinded.

In May, 1892, the fourth annual meeting of the League was held at Sunderland, where it was decided that the League consist of 28 clubs, with 16 in the First Division and 12 in the Second Division. There was keen competition among the best clubs of the Alliance and other combinations to gain a place in the leading League of the country, and among the candidates were not only Wednesday, but the newly-formed Sheffield United club, which, in the early years, had had to compete in such modest organisations as the Northern and the Midland Leagues.

The United had some enthusiastic, ambitious and determined officials in command, and they were bent on obtaining first-class football for Bramall Lane. Naturally, the rivalry and excitement created by the city's double application were very considerable. Both Wednesday and United canvassed for votes and both claimed to have obtained promises sufficient to ensure election. On the night of the meeting, fervour was intense in Sheffield and groups of people hung about the streets anxiously awaiting the result of the poll. Eventually the news came through: " Wednesday in the First Division; United in the Second." Wednesday received every possible vote and were, therefore, unanimously chosen—a substantial compliment, indeed. The voting resulted: Wednesday, ten votes; Nottingham Forest, nine; Accrington, seven; and Newton Heath and Stoke, six each. Sheffield United received five votes.

Rich as they were in tradition, national in reputation, and possessing a splendid following, it was not really surprising that Wednesday were preferred to the club which had been formed only a few years previously. One may add, however, that United were only one season in the Second Division. They beat Accrington in a " test " match at the end of the season and were promoted to the First Division, and have never been relegated.

Wednesday have shown brilliant form in the League campaigns at times, but that standard has not been consistently maintained, though always have they endeavoured to provide good, vigorous football. Twice they have won the League championship (1902-3 and 1903-4); twice have they been relegated to the Second Division, and twice have they won the championship of the Second Division. In seasons 1905-6 and 1912-13 they finished third from the top of the First Division.

Sheffield, indeed, had great years from 1890 to 1907, as the list of honours below indicates :—

1890	Wednesday	...	Cup Finalists.
1893	Sheffield United	...	Promotion from Second Division.
1894	Wednesday	...	Cup semi-finalists.
1895	,,	...	Cup semi-finalists.
1896	,,	...	Cup winners.

1897	Sheffield United	...	League runners-up.
1898	,,	,,	... League Champions.
1899	,,	,,	... Cup winners.
1900	,,	,,	... League runners-up.
1900	Wednesday	...	Second Division Champions.
1901	Sheffield United	...	Cup Finalists.
1902	,,	,,	... Cup winners.
1903	Wednesday	...	League Champions.
1904	,,	...	League Champions.
1905	,,	...	Cup semi-finalists.
1906	,,	...	Third in the League.
1907	,,	...	Cup winners.

Altogether, Wednesday, up to the end of the season 1925-26, had played close on 1,100 games in the Football League. The complete record of results up to that period is :—

Played.	Won.	Lost.	Drawn.	For.	Agst.	Points.
1,092	457	400	235	1,655	1,548	1,149

It will be observed they have won 57 more games than they have lost and have averaged more than a point per game; also they have obtained over one hundred more goals than opposing teams have against them. The record is very creditable indeed.

A thousand games in the League! What a story of stirring effort and endurance they embrace. The pity is it is only possible to take peeps into isolated periods of this section of a great club's life.

Before passing to the League campaigns it is necessary to bridge a brief period from 1887 to 1892. Wednesday won the championship of the Alliance in the first season (1889-90), after a great duel with Grimsby Town for the title. Unfortunately, the tremendous efforts in the Alliance virtually ruined their chance of overcoming Blackburn Rovers in the Cup Final, as already explained. A slump followed the triumphs of 1889-90, and at the end of season 1890-91 Wednesday figured at the bottom of the table. Local talent had begun to wane, and new players from far and near were secured. The season 1891-2 saw the club finish fourth from the top. That was the last season of the existence of the Football Alliance.

Prior to the formation of the Alliance, Wednesday had had a very good season—in 1888-89. They opened with a club match with West Bromwich Albion, the English Cup-holders. The match was lost. In their first fifteen matches Wednesday scored 74 goals and gained some notable victories. They beat Preston North End, a mighty team then, by 2—1 at Olive Grove, which result was in sharp contrast with the outcome of William Mosforth's benefit match on February 27th, 1888, when at Olive Grove the North End trounced a Wednesday & District XI. by 8—1. In 1888-9 Wednesday also overcame the famous Heart of Midlothian team by 3—0 and, incidentally, won the "Gainsborough Charity Cup" (they defeated Burton Swifts by 4—1 in the final on the Northolme ground on April 13th, 1889).

Two benefit matches are mentionable: On April 1st, 1889, Jack Hudson, a great stalwart of the club for years, was given the proceeds of the match with Blackburn Rovers. There were about 3,000 people present at Olive Grove, and the gate receipts amounted to £53 17s. 6d. "Which must have been gratifying to the beneficiary," ran a comment of the day! On Easter Tuesday of that year the second benefit match took place—Wednesday v. Staveley—and the gate-money was given to the Wednesday players. That was the season when Harry Woolhouse, in a collision with Clements, one of the Notts. County backs, was so badly injured that he had to be taken to the Infirmary.

Bootle opened the season 1889-90 at Olive Grove on Sept. 7th with an Alliance match, and were defeated by 2—1. "Mickey" Bennett should have donned the Wednesday colours, but having signed for both Wednesday and Rotherham Town he was suspended by the parent Association. The original sentence of a season's suspension, however, was reduced to one of two months. Wednesday made splendid progress and had a really good season. One achievement was the winning of the Alliance championship. It was in the Cup-tie with Accrington that "Billy" Betts had his nose broken just before half-time, yet he returned and remained till the finish of the match— one of several instances of the pluck of Betts.

Tom Cawley had a well-earned benefit, a match between
Wednesday and Stoke, which provided £132 6s. 6d. From
1880 to 1886 Cawley took part in no fewer than 28 first-class
inter-Association matches, including one North v. South.
At the close of the season, Mr. W. R. Wake presented him
with the proceeds of his benefit, at the Cutlers' Hall. The
amount from all sources was £182 8s. 6d., and in addition
to that sum the players had returned the payments that they
had received for having played in the match. A chain and
a locket were purchased for Mrs. Cawley.

The Alliance championship was won with 32 points out
of a possible 44—no small achievement, as the Alliance was
only second in strength to the League itself. The season
was as successful financially as from the playing
standpoint. The management at that period decided to
secure Scottish recruits, and the first obtained was Bob
Brandon, a centre-forward, from Glasgow Clyde,
who arrived in Sheffield in the middle of October,
1890, and was followed by his cousin, Harry Brandon, a
native of Kilburnie, who had assisted St. Mirren and Clyde.
Harry Brandon was a sterling player. Despite those
acquisitions, the club fell from the premier position to the
very lowest in the Alliance tourney in 1890-91, although the
next season they rose to the fourth place. They had
appointed Tom Brandon, of Blackburn Rovers, on a two
years' agreement, and in January, 1891, had signed on
Fred Spiksley. Another recruit was Bob (" Sparrow ")
Brown, a delightful player, and Gavin Thomson, of Third
Lanark.

A few odd incidents and conditions are singled out:
One of the matches at Olive Grove about the time was with
a party of touring Canadians. The play had not long been
in progress when " Toddles " Woolhouse and a Canadian
back, named Dalton (who later went to Sunderland), became
engaged in a sort of wrestling match. Dalton was observed
to have got a grip of Woolhouse's cheek with his teeth;
with difficulty they were parted, but neither was ordered off
the field!

Matches were fiercely fought, and grounds were quaint.
When Wednesday and Newton Heath were members of the
Alliance, the latter club played on the old North Road

ground.   In those days grass was almost as scarce there as in the later times at Clayton, and as the " Heathens " always displayed vigour in their work the fall to earth was usually disagreeable to the victim.   On one occasion Donaldson, the Newton Heath centre-forward, a raw-boned, energetic Scot, with forceful methods surpassing those of " Cockles " Appleyard, was well laid out by a Wednesday defender and probably never forgot the experience, judging by his expressions at the time.   That Wednesday defender was Tom Brandon.

Nowadays every ground with the slightest pretension to completeness has its well-appointed dressing-rooms for players and officials, but on the North Road ground there were none of those.   Players and referee had often to run the gauntlet of a hostile crowd for a full half-mile down the road to the club's headquarters, just as in those early days at Olive Grove the tramp was made along the sometimes very muddy garden-lane and over the railway-bridge to the Earl of Arundel and Surrey Hotel.

A good story is told of Birmingham St. George's on the occasion of their last visit to Sheffield for Wednesday's last Alliance match on March 26th, 1892.   The club was originally known as Mitchell's St. George's, but it had adopted the wider title in 1891-2.   The game in question ended in a win for Wednesday by 4—0 and left Birmingham St. George's stranded at the bottom of the chart with eleven points, the product of 22 matches.   However, that is not the spicy part of the pudding, for the match narrowly missed ending in a gigantic fiasco and in a fashion almost incredible in these days of well-regulated clubs, whose finances and management are run on lines closely approaching those of the most commercial and businesslike concerns.

The match had been billed in the ordinary course, and there were anticipations of the usual Saturday crowd of enthusiasts when on the Friday the Wednesday officials were disconcerted by the receipt of an intimation from the Saints' secretary to the effect that the club was " Stoney broke; cannot come."   There was what is called a " queer pickle," but Wednesday enterprisingly solved the problem forthwith by forwarding a remittance for the full amount of the players' travelling expenses.   The game was played, but the

Saints never had another chance of proving sinners, for, with the disbanding of the Alliance, the club went out of existence, if not out of memory.

One of their great players, Harry Davis, joined Wednesday, and a valiant forward he was.

Chapter Twenty-One.

*Early dangers of player-hunting—Howling mobs
—When Mr. A. J. Dickinson was attacked—
The spiriting-away of Madden.*

IN rather a casual way one has mentioned Wednesday's
acquisitions of Scotsmen.   It is difficult for modern
football-followers to realise that officials who went in
search of talent in Scotland used to take their lives in their
hands !   Often have they had to escape from football grounds
and sporting hostelries with surging mobs at their heels.
There is quite a number of prominent men in football still
who learned to their cost how angry, and, indeed, bloodthirsty, football partisans were then, when they thought
" an unscrupulous stranger " (as they put it) went to their
grounds anxious to acquire some promising player, or to
secure some established favourite whose departure would
spread grief and desolation throughout a small township,
if not over a countryside.

In those times, a player's club had no voice in the matter.
The player himself decided whether or not he would accept
the sum which the proposed new club were prepared to give
him.   His old club could not prevent him making a move,
and did not receive any money in compensation for the loss
of his services.   At that period, it was not legitimate for a
club to sue or be sued; a football club had no legal
standing.

As a club " scout " has stated : " A stranger in a
Scottish town or hamlet was then a novelty.   People moved
about very little then.   When you got out of the train, you
were a marked man.   Your speech was noted; the station-
master or the porter instantly engaged you in conversation
just to hear your accent; sometimes they could tell where
you came from.   If it was a football centre, they were
instantly suspicious ; they were suspicious, in fact, when you
had barely alighted from the train.   You were watched
right through the morning or dinner-hour, and if you went
to a sporting rendezvous there was always someone dogging

Mr. A. J. DICKINSON.

your footsteps.   There was no asking for any player's address; that would have been fatal; you would have had a mob at your heels in ten seconds.

"You went to the match and you were watched incessantly   If you made a move towards the dressing-room you were chivied about and made to understand that your purpose was known. You had to move warily, and often you simply could not get to speak to the man you had gone to see.   But you probably had gained something. You had to write and fix an appointment somewhere out of the town or village, or intercept the player on the occasion of the next out-match. That was the safest method. But if the crowd really thought you were a football agent and were sweet on a local favourite, well, you ran the risk of having your clothes torn from your back and being raced to the railway station, with a horde of bloodthirsty fanatics behind you.

"You might be besieged in a building by a mob. It isn't nice to be in a place with a roaring crowd outside clamouring for your blood. For those people really meant business. It was almost uncanny how it came about that everyone on a football ground seemed to fasten on to a man who had gone out to spy the land for promising talent. They always used to find out when they had stalked a wrong horse, but they never seemed to make a mistake when they had once settled in their own minds that the suspected one was a wrong one; or, in other words, that he had come to lure away one of their players.   I would be the last to introduce any element of theology, but I may say you had to be specially careful if you ever ventured to do any spying on a ground of a club which was run under Roman Catholic auspices. They always seemed to have bands of supporters who were especially alert and eager."

The foregoing is freely quoted, because Wednesday have an official who actually faced a bloodthirsty mob, who really underwent a rough handling in Scotland and who is the only man who has ever shed blood for the cause of Wednesday! That man is Mr. A. J. Dickinson.

It is opportune to tell the story of Mr. Dickinson's experience at Dumbarton in September, 1891, and may it be said that it was not his only adventure when in search of players for Wednesday; nor were his adventures confined to Scotland. A Lincolnshire laundress, for instance, could a tale unfold! Mr. Dickinson had gone to Dumbarton in connection with an attempt to secure two of the Dumbarton players, named Towie and Spiers (the former later went to Preston and subsequently to Derby County). Mr. John Wilson, agent, met Mr. Dickinson, and at Partick they picked up Jack Madden, of the Celtic. They arrived at the appointed rendezvous, Sinclair's Restaurant, a noted football house, and one with which every Scottish player was acquainted. Presently, Madden arrived with the players, Towie and Spiers. Mr. Dickinson had to use a great deal of persuasive eloquence to effect his purpose, and, at last, it appeared as though he had succeeded. Towie took up his pen to sign a professional form for Wednesday, and it was all but done when the door opened and in stalked some Dumbarton club officials and two or three other gentlemen with arms of muscle. The party were fairly and squarely trapped.

It was clearly one of those cases in which palaver was of no account. Physical force was the only means by which safety was possible. Wilson bolted and got clear beautifully, and Jack Madden and Mr. Dickinson were left to face the music. Without any preliminaries they prepared to depart. They scrimmaged their way down the stairs and there found a crowd of hundreds of people waiting for them! The crowd yelled like savages and made for the pair. Madden had no interest in Mr. Dickinson except that he had seen him landed in a hole, and that was good enough excuse for him, so he stuck to Mr. Dickinson like a brick. They got their backs against a wall, and Madden fought like a hero alongside the Wednesday official. But they were separated and then it was a case of Mr. Dickinson making a bee-line for the station! How Mr. Dickinson got to the station he probably doesn't know, for the crowd followed him, raining blows upon him at every possible chance. Several times they tried to trip him, and had he gone down it would have proved exceedingly awkward. As it was, he was thoroughly mauled.

At last, he struggled into the station and rushed into a train. Luckily, it was just about to start for Glasgow, his destination. In the same train the agent was seated, spick and span and comfortable, without a scratch! Mr. Dickinson was bleeding from the mouth and the nose, and felt just about used up. When his face "developed" he had two black eyes and was generally bruised. With such a face, he dared not appear in public, and for two days he stayed in his hotel in Glasgow. Then he had to send for a chemist to paint away the discolouration around his eyes before he dare venture forth as a respectable man!

There is a story about Jack Madden in connection with the power of the Roman Catholics. Madden had signed for Gainsborough Trinity in 1887, but after one season went back to Scotland and later joined the Celtic. He became prominent and represented his country; moreover, he had no superior as a centre-forward in Scotland. In 1892, Wednesday secured Madden and Brady, the latter a clever inside-left. They both turned out for Wednesday in a practice match, but Madden had been in Sheffield but two days when a Roman Catholic priest "spirited" him back to Celtic. Alec Brady, however, had been smuggled off to Boston by Wednesday, and that player remained and rendered the club yeoman service.

The days of violence passed long ago. To-day club officials do not walk in fear of howling mobs. As professional football has become the more commercialised, so has the intimate character of the relations between clubs and their supporters declined. Further, there are a thousand and one regulations in connection with the government of the game which make conditions vastly different.

In one respect, however, there has been no change and probably there never will be: Competition for the cream of the talent never ceases. The bargaining power of a big cheque was never greater than it is at present.

Apart from financial matters, the maintenance of a successful team calls for exceptional powers of diplomacy, considerable business ability and judgment in the acquisition of players; so that the strain is severe though mob law is past.

Chapter Twenty-Two.

*First League Game — Precarious situations—
A desperate rally—Arrival of Langley and
Crawshaw—Famous Albion victory.*

IT was appropriate, remembering old associations, that
the first match which Wednesday played in the Football
League was with the County team of Nottingham.
And it was good, too, that Wednesday set out on their
adventure with a victory. The match was played on the
Castle ground, Nottingham, on Sept. 3rd, 1892, and the
one goal scored in the game was for Wednesday, by Harry
Davis, the recruit from Birmingham St. George's. A
valuable goal it proved to be, so it turned out, for Notts.
County were Wednesday's opponents in their last match
of the season, and the position then was that a defeat to
either team meant a lapse into one of the bottom places in
the First Division and the ordeal of a " test " match.
Before that second game (at Olive Grove) Wednesday
had 25 points to their credit and Notts. County 24. Now
if Davis had not given Wednesday an advantage in the first
game of the season they would have been awkwardly fixed,
obviously. However, the " Blades " won both the matches,
the second one by 3—2, and the reverse led to the County's
relegation to the Second Division, in which section of the
League they remained for four seasons.

The first of Wednesday's thousand games in the League
aroused such interest and enthusiasm that 2,000 people went
from Sheffield to Nottingham to see the fun. Unfortunately,
an accident occurred which somewhat clouded the spirit of
the people—a youth slipped between a train and the platform
at the Sheffield station and he was seriously injured. The
match was witnessed by 13,000 spectators. The report in
the " Sheffield Telegraph " runs: " Long before the
advertised time of kick-off various entrances were besieged
with anxious crowds, and close on the time for starting the

crowd was so dense that part of the barriers gave way and many people got in without payment." To-day, those remarks read quaintly.

Punctuality, too, had not then become the important matter it is now, for the teams were not on the field until ten minutes after the advertised time, and then, with the spectators encroaching on the pitch, the teams retired to the pavilion. However, they re-appeared at six minutes to four, and Notts. kicked off. The first half was fast, and Wednesday deserved their half-time lead. Spiksley had netted the ball on a second occasion, but he was given off-side—yet another instance of the winger paying the penalty for his speed.

Owing to rain, the second half did not start until eleven minutes to five, at which time nowadays the majority of games have ended. It was reported that "a considerable amount of time was wasted owing to the ball being kicked out of bounds, and on one occasion being dispatched into an adjoining garden, a fresh ball having to be procured."

The teams were :—

Wednesday: Allen; T. Brandon and Mumford; H. Brandon, Betts and Hall; Dunlop, Brown, Davis, Brady and Spiksley.

Notts. County: Toone; Whitelaw and Hendry; Parke, Calderhead and Shelton; McGregor, Docherty, Oswald, Walkerdine and Daft.

Spiksley and Brady formed a superb left-wing for the Sheffield team, one of the best wings in the country, in fact, and that is interesting seeing that before the season began Mr. Dickinson had been informed by a medical man that Spiksley was suffering from "galloping consumption" and would not live the year out! [In 1925-26 Spiksley, who has had an adventurous career, was the coach of Fulham F.C., and looked the picture of health. In the summer of 1926 he entered into an engagement with a German club as coach.] However, the next season Spiksley was re-examined and the previous judgment was reversed. In consequence, the player was given a three years' engagement, though it was thought advisable to give him permission to live at Gainsborough, because Sheffield did not suit his health.

It was in 1893 that Ambrose Langley joined Wednesday from Middlesbrough Ironopolis. The rumour flew through Sheffield that the club had signed on a " crock." True, Langley had had a rather serious accident in a match at South Bank, an injury which caused him a lot of trouble. But a " crock "! His doughty deeds in Sheffield colours made the suggestion laughable. Yet Aston Villa cared not to sign him until he had had his knee examined by the club doctor, and that examination Langley would not accept. What risk there was Wednesday took—to their ultimate benefit. Langley was a great back for them for about twelve seasons. There were only two or three of the old brigade left when Langley arrived at Olive Grove. One was Billy Betts; others, the late " Toddles " Woolhouse and " Clinks " Mumford.

Wednesday accomplished in the League little that was remarkable during the years they played at Olive Grove. Their great years in that competition came after the club had moved to Owlerton. At the Grove their glory was the glory of the English Cup-ties. In the League they finished twelfth among the sixteen clubs in their first two seasons, eighth in the next two, then sixth, and in 1897-8 fifth, following which came the season of dire disaster.

Sheffield United, having won promotion at their first attempt (in 1892-3), the city had two First Division clubs in 1893-4, and there was plenty of spirited and high-class football seen in Sheffield. Both clubs had hard-and-fast supporters. Wednesday were rather unlucky. The United made an excellent start in the League; they were at the top till near the end of October, while Wednesday were hunting near the bottom, able to claim only two League victories early in December. Jack Earp was introduced into the defence, and for six years the amateur was never dropped, save through indisposition.

Wednesday continued as they began, and when the New Year dawned there seemed no hope of the club escaping one of the bottom three positions. A special meeting of the directors and players was held to discuss the precarious situation. At the time, the Blue and Whites had six League matches to play, and in order to avoid having to compete in the " test " matches it was necessary to win five of the

games. The upshot of the meeting was an announcement
by Mr. John Holmes that the directors had decided to give
the players £50 amongst them if they won the five games.

The first game of that series was against Newton Heath.
That match was won by Wednesday by 2—1; Harry Woolhouse scored both the goals.   Darwen, Preston North End
and Nottingham Forest were beaten at home by 5—0, 3—0
and 1—0 respectively.   Matches away with Burnley and
Preston North End remained.   The ten professional members
of the team thus had a thrilling chance of winning £5 each
(Earp was an amateur), and they made the issue safe by
winning at Burnley by 1—0 on Good Friday—mark the day.
The Preston match was lost, but the " Blades " had won
five matches off the reel with a goal average of 12—1.   The
team before Christmas could not have been compared with
the team in the second half of the season and when the
semi-final of the English Cup tournament was reached.
Yet they played United five times altogether that season
and did not win once, though two of the games were
drawn.

However, financially, Wednesday's first two seasons in
the League were very gratifying.

Tom Crawshaw, who played for Wednesday fourteen
seasons and was one of the finest players the club possessed,
was obtained in 1894.   It was small wonder that a player of
his ability was soon singled out for international honours,
and by attaining such distinction in his first season with a
first-class club he probably created a record.   Crawshaw
remained an outstanding centre-half for a dozen seasons.
With him in the team there was no danger of relegation in
1894-5.

On April 22nd, 1895, an incident occurred which is of
special interest.   Wednesday went to West Bromwich Albion
to settle the last League match of the season.   Stoke had
secured 24 points and stood with a goal-average of 50 for
to 67 against.   The Albion had 22 points and the match
with Wednesday at Stoney Lane still to play.   The
" Throstles' " goal figures were 45 for and 66 against, and
in order to escape the " test " matches it was necessary to
win the Wednesday match by 6—0.

One of the Sheffield defenders that afternoon was Langley. Those who remember his forceful work on the field will know how to appreciate his threat when told that West Bromwich intended to " go for " those six goals clear, so as to drop poor Stoke into the hole. " They'll do it over my dead body!" cried Langley in the dressing-room prior to the match—which showed that he had not forgotten his unfortunate experience against the Albion in the English Cup semi-final at Derby. It also proved that a good player is not necessarily a good prophet. For the Albion got the six goals; but Langley continued to grace football for years. Wednesday never gave up striving to avert the scoring of those goals. Albion, however, played irresistible football.

The season 1896-7 saw Wednesday gain the greatest number of points in the League up to that time, though, true to tradition, they, as holders, were beaten in the first round of the Cup. In that season Spiksley was awarded the match with The Corinthians for his benefit, and he eventually received the highest benefit amount paid by Wednesday up to that year.

What Spiksley has regarded as the most dangerous accident of his career occurred that season while he was playing against Bury. In jumping to head the ball just before half-time he unluckily found " a back " had been set for him. He fell with his head doubled under him and, he declares, the thoughts which passed through his mind for a second or two linger still in his memory. He always maintains that his lightness saved his life on that occasion, that a heavily-built man must have dislocated his neck.

The League items did not completely fill Wednesday's programme; occasionally " friendly " matches were played. In one they were opposed to a seaside club which gave them a guarantee of about £30. The referee was a well-known cricketer who resided in the popular resort. His duties, so the story runs, seemed to consist mainly of ruling Spiksley off-side. The match ended in a draw, and the referee, when twitted about his decisions, immediately retorted " If you think we're going to give you £30 to come here and lick us, you are sadly mistaken—at least, not while I'm alive "!

Chapter Twenty-Three.

The first Fall—Club's existence in jeopardy—
Departure from Olive Grove—Great loyalists—
An astonishing survival.

NEVER in the whole history of Wednesday has the
club been in such a melancholy plight as in the
season 1898-99—the period of their first fall to the
Second Division, and, incidentally, their last season at Olive
Grove. Troubles came not singly but in battalions, and
the surprising thing is that Wednesday survived through
the series of disasters which befel them. But how often in
history has not the hour of peril produced the man, the
leader strong, able and courageous? In the case of
Wednesday, Mr. A. J. Dickinson may safely he said to
have been the man who saved the old club. Often has it
been stated that there would have been no Wednesday club
in existence to-day but for that wonderfully enthusiastic
worker. Admittedly, he had valiant helpers, not least of
whom was the late Alderman George Senior, J.P., one of
Sheffield's grand old men, but Mr. Dickinson, as the
honorary secretary, had great responsibilities, and his word
carried tremendous weight. He was the man behind the
scenes who had the foresight to recognise the right moment
at which to guillotine arguments on land values and close
with the offer of the land at Owlerton at a price of £5,000.

There was one ray of comfort. In the hour of need the
public stuck loyally to Wednesday, as it has ever done, and
the club had £2,000 in hard cash at the bank. Yet it
needed supreme courage to remove the club bag and
baggage to a suburb of the city and which was really then
a countryside. There was precious little but green fields
beyond Hillsborough Barracks in 1899—no cars to take
followers to the ground as to-day. The people who lived
about there were not fervid Wednesday supporters as were
those who dwelt in the city and in the Heeley district.

Wednesday had to face the task of converting them to "the faith," of turning meadow-land into a football ground and of taking on trust the loyalty of supporters willing to make the long trek out to Owlerton when they could get First Division football close at hand at Bramall Lane. All sorts of obstacles had to be surmounted, and it is no wonder that at times the officials were almost in despair. It was not until June, three months before the football season was due to open, that an agreement was reached for the purchase of the ten acres of freehold land at Owlerton for £5,000.

One can imagine the anxiety which accompanied the seeking of a ground, the worry associated with the equipping of it suitably within three months. To have lost their place in the First Division and the ground they played on at the same time was a tragedy, and no club without a magnificent following and public affection would have recovered.

The season had opened under a cloud, for there was a general unsettled atmosphere, due to the fact that the club had had notice already to quit Olive Grove, which lay alongside the railway between the Sheffield and Heeley stations. The land had come into the possession of the Midland Railway Company, who required it for their own purposes. It was a worrying time for the committee, who surveyed every piece of land, likely or unlikely, within a reasonable distance of the city, wondering at the same time where the money would come from to pay for it.

The business dragged on and on. One suggestion was that Wednesday and United should share the Bramall Lane ground for League matches, the respective reserve teams to play at Sheaf House, and the men train in separate quarters. Then Sheaf House grounds were the subject of negotiations, which fell through. After that attentions were turned elsewhere, and eventually four sites were found, two at Carbrook and two at Owlerton. One of the Carbrook grounds was that of Carbrook Cricket Club and of Attercliffe Football Club, near Broughton Lane, and the other the Pheasant Inn ground; at Owlerton, the present ground and a big open space where Buffalo Bill used to disport himself, and near Wardsend Cemetery. Old readers will readily recollect the arguments on the merits of the different places, and how Wednesday asked their supporters to vote indicating into which district they would prefer the club to go.

About 10,000 supporters voted, and the figures worked out as follows :—

For Carbrook... 4,767   For Sheaf House... 16
For Owlerton... 4,115   Neutral   124

There were drawbacks to the Carbrook scheme; the piece of land in mind was not quite what Wednesday preferred, and the officials are to be complimented on the vision they eventually showed. Owlerton was country then, yet they had an impression that the city would steadily grow larger and larger; and Owlerton was one of the districts where it could easily spread out its dwellings. It is a tribute to their judgment that they foresaw the time when the locality would develop into an extensively-populated area, which it now is. To-day Hillsborough is a Parliamentary division directly represented in the House of Commons.

Obviously, the conversion scheme of the meadow land into a thoroughly up-to-date athletic ground could not be carried out by a club with a membership of less than fifty and a capital of £250, so the club was turned into a limited liability company. Mr. George Senior, one of the city's leading steel magnates, accepted the chairmanship, following Mr. John Holmes, who had been the club president, and threw himself heart and soul into the work of his new position. Many of the most influential men in the civic, commercial and professional life of Sheffield became directors, and the capital of £7,000 was quickly subscribed.

The present enclosure is one of the finest in the country.

Incidentally, the stand at Olive Grove was taken to pieces and re-built at Owlerton. It occupied the position now filled by the splendid new stand erected shortly before the war. For years it was known as " the Olive Grove stand."

It is commonly agreed that Wednesday were relegated not because they continually played bad football. They were relegated, first, because of poor refereeing, then a succession of injuries to players: Spiksley, Earp, Crawshaw, Layton and others became casualties at different

periods, and, lastly, weak play in consequence. When
Layton was hurt at Burnley the injury to his abdomen and
groin was so bad that he had to be wheeled across
Manchester in a folding chair; he could not walk. He had
actually had a narrow escape from being killed that day.
Burnley, by the way, had won the match by 5—0. Ross,
late of Preston North End, scored four of the goals.

Wednesday lost several matches by the odd goal and
through missed penalties. In a thrilling encounter with
Blackburn Rovers they were losing by 2—1, when in the
last minute a penalty-kick was awarded them for "hands,"
and Spiksley sent the ball yards wide. Layton, Earp and
Ferrier were all hurt in that match. Afterwards they ought
to have beaten Notts. County, but Earp failed with a
"spot" kick, and there were other vital instances. Nothing
would go right for them, and away from Olive Grove their
experiences were really distressing. They not only did not
win an away match, but they did not even score a goal
on opponents' grounds until December 17th, when they drew
2—2 with Newcastle United. The scorers were Wright and
Spiksley. Wright was a clever forward they had got a
month before from Bolton Wanderers.

Altogether, Wednesday played 17 away matches and
lost all save five, which were drawn, and scored only six
goals against 37. The players felt like walking in sackcloth
and ashes!

The voting, mentioned previously, took place on
November 20th, 1898, at the match with Aston Villa at
Olive Grove, and that match will be remembered on another
account. It was stopped ten and a half minutes from
time owing to bad light, at which stage Wednesday were
leading by 3—1. It was that which followed which caused
the match to be memorable, for the League ordered Aston
Villa to come to Sheffield at Wednesday's expense and play
out the remaining minutes of time.

Now the League had not been consistent in things of
that sort. Some years before Wednesday and Bolton
Wanderers had played a match on the Lancashire club's
ground and it was stopped seven minutes from time owing
to a terrible rain-storm, when the score was 1—1. The
League then ordered the teams to play the remaining seven

minutes on another date, Bolton to pay Wednesday's expenses. The proviso was made, however, that if the seven minutes were not played the match would stand as 1—1. Those seven minutes were never played.

On another occasion a Wednesday match, with Stoke, was stopped 25 minutes before time owing to a snowstorm, and the League ordered the whole match to be replayed.

The Villa lodged an appeal against the League's decision so far as their match was concerned, and it was not until March 13th that the remaining 10½ minutes were completed. Wednesday won by 4—1 : their biggest score of that season. Perhaps it ought to be mentioned that in the November part of the game the start had been delayed about six minutes owing to the late arrival of the referee. Mr. Fred Bye, a member of the Wednesday committee and a League referee, officiated to half-time,, and at the interval there was another delay until the officially appointed referee had had time to change.

When Aston Villa appeared at Olive Grove a second time, it was arranged that after the ten minutes had been played, a " friendly " game would be decided to supplement the benefit of Harry Davis, the old Birmingham St. George player. In those ten minutes the Villa had rushed off altogether to score, but Wednesday went away and obtained a fourth goal. As a coincidence, it is worth noting that 29 players actually took part in that one match—surely a record of its kind? For the " friendly " event the Villa changed their team, and Bob Templeton made his first appearance for the Villa in their League eleven. He took the place of Athersmith on the right-wing. Wednesday backs said that with Athersmith off they would get a bit of peace, but they found in Templeton a greater player still, and he caused them more worry than Athersmith would have done. He played magnificently.

The shades of relegation were then drawing nigh, and rumours were flying about the city. Coupled with the ground trouble, etc., the situation became such that the Wednesday committee felt it necessary to contradict statements that at the end of the season the club would cease to exist.

It really was an extraordinary season. During the course of it Wednesday sustained that disaster at Derby, where they were defeated by 9—o, of which Steve Bloomer scored six. It occurred about half-way through January. A week or two before then, Wednesday's players had gone to Matlock for special training. At that time Matlock was considered a good training-centre; many teams went there. Derby County and Stoke were there at the same time as Wednesday. However, the players became weary of Matlock.

Regarding the match with Derby County, rarely has there been seen such shooting as Bloomer's. Never was a man in such form as Steve was that day, scoring six goals and hitting the post and cross-bar many times. Whenever the ball went to him he would spin round and shoot without wasting time to trap it. He was unbeatable. If it had not been for some good goal-keeping by Massey, no one knows what the score would have been. After the game, Steve said he would have scored if he had never looked where the goal was, and probably he would have done, too.

Afterwards, the players were asked if they would like to go back to Sheffield, but they felt they would rather endure Matlock than the reception they would have got in Sheffield. Only Spiksley and Ferrier returned to Sheffield. They had been injured. At Matlock the next day Stoke, whom Wednesday were drawn against in the Cup, asked them to " give 'em a chance." The irony of it! Wednesday were beaten by Stoke in the replay!!

Of their 34 matches that season, Wednesday won only eight, lost 18, and drew eight. They scored 32 goals and yielded 61. It was a sorry season, for Sheffield United were third from the bottom, though they carried off the English Cup.

Wednesday finished at the very bottom of the First Division, one point behind Bolton Wanderers. They had no chance to redeem themselves in the " test " matches, for those had been abolished the year before. So straight into the Second Division they went.

On the formation of the Second Division, it had been decided that the three highest clubs in it must play the three lowest in the First Division in so-styled "test matches" to decide the right of promotion, but because the system was abused it was abolished, as already stated, in favour of the present automatic method of promotion and relegation.

The last "test match" was between Stoke and Burnley. The position was that if the match were drawn both clubs would remain in the First Division the following season. It was drawn, and the manner in which it was drawn undoubtedly led to the dropping of the system.

The last match played at Olive Grove was against Preston North End on April 22nd, 1899, and it ended in a draw (1—1).

An amusing incident is related of the side that season. Towards the end of the campaign a group photograph of the Wednesday team was sent to the ground. The sender had carefully drawn a pair of spectacles around the eyes of each player. Further, he had actually taken a pin and pricked out the eyes of each man, and underneath he had written: "The Blind Eleven!" The players did not take exception to little things in those days, but they thought that that was the limit. They took it as a great insult, coming as it did when they were in the danger zone and fighting desperately to avoid the fate which eventually overtook them.

In bidding good-bye to the old home, ardent Wednesday folk felt many a pang. It always appealed to players as it appealed to thousands of supporters. It was a most comfortable little ground. It was a place which seemed to foster friendships, and it appeared to encourage that feeling in the spectators "These Wednesday fellows are part of us."

The players were on very friendly terms with the spectators, possibly because the play was so near to the railings, and the personal link between player and onlooker then was far stronger than it is now. Maybe modern grounds and conditions are responsible for the drifting apart. Wednesday never used to train behind locked doors, behind bolts and bars: the folk could go and see them train, and the players were pleased to see them.

Olive Grove! It used to be considered one of the best grounds in existence, and the small stand one of the best, too. Yet what a contrast with modern structures! The stand's inside walls were whitewashed, there was a tiny gas-stove for the comfort of the men, and one slipper-bath for eleven players.

Many were the thrilling dramas in the English Cup-ties enacted there. However, the removal did not prove the calamity that was threatened at that moment. Brighter days were in store.

SPLENDID VIEW OF THE

N TO THE FIRST DIVISION

Reproduced from "Yorkshire Telegraph & Star."

ILLSBOROUGH GROUND.

Chapter Twenty-Four.

Rise from the Ashes—All eyes on Sheffield—
Return to First Division in splendid style—
Chesterfield's distinction.

ONE knows not what is in store for Sheffield's premier teams, but whatever distinctions they may gain they can hardly rouse the city sportsmen's enthusiasm more than they did at the dawn of the twentieth century. Successes in Cup and League came as with a flood. The light soon shone through Wednesday's gloom of 1899, and United and Wednesday together carried almost everything before them in the grand season of 1899-1900. Forgotten was Wednesday's exit from the First Division in the glamour of a glorious promotion fight. Wednesday rose triumphant from the ashes. Not only did the first season at Owlerton end in a blaze of glory, but Sheffield United nearly won the League championship (they missed it by only two points). Wednesday became the champions of the Second Division, and thoroughly won promotion.

Sheffield was the talk of the football universe. For weeks and weeks, even months and months, United and Wednesday were the leaders of their respective divisions, and their record in that direction has never been equalled. Strange that at such a time they were drawn together in the English Cup.

In spite of the accidents to their men, the suspensions of Pryce and Langley, Wednesday did not falter, and by the middle of April had made safe their return to their old sphere of action. How complete was their revival! They did not drop a single point at Owlerton; they scored no fewer than 61 goals in 17 matches and yielded only seven to visiting teams, not one of whom obtained more than one goal in any match against them. Throughout the season, they lost only five games in the Second Division and four of those were by 1—0. The biggest set-back was the 4—1

Second Division Championship Shield won
by Wednesday in 1899—1900 and 1925—26.

defeat at Small Heath. That match immediately followed the grim Cup-fights with United, and they were short of Lee, Massey, Wright, Millar and Spiksley, owing to injuries, so that they had a good excuse to offer.

Wednesday did not lose a League match until Dec. 30th —unbeaten in 14 consecutive fixtures—and only mistaken tactics cost them the points at Chesterfield on the date named. The position of Sheffield football was extraordinary; the deeds of the teams were as a beacon. What would be said to-day if two city teams went virtually through four months of a season without being conquered? For just as Wednesday were beating all and sundry, so were Sheffield United making glorious history. The " Cutlers "—for that is really the United's nick-name—played 22 games in succession without a defeat, and thus equalled Preston North End's proud record.

To the end of November, United and Wednesday had jointly won 41 points out of 46 possible, and had scored 53 goals against 15. The record to the end of the year was better still, but the figures already given are sufficient to indicate the prowess. The final readings for the season were :—

	P.	W.	L.	D.	For.	Agst.	Pts.
Sheffield United ...	34	18	4	12	63	33	48
Wednesday	34	25	5	4	84	22	54

Wednesday's performance was then a record for the Division. The Reserves, too, were very successful: they won the Sheffield Challenge Cup, the Wharncliffe Charity Cup, and Sheffield Association League; in fact, in the whole of those competitions they lost only one game and scored 154 goals against 21. The complete record was :—

P.	W.	L.	D.	For.	Agst.
36 ...	29 ...	1 ...	6 ...	154 ...	21

Wednesday's left-wing, Spiksley and Wright (the latter the inside forward obtained from Bolton Wanderers in the previous season) was a superb one, and that wing scored no fewer than 20 of the first 30 goals that Wednesday secured in 1899-1900, and made, in addition, many oppor-

tunities for their chums. As a matter of fact, Wright, in
the course of the term, scored 25 goals.

The club had obtained one or two new men. One was
Brash, another Millar, a centre-forward, who started his
career with Paisley Abercorn and had experience with
Reading and Bury. A good player he was.

Many people thought that the new ground would not
be ready in time for the first match, for it was meadow-
land and covered with dandelions. But the work was
pushed on, and the pitch put in order, though, naturally, it
was a bit rough. The accommodation, too, was limited,
but good in the circumstances, and improvements proceeded
all the time.

A new stand was erected, and by the end of the season
there was cover for 6,000 people. The directors' report
said: " One feature of the accommodation is that the
visiting teams have the same-sized dressing-room and bath-
room and a similar bath to the home team, which is an
example your directors hope may be followed by other
clubs." The players did most of their training on the old
Niagara ground, once the home of Sheffield Club.

The new ground was opened on Sept. 2nd, 1899, by the
then Lord Mayor of Sheffield, Alderman W. E. Clegg, who
is still a director of the club, and the visiting team were
Chesterfield. Chesterfield were the first who scored a goal
at Owlerton ; Herbert Munday, one of the best forwards of
his day, and who refused to be tempted by some of the
biggest clubs in the land to leave Chesterfield, was the
player who gained the individual distinction. After ten
minutes' play, Geary got away at top speed, beat Earp
excellently, and got in a hot shot at a difficult angle. The
ball hit the post and bounded right in front of goal.
Munday, following up, easily scored.

As soon as Munday had scored, people began to shout
that now Wednesday had got into the Second Division they
looked like stopping there. But the men soon showed them
they were wrong in their ideas, that they meant to get out,
and quickly. They played a really fine game, and Spiksley
equalised for them. In the end the Sheffielders won by
5—1. It was but one of several pronounced victories at
Owlerton. They beat Burton Swifts by 6—0, Small Heath

4—0, Luton 6—0, Gainsborough Trinity 5—1, Loughboro'
5—0, Barnsley 5—1, and New Brighton Tower and Burslem
Port Vale each by 4—0.

Chesterfield and Barnsley both took their whackings to
heart. Each had been beaten by 5—1 at Owlerton. Was it
not a striking coincidence that both those teams beat
Wednesday on their own grounds by 1—0?

The defeat at Chesterfield was Wednesday's first upset.
The match aroused great excitement.

Chesterfield had a good team, and that day they had a
record " gate," £163 Wednesday were much the superior
in general play and attacked vigorously. All of the men,
with the exception of Massay, strove to score, but once
again did Geary slip away and centre so that Munday was
able to score a beautiful goal—a fine shot in the corner. In
vain did the Sheffield team endeavour to draw level, and
one of the most courageous men on the field was Hancock,
the Chesterfield goalkeeper, who played brilliantly.

When Wednesday visited Barnsley, the latter also had
a record " gate," and defeat was Wednesday's portion ; but
they were short of Langley and Spiksley. Mr. McCartney,
the manager of Portsmouth in succession to Mr. R. Brown,
of Wednesday, played for Barnsley then. It is true that it
was customary for the relegated of those times to return to
the First Division within a year, yet in the Second Division
then there were several good sides : Bolton Wanderers,
Middlesbrough, Arsenal, Leicester Fosse and Newton
Heath, for example. And no matter what competition, it
is hard to win promotion. For every loss at home teams
have to make a draw and secure a win away to balance it.

That season Langley, who was the captain, scored six
or seven goals—useful work for a back. He used to go
well up when corner-kicks were taken, for he was very
smart with his head. Opponents used to say : " Watch
the big 'un "; consequently, the other players had greater
freedom, because two or three men guarded Langley.

When Wednesday lost at Bolton, Bob Jack, now the
manager of Plymouth Argyle, was the scorer of the goal.

One of the fiercest games of the term was played at
Newton Heath, and the newspapers declared that it was
stopped fifty times owing to fouls. The trouble really

started at Owlerton in the first match, when Bryant broke his wrist in a collision with Langley. A bitter feeling resulted, and that led to the Heath players trying to score off Langley and to the latter benefiting by all his physical advantages. The crowd resented Langley's vigour, and he was blamed by most for the bother.

Reverting to that first match at Owlerton with Chesterfield, it should be placed on record that Spiksley, Ferrier, Millar (2) and Brash were Wednesday's goal-scorers, and the Wednesday team were: Massey; Earp and Langley; Ferrier, Crawshaw and Ruddlesdin; Brash, Pryce, Millar, Wright and Spiksley.

The immunity from accident during the unbeaten run was remarkable. In goal no change was needed through the first four months; at back, Earp played in the first match, but Layton then took his place and stayed there to the end with Langley; at half-back there was no change at all; and in the front rank the only change was at outside-right, where Lee figured in the first two games and Archie Brash in the remainder.

The whole season was a splendid send-off for the new ground. Wednesday finished as champions with 54 points out of a possible 68, and, accompanied by Bolton Wanderers, who had fallen with them, they went back to the premier division. The Wanderers had only two points fewer than Wednesday, but had six points more than Small Heath (now Birmingham), who were third.

Chapter Twenty-Five.

Winning the League Championship—A dramatic race with Sunderland—Thrilling matches—The three L's—Riotous scenes at Roker.

AFTER Wednesday's rise to the First Division, people thought the team which had done so well in the Second Division would not be "class" enough for the senior circles; nevertheless, the club finished eighth in the season 1900-1, which was considered quite satisfactory. The team was very little changed in constitution; also in the following season, when Wednesday finished ninth, Andrew Wilson, the centre-forward from Clyde, had been secured. In each of those two seasons, the Blue and Whites were only twice beaten in League games at Owlerton, and from January 14th, 1901, to March 8th, 1902, they played 18 matches at home, won 14, and were never defeated.

In April, 1901, Wednesday beat Nottingham Forest by 4—1 at Owlerton, and it was noteworthy because, although Wednesday won by such a margin, it was a curious thing that not a Wednesday forward scored. Layton, the back, scored with a long shot; Langley, the other back, with a penalty-kick; and the other scorers were Herrod Ruddlesdin and Tom Crawshaw, half-backs. Wednesday had been unlucky with penalty kicks and about that time Langley began to take them. As captain, he thought he ought to try his hand, and, incidentally, take what "honours" came along. The match, by the way, was played in a terrific thunderstorm.

When Wednesday were awarded the kick, the crowd called out first one name, then another, of players who they thought ought to take the kick. Up to that point no goal had been scored. As Langley advanced, Linacre, the Forest goalkeeper, said to him: "Give me a chance, cockey!" Langley gave him no chance whatever.

In those days it was much harder to score from penalty-kicks, as the goalkeeper was allowed to advance to the six-yards line and so practically "cover" the goal, save

During the season 1902-3 The Wednesday won five trophies, i.e., the League Championship (Div. 1), Midland League Championship, Sheffield Challenge Cup, Wharncliffe Charity Cup, and the *Plymouth Bowl.

Back Row (left to right): Eyre Ryalls Hemmingfield J. Beech Stewart Bartlett, Thackeray, Morallee, P. Crawshaw, W. Ruddlesdin. Middle Row: J. Davis (asst. trainer), Marrison, H. Ruddlesdin, Ferrier, Layton, Langley, Lyall, T. Crawshaw, Stubbs, Burton, G. Cawley, P. Frith (trainer). Front Row: V. S. Simpson, H. Davis, Chapman, Wilson, Malloch, Spiksley, G. Simpson

* Beat Notts County in an exhibition match at Plymouth by 2—0.

for about a yard on each side of him.   He would stand only six yards away from the penalty-taker, thus the difficulty is apparent.   By his success that day, Langley became the recognised penalty-taker of the side, and he actually scored from twelve consecutive " spot "-kicks in that and succeeding seasons.   He knew not failure, and in the first championship season he was successful with five, which gave Wednesday valuable points in more than one instance.

Langley was looked upon as a " certainty " with those concessions, and Tom Crawshaw always said to him, " Go on, old lad, let 'em have it."   Mr. John Holmes, the enthusiastic official, once popped into the dressing-room to say to the men : " Now, then, don't let the result depend upon Langley's penalty-kick to-day."   The forwards did not always get the desired goals.

One may tell here also the story of how a goalkeeper presented an opposing side with six goals.   The event occurred in the first season of Wednesday at Owlerton, but when playing Notts. County at Nottingham.   Wednesday had a goalkeeper who bade fair to be another Foulke—a giant named Stubbs, who could keep the ball from passing between the uprights as if it were the job he had been born to.   In the match in question Notts. were rampant, but Stubbs guarded the goal with such brilliance that they could not score.   In the course of one scrimmage, however, Stubbs went full length and received a heavy crack on the head from somebody's boot.   He walked off the field with the others at the interval, and his comrades, knowing him to be a joker, took no notice of the fact that he kept asking them what the score was.   The kick he had received had affected his head, and to the amazement of his colleagues he caught the first shot that came in after the interval, turned round and placed the ball on the ground behind the goal-line.   He was as safe as ever with the ball, but time after time he repeated that extraordinary performance of placing the ball in his own goal, and thus presented Notts. with half-a-dozen goals.

Andrew Wilson and others are confident that that day's mishap deprived the game of one of its greatest goalkeepers.

Undoubtedly, Stubbs had been badly kicked.   He was absolutely dazed for the rest of the game, but he would not

go off the field. Mates would say, " Go off, Frank !" when
they caught him leaning his head against the goal-post.
His reply was: " I'm all right," and he would not leave.
To show how upset he was it may be mentioned that Langley
became mixed up with two or three Notts. County men,
and then Stubbs appealed to Layton thus: "Who's won
the fight?" Layton replied: " Ambrose, of course."
Stubbs had thought it was a fight. Mr. Dickinson also
states that after the match, when they were at Nottingham
station Stubbs thought he was in Sheffield.

Now to the greatest seasons of all in the League history
of the club, 1902-3 and 1903-4, when the League championship was won twice in succession, a feat which equalled the
achievement previously accomplished by only three clubs—·
Preston North End, Aston Villa (twice), and Sunderland.
Since then, of course, Liverpool have also gained the
honour, while Huddersfield created a new record in 1925-26
by carrying off the championship for the third consecutive
year.

In 1902-3, Wednesday won the League championship
and secured five trophies all told: The League Cup, the
" Plymouth " Bowl, the Sheffield Challenge Cup, the Midland League Cup, and the Wharncliffe Charity Cup. It
was, indeed, a magnificent season, and Wednesday had a
reserve team also which would be the envy of many a Second
Division club to-day. The reserves had rare talent with
Jarvis and Stubbs as goalkeepers; backs, Thackeray and
Burton; halves, Percy Crawshaw, Morallee, Fish and
Bartlett; forwards, O. Tummon, Ryalls, Harrison, Stewart,
Simpson, Hemmingfield and Beech, among others. The
figures of their performances were extraordinary, to say the
least. As for the first eleven, only two League games were
lost at home and only seven goals were registered against
Wednesday at Owlerton throughout the campaign. Yet
they did not please everybody!

One of the side made a mistake on the field. A spectator
immediately cried out: " It's time tha finished playing and
gave somebody else a chance !" Soon afterwards the same
player accomplished something brilliant. A friend of the
player asked: " He did that all right, didn't he?" To his
consternation the retort was: " Yes, he did, and didn't he

ought to do? he's been playing long enough!" That is
typical of the " reasoning " of some people.

The championship race was one of the most dramatic
on record, for the issue hung in the balance to the very last
day of the season, and there were more than one or two clubs
in the chase. All teams had had streaky passages and
astonishing revivals, and the concluding burst was chiefly
between Sunderland and Wednesday, with Aston Villa and
Sheffield United on their heels. West Bromwich Albion for
months were at the top of the League. To the New Year
they nearly always had their nose in front, and it seemed
as if Wednesday could never beat them down. Then in the
middle of January the Albion went all to pieces and did not
win a match until the last Saturday of the season, April 25th.
It was amazing. They who had led the field so handsomely
actually finished seventh down.

Wednesday headed the senior Division the opening week
in October, but for a long time they were second, and seldom
below that position. Finally, on March 7th, they led the
way again and were never displaced. For all that they had
their shakings. With the decline of Albion came the rise
of Sheffield United and Aston Villa. The Villa were fourth
from the bottom in the middle of January; they were never
in the top half of the table until half-way through February,
and were then exactly ten points worse off than Wednesday.
To their credit be it stated, they finished second in the chart,
only one point behind Wednesday and possessing a superior
goal-average.

The rise of Aston Villa started with the transfer of Brawn
from Sheffield United. Whereas before they had not gained
half the maximum points, they then won match after match.
They gained both points in twelve games out of the
remaining fifteen. The programme for the season was 34
games. Derby County were also in the hunt, and Sheffield
United were fourth, with Sunderland third.

What a duel it was with Sunderland, too! For months
they had not been thought of as likely to do well. They
were twelfth at the beginning of December, and they had
been beaten at Owlerton by Wednesday. Yet between
December 6th and March 14th, Sunderland played 11
matches, won 20 points, and did not lose a single match.

As a matter of fact, one of the striking features of the season was that while Wednesday had beaten them by 1—0 at Hillsborough on Nov. 22nd, the Wearsiders did not receive another set-back until they played Wednesday in the return match at Roker on March 21st, when the score again was 1—0 in the Sheffield club's favour.

With Sunderland it was a neck-and-neck race right from the end of January, and a real " Derby " finish. With matches in hand, people were then constantly saying that Sunderland would head Wednesday off, for they had an international defence in Doig, McCombie and Watson (who all played in the Scottish rear ranks against England at Bramall Lane, when Harry Davis, of Wednesday, played for England on the wing and was hurt on the chest. That Davis was not the old Birmingham man, but the winger obtained from Barnsley.) The writers analysed the two clubs' records and, attempting to look ahead, worked out the goal-averages to show that Wednesday had but a wee advantage in decimal calculations.

Wednesday had shocking croppers in April, especially at Bury and Derby. They thought they had lost the championship; but Sunderland almost at the same time dropped five points out of six; they drew only with Stoke at home, and lost to Bolton Wanderers and Nottingham Forest, all within four days. They lost by 5—2 at Nottingham and Wednesday breathed again. To make matters worse for them they had their ground suspended as a result of boisterous scenes after Wednesday had beaten them in the March preceding. And so it came about that on the last day of the season, Sunderland had to conquer Newcastle United at Newcastle to win the championship.

The Sheffielders had finished their programme and were at Plymouth playing Notts. County for the " Plymouth " Bowl. Wednesday's men well knew the hopes Sunderland entertained, and the northerners had every cause to be hopeful. Sunderland had never been beaten by Newcastle at Newcastle; what was more, they had never lost a point there. You can imagine the climax to the competition when Newcastle United made history by beating Sunderland by 1—0 for the first time in their lives! Wednesday won the championship by one point—42 against 41 each by Aston Villa and Sunderland.

The title was won with the aid of 22 players, and Andrew Wilson, Ruddlesdin and Langley, the captain, never missed a match in the campaign. Their comrades were stalwarts such as Lyall, Ferrier, Crawshaw, Malloch, Spiksley, Harry Chapman, Layton, Davis, V. S. Simpson, and a handful of others. Malloch missed only one match during the season. He was an admirable partner for Spiksley, yet, curiously, he never scored a goal. However, a man's value does not depend solely on the goals he scores.

Wednesday were a really good side, full of the team-spirit. One noted critic wrote of them : " Wednesday must be considered one of the fairest teams playing football. Their executive can feel they have been served by an honest and clever team."

One of the matches Wednesday lost was with Aston Villa at Birmingham by the only goal scored, on Boxing Day. It was a terrific match and the rivalry intense. When Wednesday were due to meet the Villa, the gossipers used to ask each other : " Are you going to see Athersmith and Langley next Saturday?" Not " Villa v. Wednesday " you will note.

The first game Wednesday lost was at Newcastle by 3—0. The northern Magpies must have rejoiced at such a deed, for the visiting defence had a reputation in those days. When Wednesday went to Newcastle, folk did not discuss Wednesday as a team. They used to say : " The three ruddy L's are playing to-day. Are you going to see them?" The three L's, of course, were Jack Lyall, William Layton and Ambrose Langley."

Blackburn Rovers did well against Wednesday that season. In the League they took three points from them and defeated them in a replay in the first round of the English Cup competition at Owlerton. They had, however, a couple of disconcerting experiences in Sheffield. On the occasion of their first visit the horses attached to their drag fell down, and it was a long time before they could get them up. On the second occasion, when they were going home— after the Cup-tie replay—some of the wheels of their waggonette came off and the vehicle collapsed, but no one was hurt. The incidents show how changed are the modes of transport.

The English Cup finalists in 1903 were Bury and Derby County, and it will be long remembered that Bury gained the biggest victory in a Cup Final ever recorded. They beat Derby by 6—o. Bury put Wednesday " among the pots " all right, too, for on Monday, April 6th, they whipped them by 4—o at Gigg Lane, and the Saturday afterwards Wednesday were beaten by the County at Derby by an odd goal. Those reverses certainly placed Wednesday's championship prospects in jeopardy, but, as it happened, Sunderland also had a crash.

Wednesday began the New Year well, for they trounced the Villa by 4—o at Owlerton on New Year's Day, and a couple of days later beat Bolton Wanderers by 3—o on the same ground. Harry Davis scored all the three goals in the latter match. Harry was a scorcher.

In the course of one match, the captain told Davis to keep more on the touch-line. Harry turned round promptly and retorted : " Tha's got enough to do to look after thi own position. Ne'er mind about mine ; tha's got plenty on thi own plate." Still, Davis did hug the line a bit more, showing he did take a bit of notice sometimes.

Wednesday had experience of last-minute reverses. At Middlesbrough, where Williamson gave a wonderful display in the Tees-siders' goal, they were leading by 1—o ten minutes from time. But Middlesbrough rallied finely, drew level, and in the last thirty seconds scored the winning goal from a corner-kick. Later, at Wolverhampton, the score was 1—1 three minutes from close. Again Wednesday felt safe for a point, but Walker, the father of William Walker, the present Villa " star " forward, beat Lyall and so brought about Wednesday's downfall. That goal, also, was the outcome of a corner.

Dramatic scenes followed the great encounter at Sunderland. With the Wearsiders revealed as Wednesday's most dangerous challengers and they recalling what had occurred at Owlerton, it was plain that the laurels of champions might rest upon the winners of that match. It was a thrilling game and vary hard, rough and ready. In the first half, Andrew Wilson scored with a magnificent screw shot from twenty yards range, which completely beat Doig. Ten minutes of the second half had sped when the

trouble began.   Sunderland made a fierce attack and Lyall
and the ball were bundled into the net.   Sunderland argued
that Gemmell had scored, but Mr. Arnitt, the referee, would
not allow the point, because of the unfair charging of Lyall.
The crowd waxed greatly indignant, and the referee had a
hot time.   The players, too, came in for attention.   The
people started throwing oranges at them, and, ultimately,
the referee consulted his linesmen as to whether or not he
should abandon the match.   However, he decided to finish
it, and finished it was, with Wednesday winners by that
one goal.

Afterwards, extraordinary scenes were witnessed.   A
mob gathered outside and waited for the Wednesday
players and there was a display of hooliganism.   Wednesday
had to face a barrage of stones and various missiles.   In
their drag, the horses galloped away as fast as they could,
with hundreds of frenzied folk chasing behind throwing
stones and whatever they could lay hands on.   However,
no one was seriously hurt, though players and officials were
struck, policemen as well.   One man was arrested.   As for
the referee, he was smuggled out of the ground.   As a
result, Sunderland had their ground suspended for a fortnight, and in consequence had to play one of their remaining
matches at Newcastle.

When Newcastle United and Sunderland met in the game
which was destined to settle the championship, there was
talk throughout the land of a " squared match " and to the
effect that Newcastle were going to let Sunderland win and
so gain the championship for the second season in succession.
But rumour was ever a lying jade.   Newcastle triumphed,
and incidentally did Wednesday a good turn.

That season Wednesday had done a lot of " missionary "
work.   They had played matches in the Heavy Woollen
District at Portsmouth, and on the last day of the term
were at Plymouth, as already stated.   It was while the
players were driving from the ground at the last-named
place that they heard the news that they were the League
champions, and they startled the good folk of the South not
a little by their enthusiastic reception of the tidings.

Chapter Twenty-Six.

Another wonder season—Passing of Langley and Spiksley—Magnificent home records—Powerful Reserves—Bradshaw's eight goals—Batch of amazing matches — Advent of McLean — Continental Tour—Memorable season of 1912-13—War-time football.

WEDNESDAY'S successes did not end with the triumph of season 1902-3. They won the championship again. The term 1903-4 was another wonderful one for Sheffield football. Both Wednesday and United were at the top of the League for half a season. From the beginning of the season to the end of December, there was only one week-end when Wednesday or the United were not at the top of the First Division. Though United fell away in the second half of the campaign, Wednesday carried on and retained their title with a stronger claim than before.

Up to October 30th the two Sheffield teams together had met the whole of the clubs in the First Division bar Aston Villa, and had defeated them all save Blackburn Rovers, with whom Wednesday drew 0—0. In 17 matches they won 30 points and scored 38 goals. Wolverhampton Wanderers beat Wednesday 2—1 at Wolverhampton, but the United trounced the " Wolves " 7—2 at Bramall Lane. Wednesday eventually overpowered the Villa, so that the Sheffield teams between them that season were successful against every team in the Division.

In the Cup, Wednesday reached the semi-final and United were not knocked out till the third round. The Cup conquerors of Wednesday were Manchester City, who not only won the trophy by virtue of Meredith's much-discussed goal against Bolton Wanderers, but ran Wednesday tremendously close for the League honours.

Defence always plays a big part in championship contests, and Wednesday were blessed with excellent strength
in that department. Wednesday yielded only seven goals
in the course of their first twelve matches, and fewer than
a goal a match throughout the season. The value of a
grand defence was demonstrated when there came a period
in which Wednesday played twelve matches and did not
score more than one goal in a game. The best marksman
they had was a half-back, a fine one, too—the late Herrod
Ruddlesdin.

It was not ever thus, of course, for afterwards the late
Harry Chapman scored some glorious goals and was one
of the greatest inside-forwards in the game, while the late
Vivian Simpson was a vital factor as well. Andrew Wilson,
James Stewart and George Simpson also shone. The club,
too, had superb reserves. To the middle of February the
latter had played 36 games in the Midland League, Wharncliffe and Sheffield Challenge Cup competitions, and had
scored no fewer than 111 goals. The " bag " for the season
was close on 150.

Wednesday were so powerful at Owlerton that not a
match of any kind was lost there and not a penalty-kick was
awarded against the first team. The constitution was very
much the same all through the season, though Langley
played in only about ten games and Fred Spiksley also left
First Division fields. No man is specially singled out,
though Crawshaw and Ruddlesdin were " capped " twice
for England. The side played great football. The season
saw a successful new left-wing, G. Simpson and Stewart,
and a new " star " back, Harry Burton. Harry Davis,
nick-named " Joe Pluck," and Chapman formed a right-
wing which became very conspicuous.

The championship was won by 47 points against 44 by
Manchester City, who had twice been beaten by Sheffield
United. Wednesday had also taken three points from them.
The allocation of the honours was not settled until the last
day of the season: on that day, if Wednesday had lost to
Derby and Manchester City had won at Goodison Park
against Everton, the Owlerton men would have been
deprived of the championship by one point. But Everton,
who contributed to Liverpool's relegation to the Second

Division that year, overcame the Mancunians, and Wednesday won at Derby by 2—0. Everton, incidentally, upset a lot of applecarts that term.

It was in that season that an amazing rumour was spread that Andrew Wilson had died ; one shopkeeper went so far as to announce the " news " in his shop window. Wilson soon showed how " exaggerated " was the story, however. Sunderland, the scene of so many dramatic events, was also the place which led to the close of Langley's playing career. He was hurt in the ribs, and, though he played once again against Newcastle United at Owlerton and scored the equalising goal with a penalty-kick, he had virtually finished. Harry Burton took his place and became one of the finest backs in the League. He was a splendid kicker with both feet, and the fastest back playing football at the time.

When Wednesday won their first championship, Mr. E. C. Tagg named his racehorse " Sheffield Wednesday " in honour of the event. The first time the horse ran under its new name, it won ; its jockey was G. Lyall.

In the second championship season, Wednesday had no more than 28 goals scored against them—the best defensive record of any championship side. The only games in which Wednesday surrendered above one goal were against Liverpool (a) 3 goals ; Derby County (a) 2 goals ; Aston Villa and Small Heath, both home engagements, 2 goals each.

It was a magnificent achievement.

The champions went off with such a burst in 1904-5 that the winning of the title for a third successive year was regarded as a very probable event. The first seven matches were won outright, and it was not until Sunderland was visited in October that so much as a point was lost. That coincided with the loss of Harry Chapman, whose absence from the right-wing had a great deal to do with Wednesday's relinquishing of position and ultimate failure to retain the championship. From October 15th to December 26th little but defeat was experienced, and of ten games only one was won and no fewer than seven were lost.

However, there were one or two consolations. Jack Lyall kept goal for Scotland at Crystal Palace, and Ruddlesdin figured in the England team in the same match.

Those were the only international honours secured by
Sheffield players that season. But Wednesday carried off
the Sheriff of London Shield by beating The Corinthians.
They finished ninth in the Division.

One match is worth special mention, that with Arsenal
on October 22nd, 1904, at Owlerton. Arsenal won by 3—0.
Crowe, a youngster, who scored two of them, was playing
in what was his first match in League football. In the
same game Chapman was badly hurt. The success of
Arsenal was the sensation of the day. It was the first
defeat Wednesday had sustained at Owlerton since
December 13th, 1902, when Derby County had won by 1—0;
never before had Wednesday lost three goals in a First
Division match on that ground, and it was only the eighth
defeat on that enclosure in the course of 77 First Division
matches.

The next season, Wednesday rose to the third position
in the Division. They played exceptionally well until
January and February, when, distracted by Cup-ties, they
floundered. Liverpool won the championship easily. Still,
Wednesday had a grand reserve eleven which won three
trophies. That team had the following Midland League
record: Played, 34; won, 25; lost, 4; drawn, 5; goals, for,
116; against, 28; points, 55. In various competitions they
gained exceptionally big victories such as 9—0, and on
January 20th, 1906, in a Sheffield Challenge Cup-tie they
swamped Hoyland Common to the extent of 18—0 at
Owlerton. Frank Bradshaw, who became such a prominent
forward, scored eight of those goals, one of the highest
individual scoring performances in the history of the club.
Other scorers were Rollinson 5 goals, Tummon 2, Holbem,
Reynolds and Marrison one each.

A thousand games in the League! Perforce, one can
only pick out odd engagements of special historic value.
One such occurred on November 14th, 1904. A most
astonishing affair it was, too. Everton and Wednesday
were battling with each other at Owlerton, and the
"Toffeemen" were leading by 5—1 at the interval. The
first half gave no indication as to what was to happen in
the second. The Everton combination was brilliant, so fine
indeed that time and again the home halves and backs were

actually yards away from the ball; the backs seemed to stand irresolute, while the Everton forwards brought up the ball and scored. Young, Settle (2), Hardman and Abbott were the marksmen.

That Everton held all the aces was the thought of all. But football is full of uncertainties. Wednesday recorded one of their most sensational rallies, and actually drew level. At the start of the second half, V. S. Simpson and Stewart changed places. No goal came until sixteen minutes had sped. Wednesday were then awarded a penalty-kick for a foul on Simpson. It was taken by Stewart, who shot straight at the goalkeeper. The ball went up into the air off Scott's hands, and as it came down Stewart rushed forward and scrambled it into the net. Scott was hurt in the collision, but did not retire just then.

Then came another Wednesday charge; Scott and George Simpson reached the ball together; the Sheffielder's foot found the ball first, and, though both men were well wide of the goal and almost on the goal-line, the ball screwed into the open goal and dribbled slowly through. Such was the remarkable character of Wednesday's third goal. Two goals inside four minutes, then Everton became short of their goalkeeper. Scott had to leave the field and Abbott took his place. Wednesday's resolution was at that stage in marked contrast to their previous ineptitude, and in a furious assault Vivian Simpson registered their fourth goal. The tension and excitement were extraordinary. Would Wednesday draw level? Would Wednesday win? Seven minutes to go. A bout of fisticuffs. Fiery little Davis had struck Hardman full in the face of everyone. Off he had to go. Thus both teams had only ten men left. Two minutes remained—thirty seconds. Virtually the last kick of the game was a beautifully-placed free-kick by Ferrier on the right wing. The ball was scrimmaged through and thus did Wednesday equalise in as dramatic a match as anyone could wish to see.

The teams on that occasion were :—

Wednesday: Jarvis; Layton and Burton; Ferrier, Crawshaw and Ruddlesdin; Davis, Stewart, Wilson, V. S. Simpson and Simpson (G.).

Everton: Scott; Balmer and Crelley; Ashworth, Taylor and Abbott; Sharp, McDermott, Young, Settle and H. P. Hardman.

On January 27th, 1906, there were surprising scenes in Sheffield, following a somewhat ill-conducted match between the " Blades " and Preston North End at Owlerton. Tempers of players were frayed, and " Dicky " Bond created sparks with fired passions, so that the crowd was worked up. Hundreds of spectators became incensed, and North End officials and players had to undergo a somewhat rough handling when they left the ground in a drag for the station. It may be said, however, that the North End party were somewhat indiscreet.

The matter was reported to the Football Association, and as a result the Owlerton ground was suspended for a fortnight from February 26th, though the Commission declared that the Wednesday directors had done all that they could to ensure the proper conduct of the game. However, the spectators had to be taught that misbehaviour at the conclusion of a match could not be tolerated.

For five hours the case was thrashed out at the Royal Victoria Hotel, Sheffield. Many witnesses were in attendance. There were other decisions apart from the suspension order. The players of both teams were censured; the referee and linesmen were censured; a Preston North End director was suspended from football management for a month, and as it was impossible to discover who of the Preston players had misconducted themselves a fine of £1 was imposed upon each of the visiting players.

Wednesday have had many sensational matches with Aston Villa, as already indicated, and two terrific defeats of the " Blades " are on record. The first occurred in February, 1907, when the Villa trounced their visitors to the tune of 8—1. Wednesday won the Cup that year, and they had just had duels with Southampton. They were tired after their exertions, and against the Villa they could do nothing right; on the other hand, their opponents could do no wrong, and after the interval they had Wednesday well on the run. Harry Davis says that if it had not been for Lyall's brilliance in the goal the score would have been 38—1. The Villa men figuratively plastered the woodwork with shots.

Still, Wednesday obtained the first goal of the match. Davis declares that he scored it with a penalty-kick in the following fashion (though a newspaper credits Chapman with it) : " The ground was fearfully heavy owing to a thaw consequent on a severe frost. I placed the ball on a little mound. When I prepared to kick, George, the opposing goalkeeper, knew in what direction I was going to shoot, and as the shot was made, he fell full length to save; then he could not move for a few seconds because of the mud. Now I had made a miskick, hitting the sludge as well as the ball, and while George was lying on the turf the ball simply trickled over the line a few inches and stopped."

The Villa goal-scorers were: Hampton 3, Bache 2, Cantrell 2, and Millington. Those who took part in the match were :—

Wednesday: Lyall; Layton and Slavin; Brittleton, Crawshaw and Bartlett; Davis, Chapman, Wilson, Malloch and Simpson (G.).

Aston Villa: George; Miles and Logan; Greenhalgh, Buckley and Codling; Millington, Cantrell, Hampton, Bache and Hall.

Aston Villa five years later inflicted upon the " Blue-and-Whites " their record League defeat. It was a " bombshell," for Wednesday had a good team and they had won four matches off the reel in the September and had drawn one (3—3) with Manchester United at Owlerton. Who fails to recall that 10—0 disaster on October 5th, 1912? It was a nightmare of a game for Wednesday, and it will go down in history as one of the most curious upheavals in football. It was a peculiar match, for actually Wednesday attacked oftener than the Villa did, but their work near goal was marked with hesitancy. The men were afterwards likened to Boy Scouts, so gentle were they.

The Villa wasted no time whatever. They never made a prolonged attack, for the one and simple reason that every time they got near the goal they scored. Their shooting was extraordinarily good, and besides the shots which counted the ball was only inches wide many times. Everything " came off " for them, and Wednesday players have declared that they recall no match in which there has been so much accurate shooting.

Wednesday were without David McLean and Glennon; Wright and Lloyd played in their stead. The table of the scoring is interesting :—

After 4 mins.	Halse.	After 38 mins.	Stephenson.
,, 14 ,,	Hampton.	,, 48 ,,	Hampton.
,, 28 ,,	Hampton.	,, 55 ,,	Bache.
,, 30 ,,	Stephenson.	,, 60 ,,	Hampton.
,, 36 ,,	Hampton.	,, 78 ,,	Bache.

The teams were :—

Wednesday: Davison; Worrall and Spoors; Brittleton, McSkimming and Campbell; Kirkman, Lloyd, Wilson, Wright and Robertson.

Aston Villa: Hardy; Lyons and Webster; Whittaker, Morris and Harrop; Hall, Halse, Hampton, Stephenson and Bache.

In the year that Wednesday won the Cup and lost to Villa 8—1 they were thirteenth in the League, but they ought to have finished higher, because from Sept. 1st to Dec. 15th they lost only one match and that at Newcastle, where the United won 5—1. Newcastle won the championship that year.

Boxing Day, 1911, will long be remembered by followers of Wednesday by reason of their 8—0 triumph over Sunderland at Owlerton. Such an event had not occurred in First Division football for three years. There was nothing to indicate such a sensation, for before the game the records of the two clubs were identical. However, as soon as the match began it was obvious that the home forwards were in great fettle. The goals were scored as follows :—

After 4½ mins.	Kirkman.	After 37 mins.	McLean.
,, 25 ,,	Kirkman.	,, 40 ,,	Glennon.
,, 30 ,,	McLean.	,, 43 ,,	McLean.
,, 35 ,,	Glennon.	,, 55 ,,	McLean.

Thomson, the Sunderland pivot, having strained himself, was off the field very early, and retired altogether after 25 minutes. Wednesday, against the ten men, played wonderful football, and scored six goals in 18 minutes. They eased up in the second half, but they were always masters, and in any circumstances they would have won, so brilliantly did they play.

Ten minutes from the finish, having had a magnificent shot saved by Scott (in goal), Robertson, who could not stop himself, collided with the goalkeeper, who had to be carried off. Scott was unconscious for some time in the dressing-room and had to spend a night in the Sheffield Royal Infirmary. Holley went into the goal. That victory concluded a hot spell for Wednesday, who had won four consecutive home matches, in which they scored 19 goals against 4, of which McLean claimed ten.

The players on that Boxing Day were :—

Wednesday : Davison ; Worrall and Spoors ; Brittleton, Weir and Campbell ; Kirkman, Glennon, McLean, Wilson and Robertson.

Sunderland : Scott ; Forster and Martin ; Cuggy, Thomson and Tait ; Mordue, Buchan, Young, Holley and Bridgett.

In the summer of 1911, by the way, Wednesday took part in their first Continental tour. Orgryte, a Gothenburg team, were beaten by 5—0 ; and a Swedish eleven by 2—1. At Copenhagen, Wednesday had the honour of playing before the Crown Prince and Princess of Denmark and at the same time opening a magnificent new ground, owned by the Corporation. A Danish national team was defeated by 3—2. The Prince handed silver scarf-pins to the players. A day or so afterwards a picked eleven of Copenhagen was overcome by 3—2, and the same result was arrived at when a third match with a national eleven was played. The tour was a great success ; the party was royally received everywhere.

The party consisted of : Mr. A. J. Dickinson (hon. secretary), Mr. Herbert Nixon, Mr. J. H. Thackray and Mr. J. B. Gunstone (directors) ; players : Davison, Spoors, McSkimming, Brittleton, Lloyd, Weir, Campbell, O'Connell. Kirkman, Paterson, McLean, Wilson, Glennon and Robertson ; trainers : C. Parramore and John Davis.

The names bring back stirring displays. George Robertson joined Wednesday in March, 1910, just a few days before Herrod Ruddlesdin died. With him came George Murray. But an equally important move was made in February, 1911, when Wednesday signed on David McLean, who became one of the most noted scoring centre-

forwards in the history of Sheffield football. Wednesday
had had a poor season and there was talk of relegation.
Nothing but the lack of a good centre-forward had stood
between the team and success.   Conscious of the weakness,
Wednesday endeavoured for a long time to remedy the
defect and then got a first-class man in McLean, from
Preston North End.

The season 1910-11 was notable because of the number
of changes in the team.   Up to February 16th, 1911, they
totalled 43.   The club failed to keep one man in the same
position all the season.   There had been, up to that point,
two goalkeepers, two right-backs, three left-backs, five
centre-halves, three left-halves, three outside-rights, seven
inside-rights, ten centre-forwards, three inside-lefts and
two outside-lefts.

In 1912-13, however, when Wednesday finished third
from the top, the directors called on only sixteen players;
the team—with appearances in parentheses—were usually:
Davison (38), Worrall (36), J. Spoors (36), Brittleton (34),
McSkimming (36), J. Campbell (38), Kirkman (36), Glennon
(34), McLean (36), Wilson (37) and Robertson (33).   That
was a splendid set of players, and the figures are remarkable.   Davison completed a run of 102 consecutive
appearances without taking into account the games on the
Continent, and Campbell had not missed a match since his
first appearance in the team—a record of 97 consecutive
appearances.

Campbell, like McLean, never played in the reserves up
to that time, and the centre-forward missed only three
games in the course of two and a half seasons and once he
was playing for his country.   Andrew Wilson, who had
been playing with the club thirteen seasons, missed only
one match.   In the last two seasons he had missed one
match each time, but only to play for Scotland.

The season 1912-13 was made notable because David
McLean headed the list of goal-scorers in the League with
30.   That was not a. record, for Freeman had registered
38 in one season, and since then that number has been
surpassed.   But in Freeman's great year, the Everton man
did not score any goals in Cup-ties, whereas in 1912-13
McLean had eight in the knock-out tournament, so that he
equalled Freeman's total for a season.

LATER-DAY STALWARTS.

Top Row: Worrall, Davison and Spoors.
Middle Row: Brittleton, Weir, Campbell, O'Connell.
Bottom Row: J. Davis (Asst. Trainer), Kirkman, Glennon, McLean, Wilson, Robertson and Ted Kinnear (Trainer).

McLean was greatly helped by his unselfish colleagues, and the triangle of Wilson, Robertson and Campbell was a superb one. Glennon and Kirkman, a fine wing, secured 12 goals each. Wilson scored 11 goals and Robertson 10. In fact, Wednesday had an all-scoring forward line. In all matches the regular forwards accumulated 83 goals, and Wednesday, by scoring 76 in League games, were credited with more than they had ever had before in the First Division; while their total points, 49, exceeded their previous best in that Division. That season, the brilliant Sunderland team won the championship with 54 points— then a record—and reached the Cup Final, wherein they were beaten by Aston Villa, who were the runners-up of the First Division with 50 points.

Wednesday were not beaten at home until December 21st, when Everton sprang a big surprise, and Sunderland administered a second defeat (2—1) on Christmas Day in a magnificent game. The Villa, who had beaten them by 10—0 at Villa Park, were held to 1—1 on February 8th, when a record crowd, 45,000, assembled. Only three games were lost at Hillsborough all told.

The crowning triumph of the season was a 2—0 victory over Sunderland at Roker Park. More than once Wednesday headed the First Division table, but at the end it was a case of " so near and yet so far."

The trainer that season was Ted Kinnear, who had won laurels on the track in his younger days.

The season 1913-14 was the one in which the ground was greatly improved and the handsome new stand was brought into use—a stand erected at a cost of £18,000, but to-day worth many thousands of pounds more. Then was made the change in the name of the ground from " Owlerton " to " Hillsborough."

It is curious that Wednesday have become dubbed " The Owls," apparently because outsiders thought of an owl when they read of *Owl*erton. It showed a lack of knowledge of the way to pronounce " Owlerton." The correct nick-name of Wednesday is the " Blades," and the latter is the one much preferred.

One point is noteworthy, and that is that in spite of the disaster which attended the Wolverhampton Wanderers

Cup-tie, the fourth-round encounter with Aston Villa on March 7th, 1914, attracted what, up to that time, was the biggest crowd ever seen at a football match in Sheffield—57,143 paid for admission.

The 1914-15 season provided a League struggle of intense interest, for after Wednesday, Manchester City and Oldham had made most of the running—Wednesday headed the table on March 13th—Everton came with a rush and carried off the championship by a point from Oldham Athletic.

With the outbreak of war in August, 1914, the first grave question which faced the football authorities was: Should football be closed down? After great discussions it was decided to " carry on," and the policy was justified to the hilt. But it was hard to do, and many clubs became hopelessly insolvent. However, the Management Committee of the League formulated a scheme to help clubs to get through: the rich clubs helped the poor. Then in 1915 professionalism was suspended, but the need to carry on was just as great, and, despite the critics, the game lived. Sectional competitions were arranged, and, though players popped on and off, the matches were completed. Wednesday pulled through those terribly trying days, though at a price.

Details of the matches played by Wednesday will be found in the Appendix, and of the play it is not necessary to write. But tribute should be paid to the splendid work of Mr. Clegg, Wednesday's chairman and now the Football Association President; and the Management Committee of the League, notably Messrs. J. McKenna and C. E. Sutcliffe.

Clubs responded loyally to calls, so did the players, who for three and a half seasons sacrificed their pay, except for a few shillings for their Saturday dinner and tea. Football grounds were used for recruiting purposes, charities were aided, and many thousands of pounds were raised for the Prince of Wales' Fund. The survival of first-class football was a magnificent testimonial to those in authority.

Chapter Twenty-Seven.

*The Second Fall—Tragedy of Welsh—Season of
Despair—A clean sweep—Wilson's rise to fame
—McIntyre's purple patch—Long and thorny
path.*

WHEN Wednesday first descended from their high
estate (1898-9) the causes of their downfall were
declared to be bad luck, bad refereeing and bad
play in the order named. However, there can be no
shirking of facts in connection with the second fall—in the
season 1919-20—the first season after the war. Bad forward
play was the principal cause of that drop into the Second
Division. Nevertheless, extenuating circumstances can be
quoted. The club undoubtedly suffered by reason of their
loyalty to old players who had served with the colours
during the war, and further were affected because David
McLean had to be transferred. If there had been only one
good marksman in the side, a different record might have
been created.

The trouble in the McLean case cropped up immediately
after the first match, and thereafter there was not a man
in the vanguard able to take advantage of the many glorious
scoring opportunities which were made. Many matches
were lost and drawn when a goal-getter would have weighed
the scale in Wednesday's favour. Nine contests were
drawn and eleven were lost by an odd goal. Altogether
26 matches were lost, a dismal record which had never been
placed to the name of any club in the First Division in the
history of the Football League.

The home and away record of the team was:—

HOME.						AWAY.					
			—Goals—						—Goals—		
W.	L.	D.	For.	Agt.	Pts.	W.	L.	D.	For.	Agt.	Pts.
6	11	4	14	22	16	1	15	5	14	40	7

A Wednesday triumph was secured at The Hawthorns
against the League champions, West Bromwich Albion. It
was a very fine performance, equalled that season only by
Barnsley (in the Cup), Aston Villa and Sheffield United. It

is passing strange that Wednesday have never been beaten in a League match at The Hawthorns for about 26 years. That success, however, was almost the only radiant gem of the campaign.

The Wednesday officials sought to strengthen the eleven in the second month of the season and at the historical disposal of the Leeds City players at Leeds they secured Arthur Price and J. Edmondson, two reputably smart players, Edmondson a young centre-forward, and Price, experienced, able to play at half-back or forward. H. O'Neill, a tall half-back from the North, was obtained about the same time, and on October 25th, when McLean was transferred to Bradford, it was announced that James Blair, the international back, was to return from Alloa. A " star " outside-right was discovered, namely, Lieut. W. H. Harvey. The new men were placed in the side, and Blair became a sound and brilliant defender throughout the season. Unfortunately, Price, Edmondson and O'Neill did not bring success. Further acquisitions were two Heart of Midlothian players, C. Mackay and B. Eggo, and still there was no material improvement. Parkes, the old pivot, was brought back from Stourbridge, and in January, 1920, Wednesday signed Fletcher Welsh, of Raith Rovers, then the leading goal-scorer in the Scottish League. Welsh's experience in English football was a tragedy. Next W. H. Harvey was injured in the Cup-tie at Darlington and never fully recovered, though he eventually went with the F.A. tourists to South Africa.

The situation became more and more dangerous. Team changes were a weekly occurrence. Andrew Wilson, who had first turned out for the Wednesday twenty years previously, was called on to play at inside-left on March 10th at Anfield Road, Liverpool (his last first-team appearance for Wednesday); Tom Brittleton was asked to play in his original position as inside-right; (the late) James Campbell was moved from the half-back line to inside-left; and so the shuffling and re-shuffling of players went on, all to no purpose.

The younger men did not advance quickly enough, and the older men were " going back." Again was more money spent. At the time when Blackpool created a sensation by transferring their noted players at record fees, Wednesday signed on George Wilson, the centre-half, who was destined to become England's greatest pivot of his time and his country's captain. After that bold stroke, Wednesday obtained John McIntyre, of Fulham, another fine player. But harmony and effectiveness were still absent.

In the direction of injuries the club suffered, and those mishaps contributed to the disasters. Kirkman was damaged in the opening match of the season against Middlesbrough; Pearson was injured at Ayresome Park in the return game, and in turn McSkimming, Brittleton, Harvey, Price, Mackay, Spoors and Burkinshaw were " in dock.''

There were runs of weeks when Wednesday did not win a match. They did not succeed in one of their first six matches. Then they beat Sheffield United at Hillsborough, but went another six weeks without a victory. They beat Burnley by 3—1 at Hillsborough on January 24th, and did not obtain another success until the last day of the season, when they conquered Oldham Athletic by 1—0 at Hillsboro'. In that last-named period they lost eleven of sixteen games, and scored only six goals!

The list of scorers shows the poverty of the attack in striking power: Gill 8, Welsh 4, Mackay 3, Brittleton 2, Edmondson 2, Price 2, Bentley, Campbell, McIntyre, Spoors, Binney, W. H. Harvey and W. Taylor, one each; total, 28.

It was not surprising, after such a disastrous season, that drastic alterations were made. First came the clean sweep of players: the following 21 were placed on the transfer list :—

Brittleton	Stapleton	Bentley
Lamb	Parkes	Kirkman
Edmondson	Gill	Mackay
Robertson	Platts	McSkimming
Spoors	Pearson	Burkinshaw
Campbell	Cooper (Anthony)	Cooper (Alf.)
Whalley	Armitage	Bretnall

Only two players who had served the club in pre-war days were retained, namely, Davison, the goalkeeper, and Blair.

Another important step taken, too, was the appointment as secretary-manager of Mr. Robert Brown, who, previously connected with Wednesday in their hey-dey, came from Portsmouth, where he had enjoyed considerable success as manager of that club. Two of the new players he acquired were Kean, a Sheffield boy, a product of Hallam F.C., playing with Portsmouth, and J. Lofthouse, of Reading.

No fewer than 41 players appeared in the first team that season, viz. :—

Brittleton	30	E. L. Harvey	9
Gill	27	Shelton	9
Blair	25	Parkes	8
Campbell	23	Taylor (Stan.)	7
Capper	21	O'Neill	7
Birch	21	Kirkman	6
Davison	20	Whalley	6
Stapleton	20	Robertson	5
W. H. Harvey	19	Eggo	4
Price	19	McLean	3
Burkinshaw, J. D.	18	Armitage	3
Spoors	17	Cooper, Alf.	3
McSkimming	16	Lamb	3
Bentley	16	Taylor, W.	2
Edmondson	15	Sykes	2
Binney	12	Pearson	2
Reed	11	Hinchcliffe	1
Mackay	11	Cooper, A.	1
Brelsford	10	Wilson, A.	1
Wilson, G.	9	Kite	1
McIntyre	9		

The season 1920-21 in the Second Division provided anxious times. There were periods when the outlook was so grave that a good many people began to think the management had not the ability to grapple with the situation. Wednesday sank to the bottom quarter of the table, and week after week there was little change in the position. Still, the loyalty of the supporters was magnificent. Two or three times the public was assured that the officials were not fiddling while Rome was burning. The public was told of the continued quest for players, of exaggerated prices for second-rate men, veterans and striplings; and of remarkable demands for first-class players. It will never be known how many thousands of miles the directors and officials travelled in search of talent.

The team was a young one, lacking the stability which one or two experienced players would have provided. Many of the young players were not good enough to hold their own in first-class football. Dunn, a back from Luton, did not fulfil expectations, and Welsh, the centre-forward, was shortly transferred, together with Blair, who went to Cardiff City. In goal, however, Davison played as well as he had ever done, and the halves were effectual, particularly Eggo, Brelsford and Wilson, supported by Price and Sykes. So well, in fact, did Wilson play that in March and April he was unanimously voted the best centre-half in England and played for England against Wales and Scotland.

With the departure of Blair, there was weakness in the back division, though Bellas showed great promise. Again, there was ineffectiveness in attack (the right-wing was notably weak). Many experiments were made; altogether eight players figured at outside-right during the season. When Welsh left Hillsborough McIntyre was brought from left-half to centre-forward, and for a time it looked as though he was going to solve Wednesday's problems. In the first three matches of the term, Wednesday had failed to score. When the Scot became the centre-forward, he obtained ten goals in six matches. By then, however, his fame had spread, and he was closely watched by opponents, and in the succeeding fourteen games he registered only three goals. His comparative impotence coincided with Wednesday's worst period of the season.

Wednesday underwent a very trying time from Oct. 16th to Jan. 15th, during which they played fifteen games, won only one and lost 12, and registered 6 goals against 26. Be it understood, however, that McIntyre did not always play at centre-forward; he figured on the wing during that middle spell.

A change for the better came with the acquisition of Samuel Taylor, centre-forward, a product of Atlas and Norfolk Works, Sheffield, who eventually reached Huddersfield Town and in 1919-20 scored 35 goals for that club, when the Town, threatened with extinction, won pro-

motion and reached the Cup Final. Ambrose Langley, the
old Wednesday back, was the Town manager that season.
The fee Wednesday paid for Taylor was a club record.

Taylor accomplished no miracles, he did not score the
goals expected from him, but he steadied the attack,
distributed the ball well, and should be given some credit
for the fact that from January 15th to the end of the season
Wednesday won 24 points in 18 matches by scoring 29
goals against 14. The left-wing, McIntyre and Lofthouse,
became a strong one, and from Feb. 12th to April 11th
Wednesday were not defeated.

Taylor contributed to McIntyre's success, for the season
1920-21 was the one in which the Scot obtained 27 goals—
more than all the rest of the team combined. The scorers
were : McIntyre 27, Taylor (S.) 8, Lofthouse 3, Smelt 2,
Binney 2, Wilson 2, Dent, Kean, Hall and Price, one each;
total, 48.

In some respects the season 1921-22 was like the one
just reviewed—a bad beginning followed by a splendid
finish, in which final rally 13 points were won out of 16
possible. Wednesday finished only eight points behind
Stoke and Nottingham Forest, who were the promoted clubs
that year. The pity was that the same form had not
prevailed when the campaign opened.

The management signed on new men, among them
Arthur Lowdell, Charles Petrie and James Trotter, but the
club endured many trials. One cause for disappointment
was the friction which led to the transfer of McIntyre to
Blackburn Rovers. Then were there mishaps to players.
Bellas had a knee injured at Bury, which necessitated an
operation, and he never again played regularly in the first
team. Later came the plague of influenza, which put out
of action nearly a whole team at once. Players. were
injured : Price, Ratcliffe (a forward obtained from Blackpool),
Thompson, Trotter, Petrie, Ramsbottom and Binney were
some of the casualties, and it is a remarkable fact that no
fewer than nine players had to undergo operations of various
kinds.

A serious weakness was in the back division, apart from
forward failings, and that was somewhat extraordinary
seeing that the club could have put a team of backs into the

field. It was not until the closing stages that Gray and Prior struck a happy partnership. As a rule, the attack lacked "punch," and experiments failed. Lofthouse, the outside-left, did not miss a match, but eight men were tried at outside-right, six at inside-right, seven at centre-forward and six at inside-left. Lofthouse and McIntyre with eight goals each were the leading scorers. The next best had four goals to his credit. One bright event, however, was the scoring of three goals by Binney at Hillsborough against Coventry City—the only "hat trick" of the season.

There were one or two individual successes. Davison, for instance, was selected to keep goal for England against Wales at Liverpool, and Wilson was the England centre-half against Ireland and Scotland. Wilson also played for the Football League against the Scottish League.

It was not surprising that the balance-sheet revealed a serious "slump," but in considering that it must not be forgotten that during nearly every home match the weather was wet. It was sure to rain when Wednesday had a home fixture! The receipts dropped to the disconcerting extent of £12,251, and the club's net loss on the year was £5,572. The total income was £18,561, against £33,842 in 1921, and the wages were £12,956, nearly £2,000 more than in the preceding term.

Chapter Twenty-Eight.

Chasing a Will-o'-the-Wisp — The storm of October, 1923—Death of Armitage—Touching rock-bottom—Darkest hour before dawn.

RARELY nowadays can ex-First Division clubs fight their way out of the Second Division in one season, or in two. Wednesday continued to tread a path of thorns in 1922-23. The club's resources were again unequal to the task; the team never got rid of erratic tendencies, and were barely any nearer their objective. The improvement was but one or two points on the preceding season and a couple of places in the chart. They were eighth. The players never inspired confidence until December, when the Smailes-Henshall wing was organised and flourished romantically for a few weeks: romantically is a term used advisedly, for Henshall was really a coach and a veteran. Leicester City were whipped at Hillsborough, and a splendid success was achieved at Barnsley, where a half-time deficit of 2—0 was converted into a glorious victory of 4—2. Sam Taylor was markedly prominent in that game.

Whatever hopes Wednesday had of winning promotion were dashed to the ground in the period from Dec. 23rd to Jan. 6th inclusive. During that stage they lost seven extremely valuable points which they ought to have won. In not one of six games did they achieve victory. Not for the first time did the Yuletide Festival programme results prove disastrous. Later came a rally, and once again a good end to the campaign, but odd points had been thrown away when they had a double value. It was passing strange how the weaknesses were of a will-o'-the-wisp character. In the first ten games, with Gray and Prior as backs, only six goals were yielded; but the forwards could not score goals. Next Prior was hurt at Fulham, and Gray had his first-class playing career terminated at Hull by reason of a knee injury. Those men were never adequately replaced for some time.

To obtain scoring effectiveness, Wednesday signed on Andrew Smailes, and to Smailes' credit, be it said, he scored some brilliant goals. The van got goals then—22 in a

dozen games. But alas! the defence had " come unstuck."
It was penetrated materially 21 times in the same number
of matches. Could anything have been more exasperating?
The management had to come back to the defence problem.
Something had to be done. First Felton was obtained
from Grimsby Town and soon afterwards Blenkinsop from
Hull City. Those two backs first played together on
Jan. 27th at Gigg Lane and a dismal baptism they had—
Bury won by 4—0. Still, they had shown promise, which
was amply fulfilled later.

Meanwhile, the attack was not consistent. The policy
of sending Binks away on solo runs was overdone. He
became " known." Several brilliant individual efforts he
made, efforts which were masterpieces in their way, but he
could not command success every time. The Cup-tie at
Derby, where the ground was so heavy, smashed up the
Smailes-Henshall wing. The failure there was amazing.
Lofthouse shortly afterwards was transferred to Rotherham
County, and Harron, of York City, was acquired. Both
were little and whole-hearted players, yet not quite good
enough for the work required.

One young and new man did shine, however, and he
was Rees Williams, the Welshman—a craftsman beautiful
at outside-right, who played for Wales against Scotland.
He had alternate partners in Lowdell and Sam Taylor.
Binks was the regular centre-forward. The safe and great
stratum was the half-back line. Wilson played for England
against Scotland, Wales, Ireland and Belgium. Kean,
converted into a right-half, rose to such heights that he,
too, was a representative of England against Scotland and
Belgium; in fact he was the first Sheffield-born player
" capped " since Crawshaw's heyday. Brelsford was a fine
left-half. Davison kept goal extremely well on the whole,
and he made one of the finest and most spectacular saves
of his career in Waller's benefit, when he ran out, fell full
length and fisted the ball after a terrific ground-shot by
Tunstall. The ball went straight into the air about 40
yards.

That was the season in which Petrie was operated on for
appendicitis. Petrie was taken ill at Hull while a reserve
player, and a rather amusing story is told in connection

with his journey home.   A Wednesday director took charge
of him; the train stopped at several stations and people
insisted on entering the compartment where Petrie lay in
considerable pain, and the only way in which the official
could get them out was by saying, in tones of deep
sympathy: " I'm sorry, gentlemen, but this poor lad is
suffering from scarlet fever "!   Towards the end of the
term, Petrie returned and was a very useful partner to
Harron.

The reserves won the Midland League championship and
so provided a good case for their admission to the Central
League, which took place the following close season.   J.
Brown, the goalkeeper of Worksop Town, made one
appearance that season in the first team.   Wednesday's
chief scorers were Binks, Smailes and Taylor (S.), with 13
goals each.

When a club such as Wednesday have a succession of
failures, supporters, naturally, are grieved, even angry and
bitter, and one of the features of the season 1923-24 was the
great airing of public views in the month of October.
Stinging comments were made by contributors to the local
Press, yet the old club kept its place in the hearts of its
army of friends.   Into the domestic affairs of the club it is
not intended to pry; one, therefore, gives only the official
statement issued by Wednesday, which was:—

> The directors of The Wednesday F.C. have made
> full inquiry into matters affecting the club and find
> that there were some minor matters which have
> caused friction.   These have now been satisfactorily
> dealt with, and, it is believed, will not recur.
> The directors desire to express their strong con-
> demnation of the paragraphs suggesting the
> probability of George Wilson and Fred Kean leaving
> the club, as there is no foundation for such sugges-
> tions, which can only cause mischief.

Another event caused sadness that season.   A tragedy
cast profound gloom over the Wednesday camp.   T.
Armitage, Wednesday's reserve forward, died following an
injury in the Wharncliffe Charity Cup-tie with Rotherham
Town at Hillsborough on Christmas Day.   After about
fifteen minutes' play Armitage shot at the Rotherham goal

from a distance of about seven yards. The shot was a hard
one, and the ball rebounded off the goalkeeper and hit
Armitage on the left side, just above the hip. William
Betts, the old Wednesday player, attended him in his capacity
of assistant trainer, and the victim played on for another
half-an-hour. During the interval he complained that the
pain in his side was becoming more acute. He was
removed to the Sheffield Royal Infirmary and an operation
was performed the same night. The left kidney was
removed, but the player died on Dec. 30th. A coroner's
jury said that they had no hesitation in saying that the injury
was caused through a pure accident, although it was a
very uncommon form of accident. A verdict to that effect
was returned. Armitage was very popular and of a kindly
and genial disposition.

After four seasons' toil in the Second Division, it could
not be said in May, 1924, that Wednesday were any nearer
the achievement of their ambition—promotion. Their performances were beyond understanding. There had been a
period from October to the end of January in which the
team appeared to be as good as any in the Second Division ;
at Hillsborough, in those months, it is questionable whether
any team would have defeated them. The only match they
lost at home that season was, ironically enough, their
1,000th game in the League, played on March 23rd, 1924,
against Oldham Athletic. The result was 2—1. Watson
and Blair scored for Oldham Athletic and S. Taylor for
Wednesday, all in the second half. The teams were :—

Wednesday : Davison ; Felton and Blenkinsop ; Kean
(captain), Froggatt and Levick ; Lowdell, Walker, Eyre,
Taylor and Harron.

Oldham Athletic : Matthews ; Wynne and Grundy ;
Bassindale, Pilkington and Naylor ; Douglas, Longmuir,
J. E. Blair, Hargreaves and Watson.

However, while Wednesday were so formidable at home,
they were oft as lambs led to the slaughter on foreign soil.
Their difference in form is strikingly shown as under :—

HOME MATCHES.						AWAY MATCHES.					
—Goals—						—Goals—					
W.	L.	D.	For.	Agt.	Pts.	W.	L.	D.	For.	Agt.	Pts.
15	1	5	42	9	35	1	13	7	12	42	9

The only League victory away from home was obtained
at Bristol. Yet at Bristol the City, " wooden-spoonists "
of the Second Division, dismissed Wednesday in the second
round of the Cup in a replay.
The forwards shot 54 goals, the same number as in
1922-23; the defence yielded four goals more—51 against
47. The team again finished in the eighth position.
Wednesday had made a bad start. To general surprise,
Brown, the goalkeeper obtained from Worksop Town,
appeared in the first match to the exclusion of Davison. In
the first nine matches, Wednesday surrendered 18 goals,
though the blame is not placed on Brown's shoulders alone.
Since then, he has proved a praiseworthy successor of
Davison. At that time he had had little experience.
Davison was brought back, and it was significant that in
the succeeding eleven matches opponents registered only
seven goals. At Coventry, Davison had five goals debited
against him, but in the next 14 games only eleven. The
long-service goalkeeper thus again demonstrated his useful-
ness.

Then there was the tragic comedy at Port Vale at the
start of the campaign, when Kean had to play back and
Jeremiah Jackson, the trainer, at 46 years of age, had to
complete the side owing to Felton and Williams having
missed their train. Jackson showed splendid pluck in
remaining on the field all the first half. The offending
players were each fined £5 by the Management Committee
of the League. So handicapped, it was no wonder that
Wednesday were defeated.

Blenkinsop was the only man who did not miss a match,
but changes had to be made in the other main defensive
position owing to uncertain form. The halves were again
strong, though Kean and Wilson were not quite so powerful
as previously. Nevertheless, the two again played for
England. Tom Brelsford, who had had a leg broken, did
not reach his former strength, but Levick and Froggatt
responded fairly well.

Petrie scored 15 goals, and two-thirds of them were
from headers (at that time he was about the best in Sheffield
at heading the ball near goal). Binks, of whom so much
was hoped, declined, and his individual successes became

very limited. Smailes dropped out. Taylor was uncertain
and Rees Williams played weakly away from home. Binks
scored 16 goals, Petrie 15, and Taylor 9. Trotter scored 12
for the reserves, who finished eighth from the top of the
Central League—their first season in that competition.

Wednesday's trials were not yet over, and in 1924-25
they actually came within the relegation zone, and people
talked of Third Division football for 1925-26! Throughout
the season, the club did not once figure higher than ninth
in the chart, and were actually placed 17th on April 1st.
They finished in the 14th position, but only after a fine rally.
New men at the start of the season were Ayres, of Charlton
Athletic; W. Collier and Inglis, two Scots from Raith
Rovers; Marsden, a forward from Sunderland; W. M.
Powell from Notts. ; Prince, of Port Vale, and G. Toone, of
Watford.

Ayres did not fully rise to expectations, nor did Marsden
as a forward, and Collier, an excellent half-back on his day,
was a bit too slow. Inglis, however, rendered sound, hard
service, and Powell promised to become a useful left-half.
Prince was uncertain at outside-left, but Toone was a
tremendous and tireless worker in the half-back line. He
supplanted Kean after the latter had revealed feebleness
of form against Blackpool on Christmas Day, when the
" Seasiders " won by 6—2 at Hillsborough and when Mee
could not be held.

Twenty-eight players were tried altogether, and with
Binks transferred to Huddersfield Town, in exchange for
Richardson, Trotter had his first real opportunity since his
injury in his fourth match after his arrival. Trotter scored
17 goals in 24 matches. He, at all events, was a success.
The next highest scorer was Harold Hill, transferred from
Notts. County early in the season, in rather dramatic fashion
following an early-morning adventure.

There is no occasion to go through the season too
critically, with its ups and downs. The 5—0 victory over
Hull City ; the 5—2 win against Portsmouth at Hillsborough
on Dec. 13th (when Trotter scored all the five goals and
created a League record for the club) contrasted with the
disaster against Blackpool and the deep humiliation at
Leicester on Feb. 7th, when Wednesday were beaten by

6—1. Suffice it to say that in the middle of March, Wednesday were in an awkward situation. Then it was that they strengthened the attack by signing on M. Barrass, the captain of Blackpool, and Sam Powell, of Leeds United, both inside forwards. They made their first appearance at Middlesbrough on March 21st, a terrible snowy day. The ground, too, was awful, and Wednesday were beaten by 2—0. It was George Wilson's unlucky day, and he lost his place in the side to Frank Froggatt. However, the lowest depths had been reached. Seven matches remained to be played. Of those, three were won and three were drawn, so Wednesday were saved. The new men played their part, but it may also be pointed out that Lowdell and Marsden had been converted into most serviceable half-backs.

Davison kept goal in 20 matches and Brown in 22, and the season marked the passing of the former as the recognised first-team goalkeeper. He was the last of the pre-war players on the club's books.

Chapter Twenty-Nine.

*A Rainbow Trail—Promised Land reached—
Season of Records and Thrills—Team of great
triers—Part played by management.*

IT is too soon here to write of painful situations which
followed the disappointing and unsatisfactory team
work of 1924-25. As is nearly always the case at such
times, it was not possible then for the sporting public to be
informed of everything which had transpired over a considerable period; it is not possible to-day. One or two
remarkable disclosures were made; matters far more
remarkable were not disclosed and probably never will be.
The necessity does not exist. The least said the better; the
storm is past; a championship success is as a rainbow in
the sky appealing to the best that is in all of us and sug-
gesting that all's well with the world.

In arranging for the season 1925-26, Wednesday decided
upon what was called a sliding-scale of wages, founded on
the system of increased payments by merit and in keeping
with the regulations. Several of the players did not find
the offers acceptable to them. One was George Wilson, the
captain; others included S. Taylor, G. Toone, W. Collier,
W. Inglis, F. Kean and R. Williams. It is only necessary
to record that Wilson was transferred in July, 1925, to
Nelson, the Northern Section club, and that Kean and
Williams eventually signed on again.

No one seriously believed in the month of August that
Wednesday had a championship team in the making; no
sensational acquisitions had been made. Still, the escape
of the hot air had produced a happier atmosphere, and an
important decision had been the appointment of Chris. Craig
as trainer. Craig had done exceedingly well as trainer of
the reserve team the previous season. Worthily did he
fulfil his duties with the seniors, for one of the characteristics
of the team, which was so successful, was the power of
endurance; also the ability and courage to rally splendidly
in the later stages of critical games.

MAIN MEN IN PROMOTION FIGHT 1925-1926

Standing: F. Kean, A. Lowdell, W. Felton, J. Brown, F. Froggatt (Capt.), E. Blenkinsop, W. Marsden.
Seated: R. Williams, M. Barrass, J. Trotter, H. Hill and A. Prince.

The march back to the promised land—the First Division—which had been viewed from a distance so long, restored all the old enthusiasm of Wednesday followers. There was unfeigned pleasure everywhere, and the campaign will be recalled often by its happy memories and a fine triumph which compensated for many failures and trials. Probably not for a score of years had the supporters followed progress so closely, nor travelled in such numbers to away matches near at hand. It was calculated that about 5,000 Sheffield people went to Derby for the return match with the " Rams " on the Baseball ground, and it was said that close on 10,000 from Sheffield went to see the game with Barnsley at Oakwell. At all events, the attendance at Oakwell was 28,149, and the receipts were £1,640, which figures constituted a record for a League match at Barnsley. There were over 10,000 more people present at Oakwell that day than at any previous Barnsley match that season. As for Hillsborough, a splendid balance-sheet was fully expected.

Several records were broken. By scoring 88 goals and winning 60 points, Wednesday surpassed all their previous feats; and James Trotter, with 37 goals, was the leading scorer in the Second Division, and also broke the record for the club of 30 League goals by an individual in one season, set up by David McLean in 1912-13. The centre-forward also repeated his record performance of having scored five goals in one match, which he did against Stockport County at Hillsborough.

It was a season with many attractive features. The regaining of the lost status coincided with the Diamond Jubilee year of the club and with the appointment of a Sheffield-born player as the captain. Frank Froggatt, who succeeded Wilson, is the first native of the city to act regularly as captain since Crawshaw. Under Crawshaw, Wednesday gained their previous renown—as Cup-winners in 1907—and prosperity and honours were renewed with another Sheffield man at the helm on the field.

Froggatt led a team which was extremely whole-hearted and of good spirit. The men were a band of triers; ninety-minutes men, and not a star, in the national sense, among them; yet, on their day and especially at Hillsboro',

Mr. R. BROWN.
Secretary-Manager of Wednesday.

Mr. C. CRAIG.
Trainer.

Mr. S. P. STEPHEN.
Assistant Secretary.

no team was more formidable in the Second Division. And one does not draw the line at Derby County, for though Derby County twice whipped the Sheffield eleven by 4—1, the first game would most probably not have resulted so if Marsden had not been hurt a few minutes before the interval. If Wednesday had shot better that day, they must have made the points safe before half-time. They had called the tune for forty minutes.

The team was exceptionally fast, the shooting very effective on the whole, and though there were occasional lapses steadiness was maintained with telling consistency. Away from home, more than a point per match was averaged; at home, only two games were lost; the remainder were won. At Hillsborough, 21 games produced 61 goals to Wednesday and only 17 to opponents. The defeat by Derby has been explained; the other reverse—against Port Vale—occurred immediately after the team had returned from a few days' change at Scarborough. The men had, perhaps, not been there long enough to do them good.

Admittedly, good fortune attended Wednesday's efforts, yet not out of their turn. It meant a good deal that casualties were few, though a reserve player, Weaver, had a leg broken and Hodgkiss had to undergo a knee operation. But only twenty players were utilised in the Second Division campaign. The team was not changed for weeks together; when changes were made they were invariably successful.

When the season is analysed, the success which attended team alterations becomes apparent. In the middle of October, there were signs of weakness creeping in. Derby had conquered them, a poor display was given against Nottingham Forest on the City ground. Then it was that Hill was introduced into the team, and the value of Hill's work for several weeks was immense. A " Tom Thumb " in stature, Hill is lion-hearted and very clever. He played first against Barnsley, and to the end of the year Wednesday played 11 matches, won eight, drew one (at Clapton), but lost at Port Vale by 4—3 and at Blackpool by 1—0. Trotter was absent from the last-named match owing to influenza. Hill was an inspiration at inside-left. Against Barnsley he scored twice, did the " hat-trick " against Chelsea, and in the eleven games he scored eleven goals and Trotter a dozen. The team obtained 31 against 10.

Steady progress was maintained until the Port Vale collapse in the middle of March. True, after that, Nottingham Forest were beaten, but at Darlington a serious disaster befel them, for they were thoroughly trounced by 5—1. That last reverse was on March 27th, and the situation was critical, for Derby County and Chelsea were at hand, and Swansea Town, then playing well, had to be feared. The strain was telling. Again did the directors resolve on changes, to relieve some of the men of the burden and bring in some who had not been so tried.

The left-wing of Hill and Prince, created in the October, had lost its lustre. Strength had been sapped. So Wednesday, for the game with Hull City on April 3rd, placed an 18-years-old boy, Jack Wilkinson, formerly of Wath Athletic, at outside-left, moved Barrass to act as his partner, and in the vice-captain's place at inside-right put Brough Fletcher, the Barnsley veteran, who had virtually revolutionised Wednesday's ineffective reserve team. Kean replaced Lowdell at right-half, and Walker, a back secured from Bradford City, was chosen instead of Felton at right back. Those decisions were some of the most vital taken throughout the season.

It will be recalled that Fletcher gave the men renewed steadiness and confidence. He had a hand in the first goal scored after nine minutes' play. Then Wilkinson was a big success. He was a tremendous favourite with the people and sealed the victory with a magnificent goal seven minutes from the end. That lad, in his first League match, had the intelligence, the ability to beat a seasoned Irish international, O'Brien, " off his own bat," and then scored. Kean was also delightful at half-back.

One or two further alterations were made later, and Lowdell shone as an inside-right, but the re-organisation for the Hull City match had saved the situation. In the concluding seven League matches 13 points were grasped; the only one dropped was at Chelsea, where Brown proved that he was a first-class goalkeeper, for he stopped some free-kicks (by Barrett) which nearly drove him into the net, so powerful were they, and made a wonderful and dramatic save from a penalty-kick by the same back two minutes from the end. Only one goal was sacrificed in those seven games.

At the last, Wednesday won the title easier than was
expected; nevertheless it was a hard-fought campaign. From
the start, Derby County demonstrated their strength and in
turn Middlesbrough, South Shields, Oldham Athletic,
Swansea Town and Chelsea made spirited challenges. But
Wednesday were always round about the top of the Division.
They began the season well, and at Christmas and Easter
played so splendidly that they won the six points possible
on each of those holiday occasions. At Christmas, when
Bradford City were beaten 4—1 at Valley Parade and 5—1 at
Hillsborough, and Oldham Athletic by 5—1 at Hillsborough,
their football rose to brilliant heights.

The last match of the season provided an inspiring finish.
Binks, the former Wednesday centre-forward, was captain
of Blackpool, who fought gamely. The play and the subsequent scenes were more in keeping with a fierce Cup-tie.
Men were dressed in Wednesday colours, there were mascots,
and on the terrace of the grand-stand an enthusiast with a
cornet played such melodies as " See the Conquering Hero
Comes." When the game was over, the people leaped the
fences and rushed towards the grand-stand. Kean was
carried off shoulder-high, and then the players assembled in
the directors' box to acknowledge the plaudits of the excited
throng. Some of the supporters carried away bits of the
goal-nets as souvenirs!

The men who took part in the promotion fight were:—

	Matches.		Matches.
Froggatt	42	Hill	21
Brown	42	Kean	19
Marsden	42	Powell, S.	12
Blenkinsop	41	Bedford	11
Trotter	41	Wilkinson	7
Williams, R.	41	Walker	7
Barrass	40	Ayres	5
Felton	35	Fletcher	2
Lowdell	28	McIlvenny	1
Prince	24	Williams, L.	1

The scorers were: Trotter, 37; Barrass, 14; Hill, 12;
Prince, 6; Ayres, 4; Blenkinsop, 4; Wilkinson, 3; Bedford,
2; Powell, S., 2; Lowdell, 2; Kean, 1; Williams, R., 1.

Shooting feats were: Sept. 12th, v. Preston North End (h), Trotter, 4 goals; Sept. 21st, v. Stockport County (h), Trotter, 5; Nov. 14th, v. Darlington (h), Trotter, 3; Nov. 28th, v. Chelsea (h.), Hill, 3.

All wish the old club good luck in the First Division.

PART V.

An Illustrious Company.
Chapter Thirty.

Mosforth, " The Little Wonder "—The old guards of the '8o's — William Betts — Tom Cawley—Harry Winterbottom—Jack Hudson— Jim Smith.

WHAT of the brilliant exponents of the game who have figured in Wednesday colours in the course of sixty years of football? They form an illustrious company, and already readers have become acquainted with their great and glorious deeds. The formidable stalwarts of the 'seventies have already been reviewed—the Cleggs, the Staceys, the Butterys, J. J. Lang and others. No more suitable leader of the notable group now to be paraded could be found than William Mosforth, always referred to in his day as " The Little Wonder." Possibly no Sheffield-born player earned such fame. Playing regularly in Sheffield's representative inter-Association matches, he also gained nine international caps for England, five against Scotland and the others against Wales. Matches with Ireland did not begin until February, 1882, Mosforth's last season as an international.

Mosforth was a great personality of his time. He was a son of the people, by trade an engraver, and there are many authorities who consider that England never had a finer outside-left than Mosforth, even including the wonderful Fred Spiksley. When he first played for England against Scotland in 1877, he was only 19 years of age, and the English team on that occasion consisted of University men or Public School boys, with the exception of " Billy."

Although but 5ft. 3ins. in height, he was a terror for his size, and a thorn in the sides of all defenders. He was essentially an individualist—the style of play which dominated in his day—and he was remarkably agile and very strong. His wonderful screw-efforts from the corner-flag and his unerring aim were never forgotten by those who saw him play. He used to take the ball right into the corner repeatedly, and was always the more dangerous when he did so. Many a time he knocked down a corner-flag in making his final shot, and many a time that shot beat the goalkeeper all the way. Wonderful shots were those, full of superb screw and accuracy. We do not see their like to-day. And he could put them in when travelling at full speed. In short, he was marvellously skilful though small; hence his nick-name, " The Little Wonder."

As a hurdle racer he gained prominence and accumulated over 200 prizes; while as a cricketer he did good work for Hallam, especially as a bowler. The zenith of his international fame was reached when in April, 1879, Scotland was beaten 5—4 by England at the Oval. He gave a brilliant exhibition, and so wound up the spectators that he was carried shoulder-high to the pavilion. It was the first defeat the Scots had sustained against this country for five seasons, and after that memorable match they went through eight more seasons before again lowering their colours to the Saxons. Mosforth is also the only English player who has been " chaired " at Hampden Park, Glasgow; that incident occurred after another superb wing display—on that occasion for Sheffield against Glasgow.

Mosforth played about twelve years for Wednesday, but finished his career with Sheffield United.

The late Bob Gregory, who died in 1910, was another of the old guard who played sterling football for Wednesday and the city, though his highest honour was a place in the North team against the South in 1881. A lovable fellow, Gregory was a centre-forward above the average standard, hard to knock off the ball and a charming and confident dribbler. In spite of apparent lack of speed, he got over the ground very well and made an admirable leader. For a long time he was Sheffield's centre against Glasgow. As a cricketer, he played for Hallam and once turned out for the Colts against Yorkshire. One of his chums was Harry Winterbottom, a right-winger of considerable distinction, very fleet of foot, a fine marksman, and a man who could

centre on the run with exceptional ability.   His centres were
ideal, and Cawley scored innumerable goals from them.
Winterbottom, of good build and strength, was a tremendous
worker and was always very conscientious on the subject of
training.   Born in Sheffield, he was ever a great favourite
and is still fondly remembered.

The old players were intensely loyal to their club, and
to-day their affection for Wednesday is unchanged.

Jack Hudson was a great half-back most difficult to pass.
In 1881-2-3 he was "capped" four times for England.
Hudson, who lives not far from Wednesday's ground,
occupied various offices in his time.   He was a committee-
man, once the hon. secretary, and also captain of the team.

Tom Cawley was a delightful player, who could adapt
himself to any position, though he was chiefly a forward in
the early years of his career.   How he played regularly
year after year for Sheffield has been told.   He was a player
who depended upon skill rather than force, clever in ball-
control and accurate in passing.   Tom is to be seen regularly
at Hillsborough still, and is always willing to give the club
the benefit of his experience.   In various capacities since his
playing days he has rendered Wednesday good service.

Many names famous in Wednesday history crop up in
relation to the early years—H. Housley, " Sandy " Charles
(now more interested in steel), " Nudger " Anthony (a very
clever and tricky player on the small side), Fred West (gritty
and good), Jack Jeeves (long and strong), Willis Bentley
and Maurice Naylor.   Carl Hiller, his brother Percy, and
Walpole Hiller—the last-named a well-known solicitor, who
has dabbled in nearly all kinds of sport, but who had great
preference for cycling and swimming.   There are, too, Tom
Moss, of Heeley ; George Groves, a grand little sportsman ;
Jack Dungworth, a splendid mile runner ; Harry Wilkinson,
who played for the North in 1883 ; George Ulyett, who very
often kept goal in the old days, but who won fame as an
England and Yorkshire cricketer ; Fred Newbould, Laurie
MacLaughlen, Talbot Wilson, Fred Sheel, Walter Sugg,
the noted cricketer, and his brother Frank, now a first-class
umpire on county fields.

In 1883, " Teddy " Brayshaw joined Wednesday, and
Christopher Porritt (afterwards a great political figure), and,

about the same time, Leonard Clegg, Sheffield's present Official Receiver. Not to be forgotten, either, are C. L. Stratford, W. O. Stratford, B. L. Shaw, and " Daff " Davy.

Big Jim Smith, who used to keep goal for All Saints Wanderers, joined Wednesday in 1883, and for ten years played magnificently. The reports of Cup-ties tell of his prowess. He was not a showy custodian, yet very sound. Smith was also a fine cinder-track runner, a winner of events at distances from 100 to 300 yards (the last was his best distance). A splendid sportsman, he had a well-earned benefit in 1893 at Olive Grove and altogether received about £120.

The name of " Billy " Betts recalls many a hard-fought field, Floddens and Bannockburns, and the grand little centre-half, a fine man with his head, is an imperishable figure in records. The " old war-horse "—as everybody knew him in those days—had a particular fancy for training in the Gas House at Neepsend, and even although his pale face would not suit the fancy of the present-day director or manager of teams, there was no getting away from the fact that Betts always played his best games after he had made a hurried rush from the stoke-hole and changed into football without the preliminary ablution.

Old followers of the game in Sheffield have a lingering affection for him. Betts played for England against Wales in 1889. They can recall how he used to smash up the movements of the sturdiest forward-lines. Men like Fred Dewhurst, John Goodall, Dennis Hodgetts, " Skimmy " Southworth and Tinsley Lindley could all tell the tale of the grave-looking centre-half's persistent hanging-on to the man and the wily movement toward the ball. He would shoot out a foot when least expected; would hang around and rob the opposing forward of what that confiding individual had presumed to be his prerogative.

In the battles with Nottingham Forest, Betts played his part repeatedly. One of his mates, Jack Dungworth, had a prominent career as a half-back, although it was rather brief. He had a speed seldom seen amongst half-backs to-day. A half-back to be included also is George Waller, who figured in the North side in 1890. Waller has had a surprising life in sport. He has the distinction of having played for both

Wednesday and United, has been football player, cricketer, and football trainer, and consultant to all and sundry. Athletes have called on him from far and near to have their injuries overhauled by Waller, who has been connected with Sheffield United over thirty years.

Extremely versatile as a player, Waller did not confine himself to half-back play; he figured in every position on the field, including the goal, at one time or another. He played cricket for Yorkshire in 1893-6. It has been said that the half-back line of Waller, Betts and Dungworth could play for a week and never tire! Just as Waller is affectionately regarded by many, so was Teddy Brayshaw, a fine and vigorous back, one of the best defenders the club ever had. Brayshaw was fearless, one of the old " never-say-die " sort.

Of those times also was the late H. Woolhouse, familiarly known as " Toddles," and who preceded Spiksley. He was a capital outside-left, though, like the others, could apply his ability to various positions; he played, for instance, sometimes at inside-left and occasionally at centre. The story goes that once " Toddles " was ill and he wrote to the club secretary as follows :—

Dear Mr. Dickinson,

I AM ILL.

I believe you are having ox-tail soup at the ground to-day; if so I should like some.

TODDLES.

He went about on the field as though taking no notice of the hard knocks and bumps he received.

Another favourite was " Clinks " Mumford; a better all-round man in football could not be found. He could not be put in a wrong position; he was extremely versatile, loyal, and a mainspring of a team. Old-stagers remember Jack Darroch, who was noted for his tackling. He would run alongside a man; suddenly his opponent would tipple head over heels, and it was a mystery how Darroch worked the trick. Referees were much puzzled. " Billy " Ingram, a lively inside-forward, performed many a doughty deed for the club, too.

Chapter Thirty-One.

Wednesday Idols of the '90's—Spiksley and Crawshaw—Brilliant defenders and great wings— Andrew   Wilson — Tom   Brittleton — Vivian Simpson.

FOOTBALL crowds are often declared fickle in their sentiments towards players. 'Tis true. The subject of hero-worship to-day is all too frequently the broken idol of the morrow. Yet not all pass into the forgotten tombs of time. Memories of great Wednesday players of other days are cherished still, and none more so than those of Tom Crawshaw and Fred Spiksley. Those two large-hearted and loyal fellows made glorious history; they never thought of anything but winning, and in the worst of situations they deemed defeat a dream! Many of their accomplishments have already been emphasised; here the artistes are placed in the gallery of the scintillating ones.

In the opinion of thousands, Spiksley is the greatest player the Sheffield club has had. He was a marvellous outside-left—a wonder every bit as capable as Mosforth. Ernest Needham—and he is not alone in this respect—has asserted that the Gainsborough-born player was the " star " of all outside-lefts in English football. His control of the ball, his personality, his speed, his pluck and his scoring successes were amazing. Spiksley could do anything with a ball and with either foot. To-day, he is remarkably agile and seems as light on his toes as a lady! The winger, who studied football deeply and scientifically, always played the ball with the outside of the right or left foot, and could judge distances, angles and strengths to a nicety.

A feature of his play was his ability to keep the ball close to his toe when dribbling. No man could stop and start again so quickly as the Wednesday wizard. He would often set off from the half-way line, stop " dead " twice and go

on before he attempted to put in a centre.   In consequence
he out-manœuvred opponents time after time.   They would
run full-speed ahead; Spiksley would stop and before they
had pulled up and recovered he would be off again.   His
stopping and starting made him exceptionally fast.   He did
not always go to the corner; sometimes he would cut
towards the centre and there was always extreme danger
when he was working his way through to goal.   Scores of
times he was pulled up for off-side when he was well on-side,
simply because his speed was not credited by referees who
did not know him.

Being such a dangerous man he got a lot of knocks, for
he was only lightly built, and, remembering how backs and
half-backs always concentrated on him, it is astonishing that
he ever shone at all.   He was not a hard shot, but invariably
accurate, and his skill made such openings that high-powered
efforts were unnecessary.   It is well-nigh impossible to
discover how many goals Spiksley scored in a career of
nearly twenty seasons, but the total must be near to that of
Bloomer's record of 384.   Certainly his scoring achievements
have never been approached by any extreme winger.   In his
first two international matches he did the " hat-trick,"
including three goals in succession in ten minutes against
Scotland at Richmond in 1893.   No other Englishman has
performed the feat.   In all he gained seven caps.

He was introduced into senior football by Gainsborough
Trinity in 1887, and Wednesday obtained him by an
accident.   He had practically arranged to go to Accrington,
who offered £2 10s. a week and a situation.   Late one night
he arrived in Sheffield after a visit to the Lancashire town
and found that the last train to Gainsborough had gone.   He
had to spend the night in Sheffield.   At the Maunch Hotel
he met Fred Thompson, of Wednesday, and he promised
him he would not sign for Accrington until he had heard
from Wednesday.   Mr. John Holmes and Mr. A. J.
Dickinson came along, also Mr. A. Nixon, and he was
signed at the Bull and Mouth Hotel in Waingate.   His pay
was £3 a week, and he was given a berth at the " Sheffield
Telegraph " office.

After he left Wednesday, he played for Glossop, Leeds
City, Southend and Watford.   Then he took to coaching.

He has served in that capacity in Germany, Mexico and other centres. On returning to England he was appointed to the Fulham Football Club.

Next to Spiksley stands Tom Crawshaw, a son of Sheffield, a Sheffield blade, who played for England on ten occasions, a record which still stands unequalled by any Wednesday player. A lad of the Park, Crawshaw was signed in '94 and swiftly became the finest centre-half in the land, and the best man in Britain with his head. He was captain of the team which last won the Cup (in 1907), was a member of the two championship teams and of the team which first won the Cup (in '96). He was not, perhaps, so deft and accurate with dainty passes to his forwards as recent pivots such as Joe McCall and George Wilson, but he was a glorious spoiler of the opposition and a ruthless destroyer of combination.

He was, however, speedy and a tireless worker. In heading, it did not matter whether a rival was six foot tall or more, Crawshaw could be depended upon to be going up when the other fellow was coming down! At heading a ball he was unrivalled. Crawshaw was a superb successor to the dominant Betts and every bit as big a favourite.

Spiksley was never on the losing side in an international match, and Crawshaw had a similar fortune against Wales and Ireland, but England were beaten twice by Scotland when he played. A long, lithe figure, revelling in the game of which he was so brilliant an exponent, Crawshaw brought honour to his native city.

Spiksley had as his partner for seven or eight seasons Alec Brady, an extremely clever player, who by his sterling quality and unselfishness contributed not a little to the brilliance of his colleague. The understanding which existed between those two men was virtually perfect. Just as that wing was a magnificent one, so was that consisting of Archie Brash and Bob Ferrier on the right. They played tit-tat-toe to perfection, were conspicuously skilful, and although they did not always make a lot of headway they repeatedly led opponents a pretty dance. Two light-weight forwards they were, little fellows who quickly made names for themselves. Of them it has been said: " They were miracles of quickness and cleverness; their artistry defeated burly backs, outwitted clever half-backs, set the crowd in a roar time and time again."

They had speed in plenty, daring and audacity, and oft either one or the other would nip in and score bewilderingly brilliant goals.

One little story told of Brady: Before a certain away match his wife kissed, as she believed, his left football boot, for good luck. But just before the match Brady discovered that his wife had kissed the boot of Brash!

Ambrose Langley was a splendid back and one of the mightiest defenders Wednesday have had, though he was often in hot water. Six foot high, and weighing 14 stones, Langley never knew his own strength. He played against Archie Hunter, of the Villa, in an English Cup-tie when only 16 years of age, and ended his football career as manager of Huddersfield Town. For some years he was manager of Hull City, and for a time was assistant secretary for Wednesday. He played for Wednesday for twelve seasons, during which period they gained most of their triumphs.

Hadyn Morley was a clever back, if short in stature, and Tom Brandon, a brave butting defender, a solid 12-st. back, was not without art although he made all use of his strength. Morley, of course, was the hero of that dismal first Cup Final appearance when the crowd rose to him in sympathy after a most valiant exhibition. He is now a solicitor. An amateur, he came from Derby. In a later year Wednesday had another splendid amateur back, Martin J. Earp, of Nottingham. Clean-limbed, a delightful fellow with a terrifically strong kick with his right foot, Earp eventually went to the South African war and suffered somewhat severely.

Harry Brandon, a wonderfully whole-hearted half-back, could never hang back. On one occasion in a match he had to change his boots, but as Wednesday were being badly pressed he returned to the field and played in his socks. He kicked the ball at least half-a-dozen times without his boots on until the danger was cleared. Besides being a sound half-back, he was a good back.

Jamieson was a middle-line man, exceptionally good on heavy grounds, a tireless player, a plugger all the time.

Bob Petrie was another sterling worker in the intermediate section, and has been likened to a block of granite when stripped. He was a superb athlete and commanding in appearance on the field.

The club once had a very fine goalkeeper in Mallinson, who, in a notable match, was bowled over by Bell, of Everton. When asked why he had not got out of the way, he replied, " I never saw the fellow until he was out of sight " !

Wednesday have had other clever goalkeepers, and one, named Allan, was so well off for " understandings " that the people used to say he had only " to spread his feet out " to keep out any shot on the ground!

Massey dared everything in the defence of his charge and in consequence was frequently hurt. Yet at times, that hard-working custodian rose to brilliant heights.

" Sparrow " Brown should not be overlooked—a deft and dainty forward, who could worm his way through all kinds of defences with the utmost confidence, and shoot excellently from all ranges.

Coming to Owlerton, more excellent men of merit come under notice ; for example, Harry Chapman, a Wednesday hero if ever there were one. Some believe he was the best inside-right Wednesday have had, and it has been asserted in all sincerity that for two seasons he was the best man in that position in the country, greater even than Steve Bloomer. He would assuredly have been England's inside-right if he had not been playing in Bloomer's day, at any rate. It could be argued that Chapman was a better footballer than the famous Derby international, but the latter had an advantage in his shooting powers. Chapman was a most useful man to have in a team, because he was such a grafter ; he never seemed to tire ; often he did two men's work and kept it up. He and Harry Davis the second comprised a brilliant right-wing in the championship seasons, 1902-3 and 1903-4. They used to be called " The Marionnettes," and their harmony was so good that they could inter-change positions so that a stranger watching them could never have distinguished from the play which of the two was supposed to be the outside-right. Also they were very fast. Davis would have made a good acrobat, an excellent turn as a tumbling man on the stage. When bowled over he had a knack of sliding on his back for a matter of ten yards or more, with his legs and arms in the air, and he made the crowds roar with laughter. He was a " star turn." A product of Barnsley, he joined Wednesday about 1900, and was another son of Lilliput, standing but 5ft. 4ins. ; yet he had rare breadth across the shoulders and his heart was true.

When James Stewart and George Simpson arrived on the scene for a trial they caused a sensation by their grand display as a wing. They were soon snapped up. Stewart was conspicuous for his artistic work, but Simpson was just the reverse, very fast and fearless. Many times it was remarked that it was a wonder he did not collide with the goal-posts in his dashes for goal. For a little fellow it was astonishing how he escaped injury.

William Layton, who succeeded Earp, was a big fellow in little room, and he had a peculiar way of volleying the ball, a kind of scissors-kick. A dashing right-back, he was a faithful Wednesday man, happily recalled because of his zest and reliability. He was a member of the team which twice won the League championship, and, later, the English Cup. Like Langley, he was honoured by the Football League, and appeared in the international trial match, Amateurs v. Professionals, in 1907, as did Stewart, who was " capped " against Scotland and Wales that year.

A remarkable story is told of Layton's migration to Wednesday. At the time he was working on the night-shift in the Low Main seam at Blackwell Colliery. On Monday, Nov. 11th, 1895, he was due to play in a trial match at Sheffield, and, in order to be fit and to do himself justice, he did not go to work on the Sunday night. The Blackwell explosion occurred that very night and seven men were killed. Layton evidently saw the hand of fate in that, for he vowed that if Wednesday engaged him he would never play for any other club. And he never did. To-day, he is in Australia.

The three L's, Lyall, Layton and Langley, were a formidable defence. Lyall takes his place as a leading Wednesday goalkeeper. He came from Jarrow, and when he got into the first team he never lost his position until he ended his career with the club. He was a goalkeeper who possessed splendid reach. Yet he was nervous in his greatness, and one centre-forward he never liked to oppose was the famous " Cockles " Appleyard. A smart feature of his play was that he could kick a ball out of his hands after he had taken only one step and punt it down the field. Most goalkeepers have to take three or four steps before they are able to clear, but Lyall required very little room in which to do so. Lyall, who was " capped " for Scotland in 1905—he was once invited to play for England, but an error was soon discovered—was 6ft. 1½ ins. tall and weighed 12st. 7lbs. His successor, Davison, was the smallest goal-keeper in the League, standing 5ft. 7ins. only.

Andrew Wilson, their famous international centre-forward, had much to do with Wednesday's progress, and that Scot, so big a favourite at Hillsborough, was probably the best centre-forward the club have had. It took him some time to settle down when he first came to the city (in 1900), and the crowd was not impressed with his ability. But when he came to his own, the skilful, sturdy Scot became a hero. For twenty years he served the club, first as centre-word and later as inside-left, and so fine a player was he that he appeared for Scotland on six occasions. Andrew, who went to be the manager of Bristol Rovers in 1920, was a sportsman of splendid character both on and off the field. His speciality, which gained him much distinction, was a screw-shot, with which he won many matches.

A man of powerful build—he stood 5ft. 9ins. and weighed 13st. 10lbs.—Wilson had an unusually good turn of speed, and another exceptional point about him was that he first won a cap as a centre-forward and in 1912 was honoured as an outside-left. Four times he played against England.

Transferred to Wednesday from Glasgow Clyde, he was the son of a farmer, who had a rooted objection to his boy playing football, which objection, however, was finally overcome by a Mr. Lucas, of Preston, acting on Wednesday's behalf.

Wilson had to undergo some rough experiences on the field, and once had a serious facial injury. Albert Iremonger and his brother, who had such noted connections with the Nottingham clubs, have said that he was the only player they could not knock off the ball, and, what is more, they

never once saw him knocked off it.   When he had the ball,
goalkeepers had to be constantly on the alert, because of the
habit he had of screwing the ball from apparently impossible
positions; also he was never afraid to charge goalkeepers.
Both McBride, of Preston North End, and Albert Iremonger,
with his enormous reach, have been hurled into the back of
the net by the relentless Scotsman.

Another Wednesday " star " was Herrod Ruddlesdin,
one of those who played the game fairly and honestly without
swagger, but with brains.   There is no doubt that had he
been more robust in health he would have represented his
country more times than he did.   He played against
Scotland, Ireland, and Wales in 1904, and as a half-back
earned deserved praise.   A mate of his in the middle line
was Bob Ferrier, the former forward, who continued to do
good work until the rise of Tom Brittleton.

Bartlett should not be overlooked.   Never a great half,
he nevertheless was good and reliable.   Harry Burton, one
of the second championship side in 1903-4, was fully expected
to become an international.   A back, he was one of the best
playing, a fine kicker of the ball, who possessed exceptional
speed.   Cartilage trouble, however, closed a promising
career all too soon.

One of the most remarkable players the game has known
is Tom Brittleton, Wednesday's international half-back, who
became a member of the Sheffield club in September, 1904,
after service with Stockport County and Winsford United.
He was transferred to Stoke in 1920, and in March, 1925, he
was still playing in League football, although he was within
a month of his 46th birthday.   Stoke called on him in a
crisis, and it was a tribute to the wonderfully well-preserved
powers of the oldest man in first-class football.   His life has
been devoted to the game, though now he has retired from
League football.   Brittleton first played with Winsford
Juniors (in 1896); so that virtually his playing days embraced
thirty years.

One cannot forget such men with scars and medals who
have given delight to the people.   His first appearance for
Wednesday in the League was against Bury on Jan. 14th,
1905.   At his best he was a perfect footballer, a man who
won every honour in the game, including a Cup medal and

five caps. In 1910 he was invited to go with the F.A.
touring team to South Africa, but his reply was that he
would rather go fishing !

Brittleton was a tireless half-back, though originally an
inside-right, and he could throw in the ball a remarkable
distance. A smart tackler, he had a clever way of hooking
the ball with an overhead kick, yet he never much fancied
heading it.

A Sheffield-born player, who had a distinguished career
with Wednesday, Northampton, Everton and, later, Arsenal,
was Frank Bradshaw, a product of Sheffield Sunday School
League football.   When in form, Bradshaw was truly a
great inside-forward, and would probably have been better
still if he could have avoided accidents to his knees. He had
a remarkable revival after he left Wednesday, about 1910,
for Northampton, and the fact that he continued to play in
League football until 1924 was astonishing.   When he left
Wednesday he was presumed, in some quarters, to be a
" crock."   Now he is the manager of a small club in the
South, and he is one of many fine Wednesday men who
have been a credit to the playing profession.

One of the best and most whole-hearted players who wore
Wednesday's colours was that delightful amateur forward
and charming personality, Vivian S. Simpson, who was killed
in action in France in 1918.   He was introduced into the
team late in the season 1901-2, and he had a notable share
in the club's subsequent series of triumphs.   Centre-forward
and inside-right were his favourite positions. In 1907 he
took part in an international trial, but was never " capped."

Chapter Thirty-Two.

Dazzling Davison—The sharp-shooting McLean
—Two fine wings—Blair and George Wilson.

SEVERAL fine players composed Wednesday's successful team of 1912-13, as already shown—Davison in the goal; backs in Worrall and Spoors; halves in Brittleton, McSkimming and Campbell; with Kirkman,. Glennon, McLean, Wilson and Robertson forwards. But others who had served in the intermediate periods and won their spurs were Holbem, the Heeley back and the ex-Sheffield schoolboy player; William Lloyd, the very useful forward from the North-East and who is in business near the ground; " English " McConnell, a gem of a centre-half, frequently " capped " for Ireland, on five occasions while with Wednesday; " Paddy " O'Connell, another delightful Irish pivot of skill, also an international; Frank Rollinson, a Sheffield scoring forward; Hugh Slavin, the steady, sure-kicking back, who nowadays works so devotedly for the schoolboys of Sheffield and Yorkshire; Frank Stringfellow, a pleasing attacker and still in the game; Oliver Tummon, the Sheffield schoolboy " discovery," some of whose scoring feats made history; and Finlay Weir, a grand half-back from Maryhill, Glasgow. To mention all is well-nigh impossible, but the memory of the sporting public is not so short that the names above will not remind them of stirring deeds by bygone wearers of the blue-and-white stripes.

Signed in 1908, " Eddie " Davison, for years a wonder-fully popular goalkeeper at Hillsborough, concluded his connection with the club at the end of the season 1925-26. No Wednesday man has been more popular than he. He was held in eminent esteem because he was so gentle-manly on and off the field. Such was his conduct and demeanour that it was a general, though erroneous, belief that he was studying for the ministry, and time after time after matches at Hillsborough was he asked to give addresses

in the pulpits of religious institutions in Sheffield. It was
rather embarrassing for him when such requests were made.
Davison was the beau ideal of a good sportsman, straight
as one of his own goal-posts, a bundle of pluck and entirely
modest.

His lack of inches has often been talked about; the
difference in stature between him and Lyall was so
pronounced. Probably he was obliged to be brilliant because
of his handicap, but he always fascinated the onlooker.
Some of his saves dazzled the spectator when, perchance, if
made by taller men like Iremonger, for instance, they would
not have seemed to be so much out of the ordinary. Being
the smallest goalkeeper in the League he had to throw himself about like an acrobat to cover the yawning space of
eight yards by eight feet. But as love laughs at locksmiths,
so did Davison always smile at his handicap. Good wishes
will go with him at Mansfield, where the Town have engaged
him as secretary-manager.

He had powerful arms, greater strength than
imagined, and had a marked gift of anticipation. It
was in 1922 when he received his only international cap
(for England against Wales at Liverpool). An interesting sequel to that honour occurred the same
season at Hanley, when, after a match with Port
Vale, the latter's supporters presented Davison and Peers
with a Royal Art vase, each in recognition of their having
played for their respective country. The incident was
probably without precedent. Afterwards, when Port Vale
were at Hillsborough, there were other presentations to the
men. Wednesday obtained Davison from Gateshead St.
Chad's. His complete record of appearances and the results
of the games in which he played to the end of December,
1925, was (including Reserves matches):—

Matches				Goals	
played.	Won.	Lost.	Drawn.	For.	Agst.
595	263	199	133	989	794

Davison made approximately 500 appearances for the
first team, and gave some wonderful displays for Sheffield
in the matches with Glasgow in Scotland, where he is well
remembered. He was one of the F.A. tourists to Australia

in 1925, and helped in the good missionary work done .for
Association football in that part of the world.

A figure always to be associated with the club because of
his goal-scoring prowess was David McLean, obtained from
Preston in February, 1911. As a footballer, Andrew Wilson
was the greater centre-forward, but as a goal-scorer McLean
probably had the advantage. McLean's one object was to
get goals. He did not work nearly so hard for them as
Wilson used to do, but he had a greater variety of shots
and, maybe, was somewhat quicker to realise opportunities.
How he used to go through with that stiff little trot and
fire the ball into the goal without any particular thought
regarding style will be readily recalled. He scored 88 goals
in League matches for Wednesday in four-and-a-half seasons ;
he scored four goals in a match on five occasions and twelve
times obtained three in a match. His success in Cup-ties
has beeen mentioned.

McLean was ably assisted by that strong, forceful inside-
forward, the late " Teddy " Glennon, so ruthless an enemy
to opposing defences and a rare stalwart. Glennon, who
seemed all angles physically, was brought up in a hard
school : his experience before he joined Wednesday was
gained with such teams as Denaby United, Kilnhurst, and
Grimsby Town.

Kirkman was on the right-wing then, and he was often
on the threshold of honours, for he had talent in his toes.
He and Glennon formed a formidable pair.

The left-wing in 1912-13 was Wilson and George
Robertson, and the lean outside-left was a star of lustre.
Robertson earned his international honours with Scotland
by sheer brilliance. On occasions he rose to real greatness,
and it was a pity an accident to a knee in a match with
Sheffield United was the beginning of the end of his career.
Robertson was highly thought of across the border, and
represented Scotland four times. His last season with the
club was the disastrous one immediately after the war.

In 1913 Jimmy Campbell was hailed as one of the best
left-halves in the kingdom, when critics said that he went
about his work with more airy grace than did the famous
" Nudger " Needham. Campbell came to Wednesday in
1911, and for over two years did not miss a match. He

played for Scotland against Wales in 1912-13, the season in
which, at Stamford Bridge, Wilson and Robertson played for
Scotland against England, for whom the opposing right-half
was a club-mate, Brittleton.

Bob McSkimming was engaged by Wednesday in 1910
as a back from Albion Rovers, but was converted into a
centre-half and so found his ideal position, a position he
occupied with no small distinction. He was a rare destroyer
of combination, a placer of no mean merit.

Worrall and Spoors were sound, reliable backs. Spoors,
had he not been contemporary with Crompton and Brittleton,
would surely have been awarded honours. Strong and hefty,
he could kick the ball as hard as the next man, and was a
stern and successful tackler.

It is not necessary to go into much detail about post-war
players of Wednesday. The ground has already been fairly
well covered. One should, however, include the talented
Scottish international back, Blair, a defender of polish and
smartness, whose footwork left little to be desired and whose
braininess carried him a long way. When he went to Cardiff,
Wednesday lost a valuable asset; but Wednesday's loss was
Cardiff's gain. Wednesday had obtained Blair from Clyde
just before the war and had shocks on account of his mishaps
as a result of motor-cycling.

One concludes with the record of George Wilson, the
centre-half secured from Blackpool in March, 1920. Wilson
was a prodigious worker, who developed into the finest pivot
in England. He, too, was a stylist and speedy, and of
splendid stamina in his early seasons with the club.
Undoubtedly, the strain of Wednesday's bad times and the
enormous amount of defensive work which he put in sapped
his strength later. Unfortunately, he left Sheffield on
rather an unhappy note, yet he left behind a record that
entitles him to a special niche in the club's history of great
players. It has often been said that he gave his best
displays for England. Perhaps it was so; nevertheless, he
gave many superb exhibitions for Wednesday.

The season before he left he received the club record
benefit award, £650, and, incidentally, he was the last
player who received a percentage portion of the transfer fee
when he came to Sheffield. Nowadays no man who is

transferred can receive more than £650, but in 1920 the percentage system was in operation. He got a very handsome sum.

Wilson has been styled the " souvenir king." He has in his possession international shirts representative of England, Ireland, Scotland and Wales, for he made a point of exchanging shirts with men of the other countries. While with Wednesday he played in nine games for England, four inter-League games, twice against Belgium, once against France, in six F.A. international trials, and one F.A. Charity Shield match. Besides the football caps, badges and medals, he has also the Belgian Medal of Honour won on the battlefield during the war.

To-day his post in the Wednesday team is filled by Frank Froggatt, a native of Sheffield and a half-back with a bright future.

[Thumb-nail sketches of the team which won promotion in 1925-26 appear in the Appendix.]

PART VI.

The Men at the Helm.

Chapter Thirty-Three.

Mr. J. C. Clegg—Fame as player and adminis-
trator—Mr. A. J. Dickinson, embodiment of
enthusiasm—Mr. C. Stokes—Mr. J. Holmes—
Mr. W. Fearnehough—Ald. Senior—Mr. R.
Brown.

> When I am dead, if men can say
> " He helped the world upon its way ";
> If they can say—if they but can—
> " He did his best. He played the man.
> " His way was straight; his soul was clean,
> " His failings not unkind, nor mean.
> " He loved his fellow-men and tried
> " To help them," I will be satisfied.
> —*Whittier.*

THOSE lines may be said to express the life policy of Mr. J. C. Clegg, J.P., the President of the Football Association, chairman of Wednesday, chairman of Sheffield United Cricket and Football Club, and holder of many other important offices. His life has been devoted to the service of his fellow-men and it is good to know that the impressive sacrifice of his leisure time and personal pleasures is universally appreciated. Will Association Football ever see his like again? He has had a wonderful career—the story of it would fill a book—and one full of contrasts.

In football's infancy, when the Wednesday Football Club was but a little amateur organisation, Mr. Clegg often undressed under a hedge and gave a lad a couple of coppers to sit on his clothes till the match was over so that they would not be stolen.   Jump fifty years to 1923 and think of the first English Cup Final at Wembley; think of that astonishing and unparalleled assembly of over 140,000 people clamouring to see the match.   That day Mr. Clegg was at the right hand of His Majesty the King.   There can be no greater illustration of the growth of the nation's game nor of the rise of a splendid English gentleman.

Football has long canonised him and has recognised in him what Chaucer called " the verray parfit gentil knight." Maybe, football is not the " sport of kings," but it is one of the most precious assets the nation possesses.   It is wonderfully well organised, wonderfully clean, and wonderfully built up.

It has largely fallen upon the Football Association to mould the policy on sound statesmanlike lines, and Mr. Clegg has been responsible in a large measure.   His legal acumen, his humour, his shrewdness of mind, and his well-balanced judgment have all contributed to make him an influence which cannot be over-estimated.   Yet no man is more unassuming, and he wins his way to the hearts of the humblest of people by his honesty of purpose and genial frankness.   An old professional comrade once said many years ago : " I do not believe Mr. Clegg ever knowingly did a wrong thing."   And how often has Mr. Clegg passed the remark : " Nobody ever got lost on a straight road "?

The foregoing pages have revealed a few of his activities as a player and referee, but not as an administrator.   He first became a member of the Football Association in 1886— forty years ago.   Three years later he became Chairman of the Council, a position he has held ever since, and succeeded the late Lord Kinnaird as President of the Football Association in 1923.   On June 15th, 1926, he celebrated his 76th birthday, and all sincerely hope the day is long distant when a successor will have to be found.

Mr. Clegg has always had a deep interest in and connection with the Wednesday F.C.   He became the chairman of the club at a critical time in its history—in 1915—after the death of Alderman George Senior, J.P   Mr. Clegg has stood by the club in difficult times, and Wednesday have profited by his excellent judgment and advice.   It is no small honour

Mr. W. G. TURNER, O.B.E.,
Vice-Chairman of Wednesday.

for a club to have as pilot so distinguished a gentleman as the President of the Football Association, and just as Wednesday are proud of the distinction, so is Sheffield.

Men at the helm have been many in the course of sixty years of football, and it seems only right now to refer to Mr. Arthur J. Dickinson, who was the honorary secretary for 33 years. How he virtually saved Wednesday in 1899 has been told; also how he risked serious injury to himself when seeking players for the club. Mr. Dickinson joined the Committee of the club in 1876, became honorary financial secretary in 1887, and full honorary secretary in 1891. For twenty years he has been a member of the Management Committee of the League, and was elected to the Council of the Football Association in 1919. He has served Wednesday and football faithfully and well, and is still a director and a power on the management. The club has been exceptionally favoured in having the aid of so able a man who is in the happy position of having the means to do the work out of pure love for the sport and loyalty to the club. After his school-days he was never a player, but he came to be a very good judge of the game.

One of the earliest officials and one of the founders was the late Mr. Charles Stokes, who belonged to the very finest sporting type. He was frank, open-handed and jolly, a true sportsman whom many will remember with affection. He died in 1913, and was the last member left of that committee of the Wednesday Cricket Club which formed the football section. Mr. Stokes played in those early days and helped the club to win its first Cup—the " Cromwell " Cup. In later years he was one of the founders of the Sheffield United Football Club; also he was a prominent official of the local Football Association and of the Yorkshire County Cricket Club, of which latter body he was honorary treasurer for many years.

The late Mr. John Holmes, who died in March, 1908, was another fine type of Sheffield sportsman, who followed the game with a whole-heartedness that was invigorating to all those with whom he came in contact. There was a breezy freshness about all his actions and for years the Wednesday club affairs were foremost in his mind. He joined the club in 1868 and did splendid service on the Committee in its

amateur days and as honorary treasurer. When the club
went to Olive Grove in 1887, Mr. Holmes was elected
President, and he held that position until 1899, when, owing
to failing health, the old sportsman gave way to Alderman
Senior. From the opening of Olive Grove to 1896, when
the Cup was first won, Wednesday were in the last eight
year after year, which reflected great credit on those who,
like Mr. Holmes, bore the brunt of the management. For
three years he was the President of the Football Alliance,
and at all times he was regarded as a warm friend of
professionals.

Earlier in that year of 1908, one other famous Wednesday
official passed away—Mr. Walter Fearnehough, whose son
is still on the Wednesday directorate. Mr. Fearnehough
was held in the highest esteem by friends and players alike,
and he did a great work for very many years. In 1883, he
was a vice-president of the club, and long before that he had
been prominently connected with the old club. He played
his part in the acquisition of James Lang. When the Olive
Grove enterprise was mooted the late Mr. Fearnehough was
one of those who helped to shoulder the grave responsibilities.
Associated with him were Mr. Alfred Holmes, Mr. Arthur
Nixon, Mr. Herbert Nixon, and Mr. C. H. Vessey. Mr.
Arthur Nixon took over the position of treasurer in the
'nineties, and he was pardonably proud of the financial
accounts of 1895-6, which showed a balance at the bank of
£2,140 after all liabilities had been discharged. All those
gentlemen named rendered faithful service.

And one should not overlook the earlier devoted servants
of Wednesday, such as Mr. H. Hawkesley, the President,
who died in the 1886-7 season; Mr. W. Littlehales, the
secretary for several years; Mr. Herbert Muscroft, Mr. John
and Mr. Alfred Muscroft, Mr. Herbert Newbould (so
prominent a figure in athletic circles), Mr. A. E. Bartlett,
hon. secretary to the Wanderers; Mr. W. H. Stacey, Mr.
Jack Hudson, secretary of the club for a time, and his
assistant, Mr. G. Cropper, and Mr. Wild.

In the old days many noted gentlemen were on the committee, and players too. Mr. Fred Bye was one. He kept
goal for Wednesday in 1883, and as a centre-forward was
once selected to play for London against Sheffield. Mr. Bye

became a leading referee, and took charge of a match
between Scotland and Ireland.

One would like to mention all, but that is impossible.

Alderman Senior became chairman in 1899. Till then
the club was an incorporated concern, its entire capital consisting of 50 shares of £5 each, fully paid up. It was then
turned into a limited liability company with new capital
amounting to £7,000. The alderman held the chairmanship
of the board until his death in 1915, when Mr. Clegg
succeeded him. Alderman Senior was a man of unbounded
energy and enterprise, of sterling integrity. He was a
familiar figure in the city; a man who rose from a most
humble position to the highest office and dignity a city can
confer on one of its sons. While chairman of Wednesday
he was elected to the position of Lord Mayor of Sheffield.
The phrase " from nailmaker's boy to Lord Mayor " speaks
volumes. Sheffield (and Wednesday) will never forget him ;
nor his rich vein of humour.

One story and one only is reproduced. " The reason I
got married," he once said, " was that I could not keep
myself. So I thought it could not be any worse if I got
married. If any man started straight in this world that day,
I did. I paid for everything, and when I had done that I
had nothing. Therefore, we started with nothing, with
nothing to pay and nothing to pay with if we had owed
anything."

He lived to the age of 77.

Wednesday's procession of directors who have occupied
the Mayoral chair of Sheffield has already been given.

Mr. A. G. W. Dronfield, who also died in 1915, and who
was one of the original shareholders of the club, rendered
yeoman service on the board for 17 years. It was most
unfortunate that the trouble with regard to David McLean's
agreement in 1913 was the cause of his severance with the
management. He always had the interests of the club very
much at heart, and no one could ever doubt his honesty of
purpose.

The present board consists of Mr. J. C. Clegg, J.P.
(chairman), Sir William Clegg, J.P., O.B.E., Alderman A. J.
Blanchard, J.P., Alderman W. F. Wardley, J.P., Mr. W. G.
Turner (vice-chairman), Mr. A. J. Dickinson, Mr. J. Cowley,

SOUVENIR PICTURE OF THE WEDNESDAY'S RETURN TO DIVISION I.

Top Row (left to right) : Messrs. J. Cowley, W. Fearnehough, W. G. Turner, A. J. Dickinson, A. J. Blanchard, J. B. Gunstone, W. F. Wardley and H. Nixon. *Second Row* : Mr. E. Mills, Kean, Walker, Fletcher, Marsden, Froggatt, Brown, Prince, Blenkinsop, Mr. Tom Cawley, Felton, Mr. A. Francis. *Third Row* : Mr. R. Brown (Manager), Mr. Wm. Hodgkiss (asst. trainer), Williams, Trotter, Mr. J. C. Clegg, Powell, S. Bedford, Hill, Mr. C. Craig (trainer), Mr. S. P. Stephen (asst. secretary), Lowdell, Wilkinson.

Mr. J. B. Gunstone, Mr. W. Fearnehough, Mr. H. Nixon, Mr. E. Mills, and Mr. A. Francis. They are an excellent body of sportsmen, the full extent of whose work and anxiety on behalf of Wednesday will never be known.

Two or three one-time officials may be mentioned in addition, the late Mr. J. H. Thackray, Dr. Bruce Wilson, and Mr. Walter Foulston.

The present secretary-manager of the club, Mr. Robert Brown, was appointed in 1920, and in the years of prosperity in 1903 onwards for a time he was also connected with the club. Many players destined to become internationals did he find. He has admirably assisted the directors in the great task of getting the club back into the First Division, and the sunshine which has followed the winter of disappointments he has had to pass through will be very welcome. Mr. Brown is a solid man, not a talker but a worker. His knowledge, ability and courage are well known. No man's courage has stood the test better than that of Mr. Brown. He possesses rather a unique record. When he left Wednesday the first time, he was appointed manager of Portsmouth, and saw that club win the Second Division championship of the Southern League, and, later, the Southern League championship. He was with Wednesday when the First Division championship was won, also the English Cup, and now the laurels are complete with the winning of the Second Division Shield by the Sheffield team.

His assistant is Mr. S. P. Stephen, who was appointed assistant secretary to Mr. Dickinson in the season of 1916-17. Mr. Stephen was of great service to the club in war-time, and he has been a loyal servant since. It was in June, 1926, when he received from the hands of Mr. J. C. Clegg, the President of the Sheffield and Hallamshire County Association, a prized long-service medal in recognition of twenty years' labour in administration on the Council of the Association. Mr. Stephen has done much appreciated work for the junior game in Sheffield.

The men at the helm are congratulated on having steered Wednesday into the First Division, and may they and the players continue to provide, as someone once put it, " good sport for the toiling people."

APPENDIX.

SOME FINANCE COMPARISONS.

IN 1884-5, the club's match receipts were £194 ; eleven years after the season's receipts were £7,283, eloquent of the money in the Cup.

When the Cup was won in 1907, the net gate receipts had risen to £10,347.

When promotion was won in 1925-26, the gross match receipts were £31,340.

The record receipts for a season were taken in 1920-21, when they amounted to £33,842.

From the wages viewpoint, the figures are interesting. In 1895-6 the wage-bill was £3,535 ; in 1925-26 it was nearly four times as big—£14,014—a record for Wednesday. The table below speaks for itself :—

Year.					Gross Gate Receipts. £	Wages and Bonus. £
1885	...	...	...	...	194	—
1896	...	...	...	...	7,283	3,535
1900	...	...	...	...	4,664	3,609
1907	...	...	...	...	10,347	5,262
1913	...	...	...	...	14,471	4,652
1914	...	...	...	...	17,035	5,414
1915	...	...	...	...	10,369	5,004
1916	...	...	...	...	2,779	369
1917	...	...	...	...	2,590	266
1918	...	...	...	...	3,836	241
1919	...	...	...	...	5,994	373
1920	...	...	...	...	25,085	8,789
1921	...	...	...	...	33,842	11,147
1922	...	...	...	...	18,561	12,956
1923	...	...	...	...	27,494	12,562
1924	...	...	...	...	25,764	11,833
1925	...	...	...	...	26,659	13,125
1926	...	...	...	...	31,340	14,014

When studying the profits and losses, it should be noted that the profits do not include the depreciation allowances ; the losses do. How this works out can be understood when reviewing the war seasons, 1915 to 1919 inclusive. In the aggregate in those years Wednesday had losses amounting to over £6,000, but in three of those years the actual workings of the club on the revenue accounts resulted in a profit of £1,055, while the losses in the other two years amounted to £319 only. So that for the five years named the working profit was £736.

Wednesday have invariably made substantial allowances for depreciation, and it is those allowances, together with interest on debentures—the latter small compared with depreciation—which account for the differences. Take the year 1921, when the recorded profits were £4,651. Actually the profits on the revenue account were nearly £8,000—a club record. But the club repaid £2,000 debentures and made a depreciation of assets only a few pounds short of another £1,000. The club is as sound as a bell financially.

Year.					Profit. £	Loss. £
1885	...	...	...	...	—	1/13/0
1896	...	...	...	...	*2,140	—
1900	...	...	...	...	—	579
1907	...	...	...	...	1,018	—
1913	...	...	...	...	5,382	—
1914	...	...	...	...	3,367	—
1915	...	...	...	...	—	1,564
1916	...	...	...	...	—	1,105
1917	...	...	...	...	—	1,312
1918	...	...	...	...	—	869
1919	...	...	...	...	—	1,158
1920	...	...	...	...	—	1,677
1921	...	...	...	...	4,651	—
1922	...	...	...	...	—	5,572
1923	...	...	...	...	—	4,768
1924	...	...	...	...	1,082	—
1925	...	...	...	...	—	3,265
1926	...	...	...	...	3,402	—

* Balance at the bank after discharging all liabilities.

The tremendous jump in transfer-fees in post-war seasons is a matter for special note. In seven seasons since League football was resumed, Wednesday have paid £43,615 in transfer-fees, and have received under that head £21,795.

Another item of interest is the increase of cost in travelling, training, refreshments, etc. In 1895-6, the account was £558; in 1913, it was £750. In 1925-26, the bill was no less than £2,015 15s.

TRANSFER FEES.

Year.					Paid. £	Received. £
1900	...	...	...	...	360	—
1913	...	...	...	...	386	715
1920	...	...	...	...	8,328	3,145
1921	...	...	...	...	6,856	6,675
1922	...	...	...	...	6,284	4,175
1923	...	...	...	...	7,647	885
1924	...	...	...	...	859	535
1925	...	...	...	...	7,833	1,630
1926	...	...	...	...	5,808	3,750
Post-war Totals	...	...			£43,615	£21,795

TRAVELLING AND TRAINING EXPENSES, ETC.

Year.							£ s. d.
1896	...	...	...	...	...	...	558 6 0
1900	...	...	...	...	...	...	480 5 0
1907	...	...	...	...	...	...	999 18 0
1913	...	...	...	...	...	...	750 1 0
1926	...	...	...	...	...	...	2,015 15 0

RESULTS IN ENGLISH CUP CAMPAIGNS.

Below is a complete list of results in the Football
Association Challenge Cup Competitions:—

SEASON 1880-81.

Date.		Opposing Club.				Home.	Away.
Dec.	18	v. Blackburn Rovers	...	...	...		4—0
Jan.	8	v. Turton ...	...	...	...	...	2—0
Feb.	6	v. Darwen ...	...	...	...	...	2—5

SEASON 1881-2.

Nov.	5	v. Providence (at Quibell's Field, near Hyde Park) ...	...	...	...		2—0
		Second Round : a bye.					
Dec.	28	v. Staveley	...	...	...	2—2	
Jan.	7	,, (re-play)	...	...	...		*0—0
Jan.	9	,, (re-play) at Lockwood's Grd.					5—1
Jan.	21	v. Heeley (at Bramall Lane)	...	...	3—1	
Feb.	7	v. Upton Park	...	...	...	6—0	
Mar.	6	v. Blackburn Rovers (semi-final), at Huddersfield ...	...	...	...		0—0
Mar.	15	Re-play at Manchester ...	...	...			1—5

* After extra time.

SEASON 1882-3.

Nov.	4	v. Spilsley (at Bramall Lane)	...	...	12—2	
Dec.	2	v. Lockwood Bros.	...	...	...		6—0
Jan.	6	v. Notts Forest	...	...	...		2—2
Jan.	13	,, (re-play)	...	...	3—2	
Feb.	12	v. Notts County ...	...	...	...	1—4	

SEASON 1883-4.

		First Round : a bye.					
Dec.	1	v. Staveley	...	...	...		1—3

SEASON 1884-5.

Nov.	8	v. Long Eaton (at the Flats) ...	...			1—0
		Second Round : a bye.					
Jan.	3	v. Notts Forest ...	...	...	...	1—2	

SEASON 1885-6.

Oct.	31	v. Long Eaton	...	...	...	...	0—2

SEASON 1886-7.

The club sent in its application too late.

SEASON 1887-8.

Oct.	15	v. Belper ...	...	...	...	...	3—2
Nov.	5	v. Long Eaton	...	...	...		*2—1
		Third Round : a bye.					
Dec.	19	v. Crusaders (at Leyton)	...	...		1—0
Jan.	7	v. Notts Forest ...	...	...	...		4—2
Jan.	30	v. Preston North End (at Olive Grove)	1—3		

* After extra time.

SEASON 1888-9.

Feb.	2	v. Notts Rangers	...	...	...		1—1
Feb.	9	,, (re-play)	...	...	3—0	
Feb.	16	v. Notts County ...	...	...	...	3—2	
Mar.	2	v. Wolverhampton Wanderers ...	...			0—3

SEASON 1889-90.

Date.		Opposing Club.	Home.	Away
Jan.	20	v. Swifts	6—1	
Feb.	1	v. Accrington	2—1	
Feb.	15	v. Notts County	5—0	
Feb.	22	Notts had successfully appealed because of the bad ground. Re-play ...		2—3
Mar.	3	Wednesday had protested against in-eligible players, and at Derby, Wednesday won the 2nd re-play ...		2—1
Mar.	8	v. Bolton Wanderers (semi-final), at Birmingham		2—1
Mar.	29	v. Blackburn Rovers (final), at the Oval		1—6

SEASON 1890-1.

Jan.	17	v. Halliwell	12—0	
Jan.	31	v. Derby County		3—2
Feb.	14	v. West Bromwich Albion	0—2	

SEASON 1891-2.

Jan.	23	v. Bolton Wanderers	4—1	
Jan.	30	v. Small Heath	*2—0	
Feb.	13	v. West Bromwich Albion		1—2

* Bought ground rights.

SEASON 1892-3.

Jan.	21	v. Derby County	3—2	
Jan.	28	The County protested against the match standing, and Wednesday lost the re-play		0—1
		Wednesday then protested, and a re-play was ordered for Feb. 2, Wednesday winning	4—2	
Feb.	4	v. Burnley	1—0	
Feb.	18	v. Everton		0—3

SEASON 1893-4.

Jan.	27	v. Royal Arsenal		2—1
Feb.	10	v. Stoke	1—0	
Feb.	24	v. Aston Villa	3—2	
Mar.	10	v. Bolton Wanderers (semi-final), at Fallowfield		1—2

SEASON 1894-5.

Feb.	2	v. Notts County	5—1	
Feb.	16	v. Middlesbrough	6—1	
Mar.	5	v. Everton	2—0	
Mar.	16	v. West Bromwich Albion (semi-final), at Derby		0—2

SEASON 1895-6.

Feb.	1	v. Southampton St. Mary's		3—2
Feb.	15	v. Sunderland	2—1	
Feb.	29	v. Everton	4—0	
Mar.	21	v. Bolton Wanderers (semi-final), at Goodison Park, Liverpool		1—1
Mar.	26	Re-play, at Nottingham Forest's ground		3—1
April	18	v. Wolverhampton Wanderers (final) ...		2—1

SEASON 1896-7.

Jan.	30	v. Notts Forest	0—1	

SEASON 1897-8.

Jan.	29	v. Sunderland		1—0
Feb.	12	v. West Bromwich Albion		0—1

SEASON 1898-9.

Date.		Opposing Club.					Home.	Away.
Jan.	28	v. Stoke					2—2	
Feb.	2	,, (re-play)						0—2

SEASON 1899-1900.

Jan.	27	v. Bolton Wanderers					1—0	
Feb.	10	v. Sheffield United						†0—0
Feb.	17	,, (re-play)						1—1
Feb.	22	,, (re-play)					0—2	

† Stopped soon after interval owing to snowstorm.

SEASON 1900-1.

Feb.	9	v. Bury						0—1

SEASON 1901-2.

Jan.	25	v. Sunderland						0—1

SEASON 1902-3.

Feb.	7	v. Blackburn Rovers						0—0
Feb.	12	,, ,, (re-play) ...					0—1	

SEASON 1903-4.

Feb.	6	v. Plymouth Argyle						2—2
Feb.	10	,, ,, (re-play) ...					2—0	
Feb.	20	v. Manchester United					6—0	
Mar.	5	v. Tottenham Hotspur						1—1
Mar.	9	,, ,, (re-play) ...					2—0	
Mar.	19	v. Manchester City (semi-final), at Goodison Park, Liverpool						0—3

SEASON 1904-5.

Feb.	4	v. Blackburn Rovers						2—1
Feb.	18	v. Portsmouth					2—1	
Mar.	4	v. Preston North End						1—1
Mar.	9	,, ,, (re-play) ...					3—0	
Mar.	25	v. Newcastle United (semi-final), at Manchester						0—1

SEASON 1905-6.

Jan.	13	v. Bristol Rovers					1—0	
Feb.	3	v. Millwall					1—1	
Feb.	8	,, (re-play)						3—0
Feb.	24	v. Notts Forest					4—1	
Mar.	10	v. Everton						3—4

SEASON 1906-7.

Jan.	12	v. Wolverhampton Wanderers					3—2	
Feb.	2	v. Southampton						1—1
Feb.	7	,, (re-play)					3—1	
Feb.	23	v. Sunderland					0—0	
Feb.	27	,, (re-play)						1—0
Mar.	9	v. Liverpool					1—0	
Mar.	23	v. Woolwich Arsenal (semi-final), at Birmingham						3—1
April	20	v. Everton (final)						2—1

SEASON 1907-8.

Jan.	11	v. Norwich City						0—2

SEASON 1908-9.

Date.		Opposing Club.	Home.	Away
Jan.	16	v. Stoke	5—0	
Feb.	6	v. Portsmouth		2—2
Feb.	11	,, (re-play)	3—0	
Feb.	20	v. Glossop	0—1	

SEASON 1909-10.

Jan.	15	v. Northampton		0—0
Jan.	20	,, (re-play)	0—1	

SEASON 1910-11.

Jan.	14	v. Coventry City	1—2	

SEASON 1911-12.

Jan.	13	v. Middlesbrough		0—0
Jan.	25	,, (re-play)	1—2	

SEASON 1912-13.

Jan.	16	v. Grimsby Town...	5—1	
Feb.	1	v. Chelsea		1—1
Feb.	5	,, (re-play)	6—0	
Feb.	15	v. Bradford		1—2

SEASON 1913-14.

Jan.	10	v. Notts County	3—2	
Jan.	31	v. Wolverhampton W.		1—1
Feb.	4	,, (re-play)	1—0	
Feb.	21	v. Brighton and Hove Albion ...	3—0	
Mar.	7	v. Aston Villa	0—1	

SEASON 1914-15.

Jan.	9	v. Manchester United	1—0	
Jan.	30	v. Wolverhampton W.	2—0	
Feb.	20	v. Newcastle United	1—2	

SEASON 1919-20.

Jan.	14	v. Darlington		0—0
Jan.	19	,, (re-play)	0—2	

SEASON 1920-21.

Jan.	8	v. West Ham United	1—0	
Jan.	29	v. Everton		1—1
Feb.	3	,, (re-play)	0—1	

SEASON 1921-22.

Jan.	7	v. Bradford		0—1

SEASON 1922-23.

Jan.	13	v. New Brighton	3—0	
Feb.	3	v. Barnsley	2—1	
Feb.	24	v. Derby County		0—1

SEASON 1923-24.

Jan.	12	v. Leicester City	4—1	
Feb.	2	v. Bristol City	1—1	
Feb.	6	,, (re-play)		0—2

SEASON 1924-25.

Jan.	10	v. Manchester United	2—0	
Jan.	31	v. Sheffield United		2—3

SEASON 1925-26.

Jan.	9	v. New Brighton		1—2

WEDNESDAY v. SHEFFIELD UNITED.

Below is a complete list of results of matches between
Wednesday and Sheffield United. The summary of results
is :—

	P.	W.	L.	D.	Goals. F.	A.
Wednesday	106	42	36	28	141	131
Sheffield United	106	36	42	28	131	141

LEAGUE MATCHES.

			Goals W. U.				Goals W. U.
1893 Oct.	16 at Bramall Lane	1 1		1905 Oct.	21 at Bramall Lane	2 0	
1893 Nov.	13 at Olive Grove	1 2		1906 April	18 at Owlerton	1 0	
1894 Oct.	27 at Olive Grove	2 3		1906 Nov.	3 at Owlerton	2 2	
1895 Jan.	12 at Bramall Lane	0 1		1907 April	4 at Bramall Lane	1 2	
1895 Sept.	7 at Olive Grove	1 0		1907 Nov.	9 at Bramall Lane	3 1	
1895 Dec.	26 at Bramall Lane	1 1		1908 Mar.	7 at Owlerton	2 0	
1896 Dec.	26 at Bramall Lane	0 2		1908 Dec.	25 at Owlerton	1 0	
1897 Mar.	2 at Olive Grove	1 1		1908 Dec.	26 at Bramall Lane	1 2	
1897 Oct.	16 at Olive Grove	0 1		1909 Nov.	6 at Bramall Lane	3 3	
1897 Dec.	27 at Bramall Lane	1 1		1910 Mar.	19 at Owlerton	1 3	
1898 Oct.	3 at Olive Grove	1 1		1910 Oct.	22 at Owlerton	2 0	
1898 Dec.	26 at Bramall Lane	1 2		1911 Feb.	25 at Bramall Lane	1 0	
1900 Dec.	15 at Bramall Lane	0 1		1911 Nov.	4 at Bramall Lane	1 1	
1901 April	29 at Owlerton	1 0		1912 Mar.	9 at Owlerton	1 1	
1901 Nov.	2 at Owlerton	1 0		1912 Oct.	26 at Owlerton	1 0	
1902 Mar.	1 at Bramall Lane	0 3		1913 Mar.	1 at Bramall Lane	2 0	
1902 Sept.	1 at Bramall Lane	3 2		1913 Oct.	26 at Bramall Lane	1 0	
1902 Oct.	11 at Owlerton	0 1		1914 Feb.	26 at Hillsboro'	2 1	
1903 Dec.	12 at Bramall Lane	1 1		1914 Sept.	5 at Bramall Lane	1 0	
1904 April	9 at Owlerton	3 0		1915 Jan.	2 at Hillsboro'	1 1	
1904 Dec.	10 at Owlerton	1 3		1919 Sept.	27 at Hillsboro'	2 1	
1905 April	8 at Bramall Lane	2 4		1919 Oct.	4 at Bramall Lane	0 3	

Played 44. Wednesday won 18, United won 15, drawn 11. Wednesday 54 goals,
United 52 goals.

MIDLAND SECTION WAR TIME GAMES.

		Goals W. U.				Goals W. U.
1915 Oct.	16 at Hillsboro'	0 0		1917 Dec.	25 at Bramall Lane	0 1
1916 Jan.	15 at Bramall Lane	1 1		1917 Dec.	26 at Hillsboro'	3 1
1916 Oct.	21 at Hillsboro'	2 2		1918 Dec.	25 at Hillsboro'	4 0
1917 Jan.	27 at Bramall Lane	0 1		1918 Dec.	26 at Bramall Lane	0 3

Played 8. Wednesday won 2, United 3, drawn 3. United 9 goals, Wednesday 10 goals.

MIDLAND SECTION SUBSIDIARY.

		Goals W. U.				Goals W. U.
1916 April	1 at Bramall Lane	1 1		1918 Mar.	16 at Bramall Lane	5 0
1916 April	24 at Hillsboro'	0 1		1918 Mar.	23 at Hillsboro'	2 1
1917 Mar.	24 at Bramall Lane	4 3		1919 Mar.	22 at Hillsboro'	0 2
1917 April	4 at Hillsboro'	2 1		1919 Mar.	29 at Bramall Lane	0 1

Played 8. Wednesday won 4, United 3, drawn 1. Wednesday 14 goals, United 10 goals.

ENGLISH CUP TIES.

	Goals W. U.			Goals W. U.
1900 Feb. 10*at Bramall Lane	0 0		1900 Feb. 19 at Owlerton	0 2
1900 Feb. 17 at Bramall Lane	1 1		1925 Jan. 31 at Bramall Lane	2 3

* Stopped owing to snowstorm.

SHEFFIELD AND HALLAMSHIRE COUNTY CUP.

	Gaols W. U.			Goals W. U.
1921 May 21 at Hillsboro'	1 2		1926 May 3 at Bramall Lane	1 3
1924 May 10 at Hillsboro'	0 2			

Played 3. United won 3. United 7 goals, Wednesday 2 goals.

CHARITY MATCHES.

	Goals W. U.			Goals W. U.
1903 Oct. 5 at Bramall Lane	3 1		1910 Oct. 3 at Owlerton	2 0
1904 Oct. 3 at Owlerton	0 2		1911 Oct. 2 at Bramall Lane	0 2
1905 Oct. 2 at Bramall Lane	3 3		1912 Oct. 7 at Owlerton	3 0
1906 Oct. 1 at Owlerton	3 0		1914 April 30 at Hillsboro'	0 2
1907 Oct. 7 at Bramall Lane	1 1		1914 Oct. 5 at Hillsboro'	2 1
1908 Oct. 5 at Owlerton	0 0		1916 May 6 at Bramall Lane	0 3
1909 Oct. 4 at Bramall Lane	3 1		1917 May 5 at Bramall Lane	2 1

Played 14. Wednesday won 7, United 4, drawn 3. Wednesday 22 goals, United 17 goals.

WHARNCLIFFE CHARITY CUP.

	Goals W. U.			Goals W. U.
1891 April 23 at Olive Grove ...	2 1		1894 April 26 at Olive Grove ...	0 1
1893 April 24 at Olive Grove ...	0 0			

UNITED COUNTIES LEAGUE.

	Goals W. U.			Goals W. U.
1894 Mar. 27 at Bramall Lane	0 2		1895 April 8 at Bramall Lane	0 0
1894 April 14 at Olive Grove ...	1 1		1895 April 20 at Olive Grove ...	1 1

SHEFFIELD AND DERBYSHIRE LEAGUE.

	Goals W. U.			Goals W. U.
1897 Feb. 13 at Bramall Lane	0 0		1897 April 19 at Olive Grove ...	2 1

CLUB MATCHES.

	Goals W. U.			Goals W. U.
1890 Dec. 15 at Olive Grove ...	2 1		1899 Dec. 26 at Bramall Lane	1 0
1891 Jan. 12 at Bramall Lane	2 3		1902 May 3†at Owlerton	3 0
1891 Oct. 26 at Bramall Lane	0 5		1918 April 13 at Hillsboro'	2 0
1891 Nov. 16 at Olive Grove ...	4 1		1918 April 20 at Bramall Lane	1 1
1892 Oct. 17 at Olive Grove ...	1 1		1919 April 5 at Bramall Lane	1 0
1892 Nov. 21 at Bramall Lane	3 1		1919 April 12 at Hillsboro'	0 1
1896 Mar. 2*at Olive Grove ...	0 5		1923 April 19‡at Bramall Lane	2 0
1898 Feb. 26 at Bramall Lane	4 1		1924 Sept. 18aat Bramall Lane	2 2

Played 16. Wednesday won 9, United won 4, drawn 3. Wednesday 28 goals, United 22 goals.

* Mumford's Benefit. † Ibrox Disaster. ‡ Waller's Benefit. a Nicholson's Benefit.

HONOURS AWARDED WEDNESDAY PLAYERS.

INTERNATIONALS.

1872—J. C. Clegg (E.) v. Scotland.
1873—W. E. Clegg (E.) v. Scotland.
1877—W. Mosforth (E.) v. Scotland.
1878—W. Mosforth (E.) v. Scotland.
1879—W. E. Clegg (E.) v. Wales ; W. Mosforth (E.) v. Scotland and Wales.
1880—W. Mosforth (E.) v. Scotland and Wales ; J. Hudson (E.) v. Wales.
1881—W. Mosforth and J. Hudson (E.) v. Wales.
1882—W. Mosforth (E.) v. Scotland and Wales ; J. Hudson (E.) v. Wales.
1883—J. Hudson (E.) v. Ireland.
1887—E. Brayshaw (E.) v. Ireland.
1889—W. Betts (E.) v. Wales.
1893—F. Spiksley (E.) v. Scotland and Wales.
1894—F. Spiksley (E.) v. Scotland and Ireland.
1895—T. H. Crawshaw (E.) v. Ireland.
1896—T. H. Crawshaw (E.) v. Scotland, Wales and Ireland ; F. Spiksley (E.) v. Ireland.
1897—T. H. Crawshaw (E.) v. Scotland, Wales and Ireland.
1898—F. Spiksley (E.) v. Scotland and Wales.
1901—T. H. Crawshaw (E.) v. Ireland.
1903—H. Davis (E.) v. Scotland, Wales and Ireland.
1904—T. H. Crawshaw (E.) v. Wales and Ireland ; H. Ruddlesdin (E.) v. Scotland, Wales and Ireland.
1905—J. Lyall (S.) v. England.
1907—J. Stewart (E.) v. Scotland and Wales ; A. Wilson (S.) v. England.
1908—A. Wilson (S.) v. England.
1909—E. McConnell (I.) v. Scotland and Wales.
1910—E. McConnell (I.) v. England, Scotland and Wales ; J. M. Murray (S.) v. England, Ireland and Wales ; G. Robertson (S.) v. Wales.
1911—J. Stewart (E.) v. Scotland.
1912—T. Brittleton (E.) v. Scotland, Wales and Ireland ; D. McLean (S.) v. England ; P. O'Connel (I.) v. England and Scotland ; G. Robertson (S.) v. Wales ; A. Wilson (Sc.) v. England.
1913—T. Brittleton (E.) v. Scotland ; J. Campbell (S.) v. Wales ; G. Robertson (S.) v. England and Ireland ; A. Wilson (S.) v. England and Wales.
1914—T. Brittleton (E.) v. Wales ; P. O'Connell (I.) v. England, Scotland and Wales ; A. Wilson (S.) v. Ireland.
1920—J. Blair (S.) v. England and Ireland.
1921—G. Wilson (E.) v. Scotland and Wales.
1922—J. E. Davison (E.) v. Wales ; G. Wilson (E.) v. Scotland and Ireland.
1923—F. Kean (E.) v. Scotland ; R. Williams (W.) v. Scotland ; G. Wilson (E.) v. Scotland, Wales and Ireland.
1924—G. Wilson (E.) v. Ireland and Wales ; F. Kean (E.) v. Wales.
1925—F. Kean (E.) v. Ireland).
1926—R. Williams (W.) v. Scotland.
1926—F. Kean (E.) v. Ireland.

AMATEUR INTERNATIONALS.

1920—W. H. Harvey (E.) v. Ireland.

AGAINST COLONIAL AND FOREIGN TEAMS.

1908—F. Bradshaw (E.) v. Austria.
1921—G. Wilson (E.) v. Belgium.
1923—G. Wilson and F. Kean (E.) v. Belgium.
1925—W. Felton (E.) v. France.
1925—J. E. Davison (E.) v. Australia (2).
1926—F. Kean (E.) v. Belgium.

ENGLAND TRIAL MATCHES.

NORTH v. SOUTH.

Bartlett, W. 1908	Hunter, J. 1880-81
Bradshaw, F. 1908-09	Kean, F. W. 1924
Brittleton, J. T. 1909	Layton, W. 1900
Cawley, T. E. 1885	Mosforth, W. H. 1880-81-82-83
Cowley, J. E. 1884	Ruddlesdin, H. 1904
Crawshaw, T. H. 1901-04	Simpson, V. S. 1907
Gregory, R. 1881	Waller, G. 1890
Hudson, J. 1883-84	Wilkinson, H. 1883

AMATEURS v. PROFESSIONALS.

Crawshaw, T. H. 1896-97	Stewart, J. 1907
Layton, W. 1907	Wilson, G. 1924
Spiksley, F. 1896	

WHITES v. STRIPES

Brayshaw, E. 1890	Brittleton, J. T. 1910-12

ENGLAND v. THE NORTH, v. THE SOUTH and v. THE REST.

Brittleton, J. T. 1914	Wilson, G. ... ... 1922 (2)-23-24

THE NORTH v. ENGLAND.

Davison, J. E. 1922	Wilson, G. 1921

THE REST v. ENGLAND.

Kean, F. W. 1924	Wilson, G. 1925

INTER-LEAGUE MATCHES.

Bradshaw, F., v. S., v. I. 1909	Kean, F. W., v. I. 1923-25
Brittleton, J. T., v. S. 1910	Langley, A., v. S. 1898
v. I. 1913	Layton, W., v. I. 1901
Crawshaw, T. H., v. S. 1895-97-99	Spiksley, F., v. S. 1894-1903
v. I. 1899-1902-04-05-08	Wilson, v. S. 1921-22-23
Davis, H., v. S. 1903	v. I. 1924
Earp, F. W., v. I. 1898	

BIG CROWDS AND GATES.

Feb. 29, 1896—Wednesday v. Everton (E.C.). Receipts £889 6s. 9d.*
* Record for Olive Grove.

			Attendance.	Receipts.
Nov.	30, 1907—v. Manchester United		43,143	£1,100
Mar.	7, 1914—v. Aston Villa (E.C.)		57,143	£2,302
Jan.	19, 1920—v. Darlington (E.C.)		52,388	£2,974
April	10, 1920—England v. Scotland		25,536	£4,278
Jan.	8, 1921—v. West Ham United (E.C.)		49,125	£2,815
Feb.	3, 1921—v. Everton (E.C.)		62,407	£4,445
Feb.	3, 1923—v. Barnsley (E.C.)...		66,250	£4,911†

† Record attendance and receipts.

BIG MATCHES AT HILLSBOROUGH.

April 10 1920—England 5 Scotland 4.
Goal-scorers:—England : Kelly (2) Morris, Cock and
Quantrill.
Scotland : Miller (2), Wilson and Donaldson.
Attendance, 25,536 ; Receipts, £4,278 8s. 0d.

ENGLISH CUP SEMI-FINAL TIES.

Mar. 30, 1912—West Bromwich Albion, 1, Blackburn Rovers 0 (after extra time).
Attendance, 20,000 ; Receipts £1,277.
Mar. 19, 1921—Tottenham Hotspur 2, Preston North End 1.
Attendance 43,320 ; Receipts £4,506 19s. 4d.
Mar. 25, 1922—Preston North End 2, Tottenham Hotspur 1.
Attendance, 49,282 ; Receipts, £4,687 7s. 2d.

MAIN MEN IN PROMOTION FIGHT, 1925-26.

Below are thumb-nail sketches of the main men who helped Wednesday to win the Second Division in 1925-26 :—

JACK BROWN.—Big and broad-shouldered, this native of Worksop rose to the occasion admirably. Efficient, sound and reliable in judgment, he justified the full confidence of the club. He became a goalkeeper by accident, after being a centre-forward in a minor team. Later, he joined Worksop Town, the Midland League club, and became the hero of London by virtue of a wonderful exhibition for the Town against Tottenham Hotspur at White Hart Lane in 1923, when the result was a draw. That year he signed for Wednesday. A collier, he first played for Worksop in 1919. Stands 5 ft. 10½ ins., weight 12 st. 4 lbs.

WILLIAM FELTON.—A young hearty back, who was often brilliant. Stood Wednesday in good stead in many a match. A powerful and robust defender, quick to tackle and recover. Just a little excitable. A North-countryman, he threw in his lot with Grimsby Town in January, 1921, and soon established himself. He was transferred to Wednesday in January, 1923, when but twenty years old. Born at Wardley Colliery, he played for that club before going to Grimsby. In May, 1925, played for England against France in Paris. Height 5 ft. 9 ins., weight 12 st.

ERNEST BLENKINSOP.—A back of polish and style, coolness in tackling, and a placer of kicks. He reminds some people of Howard Spencer, of Aston Villa fame. Another Wednesday " bargain." Only 24 years of age. A Cudworth lad, he played for the village team as a boy among men, alternately as a left back and inside-left, with his brother, Harry. Mr. H. P. Lewis, manager of Hull City, secured his transfer in the season 1921-22, and a season and a half later (January, 1923) was transferred to Wednesday. Received his baptism in Wednesday colours at Hillsborough in the celebrated English Cup-tie with Barnsley. Height 5 ft. 10½ ins., weight 11st. 2 lbs.

ARTHUR LOWDELL.—First, Arthur Lowdell was a centre-forward, then an inside-right. After that he tried his hand as an outside-right, and, in between whiles, he played at back and half-back. A general utility man, he was wholehearted. As an inside-right he had much to do with Wednesday's Cup triumph over Barnsley in 1923. Wednesday experimented with him patiently at right half-back in 1924-25, and later on he got into the team. Lowdell is a tremendous worker, very quick in recovery and lasts the distance. Yet another young man. He joined the army when only 15 years of age, fought at Ypres, Arras, Somme, Passchendaele, and Cambrai, and was thrice wounded. He is a Londoner and a schoolboy international, and was secured by Wednesday from Ton Pentre in January, 1922. Age 26 years, height 5 ft. 7½ ins., weight 11 st. 2 lb.

FRED KEAN.—Shared the right half-back honours with Lowdell in 1925-26. He has played in that position against Scotland, Ireland, Wales, and Belgium. A native of Sheffield, he went to Portsmouth, but was not long before he returned. In those days he was an inside right, and as a forward he joined Wednesday in 1920. Light-haired, he has often been mistaken for Wilson. On the field his upright figure reminds one of a Guardsman, striking in figure and striking in play as a rule. A dour player, he builds his game on lines akin to those of Moss, of the Villa, in that he likes a forward policy and to have a pop at the goal. A very fine half-back. Height 5 ft. 9 ins., weight 11 st. 6 lb.

FRANK FROGGATT.—The first Sheffield-born player to be skipper since Crawshaw's day. Like Crawshaw, Froggatt is a centre-half-back and a fine header of a ball. Froggatt ripened with experience. A dour tackler and thrustful player. Some of his passes to the extreme wingers are of the Barson type. A great Wednesday man, he was extremely loyal whilst awaiting his opportunity. He first played for Rose Athletic, an Attercliffe Alliance club, then going to Denaby United. He was transferred to Wednesday in October, 1921, and has played in all half-back positions. He learnt his football in the Army. Age 26, stands 5 ft. 9¼ ins. tall, and weighs 11¼ st.

WILLIAM MARSDEN.—A further example of an inside-forward being converted with success into a left half-back ; indeed, Marsden's efficiency in the position spoke well of his adaptability and perseverance, for he was a right-footed player, and had to practise assiduously to make his left foot a reliable servant. Tall and well-built ; a smart-looking athlete, Marsden tackles shrewdly and supports his forwards discreetly. Joining Wednesday from Sunderland as an inside-right in the summer of 1924, he did not accomplish much until made a half-back late on in the 1924-25 season. His success was surprising. He was picked up by Sunderland from a local team, but his possibilities were not fully realised at Roker. Age 23. Height 5 ft. 9 ins., weight 11 st. 11 lbs.

REES WILLIAMS.—The best two-footed footballer Wednesday have had for many years, Williams played some brilliant games. His ball control is excellent, and backs find his left foot trickery bewildering. He's little but very clever, and his centres are ideal. An elusive star. A self-made International, he has played for Wales four times. Though Aston Villa, Manchester United, and Sunderland had made offers, Wednesday secured him in June, 1922, from Merthyr Town. Williams has won several handicap sprints in Wales. Height 5 ft. 5 ins., weight 10 st. 6 lbs.

MATTHEW BARRASS.—The scheming of Barrass contributed considerably to Wednesday's effective forward play. Not a dominant player, Barrass nevertheless passed with rare judgment and calculation and inaugurated many attacks. He utilised the reverse pass. While not a prolific scorer, he had valuable goals to his credit. Barrass used to be captain of Blackpool, whence he came to Hillsborough, in March, 1925, to help Wednesday to get out of a desperate corner. Born at Preston Colliery, near North Shields, his early football was played with Seaham U.M. Bible Class and Dawdon Colliery in the Wearside League. He served with the R.F.A. in the War and, on being demobilised, played for Seaham Harbour. In 1919 he was transferred to Blackpool. Barrass was then 21 years old. Height 5 ft. 8 in., weight 11 st. 3 lb.

JAMES TROTTER.—The centre-forward broke records for Wednesday in the goal-scoring line. So far he is the only Wednesday man who has scored five goals in a League match, and he has done that feat twice ; moreover, he is the club's leading League goal-scorer in one season. He overhauled David McLean's records. Trotter was the leading goal-scorer of the Second Division in 1925-26. The Northumbrian has good ideas of a leader's duties, holds the line well together ; is not easily bustled off the ball when making for goal, and shoots well on the run. So far has scored 55 goals in 77 League games. A native of Newcastle, Trotter was playing for Parsons' Turbine Works in 1919, when Bury signed him, and after a fine run with the " Shakers " in 1921, he was transferred to Wednesday in February, 1922. After much ill-luck he came to his own late in 1924-25, with the departure of Binks, and never looked back. Height 5 ft. 9 ins., weight 12 st.

HAROLD HILL.—Wednesday's " Tom Thumb " is very popular at Hillsborough, for he is remarkably versatile, and can play in any of the forward positions. He is more than a match for many defenders, because of his cunning, virile footwork and tenacity. He is particularly effective in his heading. Hill continues the long Blackwell strain in Sheffield. He sprang from junior football with New Hucknall Colliery into Notts County's first team in 1919-20. After rendering great service for Notts, he came to Wednesday in October, 1924. He has scored several great goals. Height 5 ft. 5 in., weight 9 st. 7 lbs.

ARTHUR PRINCE.—Until Hill became his regular partner Prince showed in and out form, being inconsistent, but he steadily developed. Very fast and intelligent in anticipating the moves of Hill, he is a good winger at his best, a fair shot, and can centre effectively. He possesses surprising stamina and is a rare sticker on the track. Came to Wednesday from Port Vale in the summer of 1924. Before joining Port Vale in 1922 he was connected with an almost unknown junior club called Bucknall. Only young, he is 5 ft. 9½ in. in height and weighs 10 st.

TROTTER LEADS STRING OF GREAT SCORERS.

James Trotter, Wednesday's centre-forward, created a record for the club in Football League matches by scoring all five goals against Portsmouth, on the latter's first visit to the ground in a League match, on December 13th, 1924, The result was 5—2.

Wednesday have scored five or more goals in a match on 53 occasions in the League, that is together with the war-time competitions. The only players who have scored four goals in these high-scoring games are Miller, Stewart, McLean, Glennon, Binks, and Trotter. Details:—

THE LEAGUE.

Season.	Club.		Rst.	Goal-scorers.
1892-93	v. Accrington	(h)	5-2	Brown (2), Spiksley, Davis, Rowan.
,,	v. Aston Villa	(h)	5-3	Spiksley, Rowan, Davies, Woolhouse, Mumford.
,,	v. Everton	(a)	5-3	Brady (2), Brown, Spiksley, Davies.
,,	v. Newton H.	(a)	5-1	Rowan (2), Davies, Spiksley (2).
,,	v. West Bromwich A.	(h)	6-0	Brandon, Rowan, Brady, Brown, Spiksley (2).
1893-94	v. Darwen	(h)	5-0	Webster (2), Woolhouse, Spiksley, Miller.
1894-95	v. Liverpool	(h)	5-0	Spiksley (2), Woolhouse (2), Brandon.
1895-96	v. West Bromwich A.	(h)	5-3	Spiksley (2), Brady, Earp, Davies.
1896-97	v. Blackburn Rovers	(h)	6-0	Brash (2), Porter (o.g.), Brady, Ferrier (2).
1899-00	v. Chesterfield	(h)	5-1	Spiksley, Ferrier, Miller (2), Brash.
,,	v. Gainsbro' T.	(h)	5-1	Miller (4), Brash.
,,	v. Barnsley	(h)	5-1	Brash, Davies, Wright (3).
,,	v. Burton Sw.	(h)	5-0	Miller, Lee, Wright, Crawshaw, Spiksley.
,,	v. Burton Sw.	(a)	6-0	Topham, Wright, Ferrier, Ruddlesdin, Crawshaw, Earp.
,,	v. Loughboro'	(h)	5-0	Miller, Wright (3), Langley.
1901-02	v. Bolton W.	(h)	5-1	Wilson, Chapman (2), Ostick (o.g.), Davies.
1904-05	v. Everton	(h)	5-5	Davies, Stewart, Simpson (G.), V. S. Simpson, Ferrier.
,,	v. Middlesbro'	(h)	5-0	Chapman, Wilson (2), Stewart (2).
1905-06	v. Wolverhampton	(h)	5-1	Stewart (4), Wilson.
1906-07	v. Manchester U.	(h)	5-2	Simpson (G.), Craswhaw, Wilson (2), Stewart.
1907-08	v. Bolton W.	(h)	5-2	Stewart (2), Bradshaw, Brittleton, Wilson.
,,	v. Arsenal	(h)	6-0	Bradshaw (3), Wilson, Chapman, Brittleton.
,,	v. Bristol City	(h)	5-3	Chapman, Wilson (2), Stewart (2).
,,	v. Manchester C.	(h)	5-1	Bradshaw (2), Chapman, Stewart (2).
1908-09	v. Arsenal	(h)	6-2	Tummon, Wilson (3), Lloyd, Bradshaw.
,,	v. Chelsea	(h)	5-1	Rollinson (2), Lloyd, Wilson, Brittleton
1909-10	v. Notts Forest	(a)	6-0	Murray, Wilson (2), Chapman, Robertson (2).
1910-11	v. Notts Forest	(h)	5-2	Chapman (2), Kirkman, Rollinson, Wilson.

Season.	Club.		Rst.	Goal-scorers.
1911-12	v. Sunderland	(h)	8-0	McLean (4), Kirkman (2), Glennon (2).
	v. West Bromwich A....	(a)	5-1	McLean (3), Kirkman (2).
1912-13	v. Arsenal	(a)	5-2	Wilson, McLean (2), Kirkman, Glennon.
,,	v. Bradford City ...	(h)	6-0	Glennon, Kirkman, Burkinshaw, McLean (2), Wright.
,,	v. Oldham A.	(h)	5-0	Glennon, Kirkman (2), McLean (2).
1914-15	v. Aston Villa	(h)	5-2	McLean (3), Wilson, Glennon.
,,	v. Bolton W.	(h)	7-0	Parkes, Glennon, Gill, Robertson, Wilson, Capper, Bentley.
,,	v. Bradford	(h)	6-0	McLean (3), Kirkman, Glennon, Capper.

WAR PERIOD (MIDLAND SECTION).

Season.	Club.		Rst.	Goal-scorers.
1915-16	v. Derby C.	(h)	5-0	Wilson (2), Hatten, Harrop, Islip.
,,	v. Derby C.	(a)	5-1	Bentley, Cawley, Capper (3).
1916-17	v. Lincoln C.	(h)	7-1	Glennon, Burkinshaw (3), Kirkman, Bell (2).
1917-18	v. Lincoln C.	(h)	7-2	Spratt (2), Capper, Armitage, Buddery, Brittleton, Glennon.
1918-19	v. Grimsby T.	(h)	5-2	Burkinshaw (2), Glennon (2), Gill.
,,	v. Sheffield U.	(h)	5-0	Glennon (4), Burkinshaw.

POST WAR.—THE LEAGUE.

Season.	Club.		Rst.	Goal-scorers.
1920-21	v. Wolverhampton ...	(h)	6-0	Taylor (2), McIntyre, Smelt, Lofthouse, Price.
1921-22	v. Blackpool...	(h)	5-1	Lofthouse (2), Brelsford, McIntyre, Ratcliffe.
1923-24	v. Nelson	(h)	5-0	Walker (2), Taylor (2), Petrie.
,,	v. Crystal P.	(h)	6-0	Binks (4), Petrie (2).
,,	v. South Shields	(h)	5-0	Taylor (3), Harron, Walker.
1924-25	v. Portsmouth	(h)	5-2	Trotter (5) .
,,	v. Hull City	(h)	5-0	Trotter (2), Barrass, Powell (S.), Marsden.
1925-26	v. Preston N.E.	(h)	5-1	Trotter (4), Blenkinsopp.
,,	v. Stockport C.	(h)	6-2	Trotter (5), Ayres.
,,	v. Bradford City	(h)	5-1	Trotter (2), Hill (2), Barrass.
,,	v. Oldham Athletic ...	(h)	5-1	Trotter (2), Hill (2), Barrass.

WEDNESDAY'S COMPLETE LEAGUE RECORD.

	P.	W.	D.	L.	F.	A.	Pts.	Position.
1892-93	30	12	3	15	55	65	27	12th
1893-94	30	9	8	13	48	58	26	12th
1894-95	30	12	4	14	50	55	28	8th
1895-96	30	12	5	13	44	53	29	8th
1896-97	30	10	11	9	42	37	31	6th
1897-98	30	15	3	12	51	42	33	5th
1898-99	34	8	8	16	32	61	24	18th
*1899-00	34	25	4	5	84	22	54	1st
1900-01	34	13	10	11	52	42	36	8th
1901-02	34	13	8	13	48	52	34	9th
1902-03	34	19	4	11	54	36	42	1st
1903-04	34	20	7	7	48	28	47	1st
1904-05	34	14	5	15	61	57	33	9th
1905-06	38	18	8	12	63	52	44	3rd
1906-07	38	12	11	15	49	60	35	13th
1907-08	38	19	4	15	73	64	42	5th
1908-09	38	17	6	15	67	61	40	5th
1909-10	38	15	9	14	60	63	39	11th
1910-11	38	17	8	13	47	48	42	6th
1911-12	38	16	9	13	69	49	41	5th
1912-13	38	21	7	10	75	55	49	3rd
1913-14	38	13	8	17	53	70	34	18th
1914-15	38	15	13	10	61	54	43	7th

No Competition in 1915-16, 1916-17, 1917-18, 1918-19.

	P.	W.	D.	L.	F.	A.	Pts.	Position.
1919-20	42	7	9	26	28	64	23	22nd
*1920-21	42	15	11	16	48	48	41	10th
*1921-22	42	15	14	13	47	50	44	10th
*1922-23	42	17	12	13	54	47	46	8th
*1923-24	42	16	12	14	54	51	44	8th
*1924-25	42	15	8	19	50	56	38	14th
*1925-26	42	27	6	9	88	48	60	1st

* Second Division.

WAR-TIME FOOTBALL.

MIDLAND SECTION: PRINCIPAL COMPETITION.

	P.	W.	L.	D.	F.	A.	Pts.	Position.
1915-16	26	11	10	5	36	43	27	7th
1916-17	30	9	15	6	36	48	24	13th
1917-18	28	9	14	5	45	59	23	11th
1918-19	30	11	13	6	49	49	28	11th

SUBSIDIARY COMPETITION.

	P.	W.	L.	D.	F.	A.	Pts.	Position.
1915-16	10	3	4	3	10	13	9	5th
1916-17	6	2	2	2	12	12	6	2nd
1917-18	6	3	1	2	15	8	8	1st
1918-19	6	3	2	1	11	10	7	2nd